FRAMINGHAM STATE COLLEGE

D0567255

Western Influences on Political Parties to 1825

AN ESSAY IN HISTORICAL INTERPRETATION

A Da Capo Press Reprint Series

THE AMERICAN SCENE
Comments and Commentators

GENERAL EDITOR: WALLACE D. FARNHAM
University of Illinois

Western Influences on Political Parties to 1825

AN ESSAY IN HISTORICAL INTERPRETATION

BY HOMER C. HOCKETT

DA CAPO PRESS • NEW YORK • 1970

Framingham State College
Framingham, Massachusetts

A Da Capo Press Reprint Edition

This Da Capo Press edition of *Western Influences on Political Parties to 1825* is an unabridged republication of the
first edition published in 1917 in Columbus, Ohio, as Volume
22, Number 3 of *The Ohio State University Bulletin*.

Library of Congress Catalog Card Number 75-87650

SBN 306-71777-8

Published by Da Capo Press
A Division of Plenum Publishing Corporation
227 West 17th Street
New York, N. Y. 10011
All Rights Reserved

Manufactured in the United States of America

3|92

JK
2260
H7
1917a

Western Influences on Political Parties to 1825

AN ESSAY IN HISTORICAL INTERPRETATION

By

HOMER C. HOCKETT

Professor of American History in
The Ohio State University

THE OHIO STATE UNIVERSITY

Framingham State College
Framingham, Massachusetts

TO

FREDERICK JACKSON TURNER

In Acknowledgment of a Debt which but Increases with the Lapse of Years

PREFACE

This study was begun in a search for the key to the political history of Monroe's presidency, so long superficially known as the Era of Good Feeling. The quest for the unifying principle of this confused period revealed, however, that it could not be separated from the events which marked the earlier history of parties, and that it would be necessary to treat the whole question of the rise and decline of the first pair of parties in the United States—Federalism and Jeffersonian Republicanism. Due regard for the threads of continuity in this larger topic required that the operation of formative influences be traced from about the middle of the eighteenth century to the end of the first quarter of the nineteenth. The study has thus become a sketch of our party evolution down to 1825, so far as that evolution was influenced by new forces and issues released or raised by the development of new western areas.

It is hoped that the essay may be sufficiently successful to warrant a continuation of this type of study for the period since 1825.

OHIO STATE UNIVERSITY
August 12, 1916

CONTENTS

CHAPTER I

CHAPTER II

CHAPTER III

CHAPTER IV

CHAPTER V

CHAPTER I

THE ORIGIN OF PARTIES IN THE UNITED STATES

1. COLONIAL ANTECEDENTS

In Europe political parties have divided in the main along lines of social stratification; in the United States the lines of cleavage have tended to be geographical. The reason for this difference is that the parties of modern Europe have developed within countries occupying definitely fixed territories, while in the United States settlement has expanded over a continent many times outmeasuring the region which it occupied at the beginning of our national history. The origin of our parties is therefore to be sought in the variation of social types incident to the westward movement of population from the Atlantic coast, and our party history is closely connected at every epoch with the changes resulting from each stage of the westward advance. It was the development of a group of inland settlements differing in important ways from the coast communities which first gave rise to those conflicting economic interests and social ideals which have furnished the causes of party groupings throughout our history.[1]

The forces of social selection began very early in colonial days to produce differences between the older settlements and the new.

---

[1] "We may trace the contest between the capitalist and the democratic pioneer from the earliest colonial days."—Frederick J. Turner, in the *American Historical Review*, XVI, 227. The idea of social differentiation as a result of the westward movement was first set forth clearly by Professor Turner in the essay on "The Significance of the Frontier in American History," in the American Historical Association *Report* for 1893.

During the past two decades several writers working independently have produced monographs dealing with the social development and sectional struggles in so many of the colonies that it is now possible, by putting together the facts revealed by their researches, to obtain a fairly comprehensive understanding of the evolution of this group of inland settlements and of the reasons why they came into conflict with the older communities. The more important of these monographs are:

Ambler, C. H., *Sectionalism in Virginia.*

Bassett, J. S., "The Regulators of North Carolina," in Amer. Hist. Assn. *Report* for 1894.

Becker, C. L., *The History of Political Parties in the Province of New York*, 1760-1776 (University of Wisconsin *Bulletin*, History Series, II, No. 1).

Lincoln, C. H., *The Revolutionary Movement in Pennsylvania.*

Schaper, W. A., "Sectionalism and Representation in South Carolina," in Amer. Hist. Assn. *Report* for 1900, I.

The whole subject of the formation of the social order of the interior east of the Alleghanies has been summarized by Professor Turner in "The Old West," State Historical Society of Wisconsin *Proceedings* for 1908.

The first colonists were frontiersmen, wielding the axe and building their cabins and rude blockhouses in the forest clearings.
Wilderness conditions gave way with surprising rapidity, however,
to those of settled life, and the frontier line began its westward
march towards the setting sun. Long before it crossed the Alleghanies, the dominant members of the communities first settled
had worked out a measurably satisfactory adjustment between their
ideals and environment, and had set up ecclesiastical, political, and
economic systems which they desired to perpetuate. The hunters,
fur traders, and farmers upon whom fell the chief task of settling
the interior came, on the other hand, from those elements of the
population which were more or less in ill-adjustment with the coastal order. Thus it came to pass by the middle of the eighteenth
century that two contrasting societies dwelt between the mountains and the sea, the one occupying the coast lands, the other the
"back country," and thus was prepared the stage for the first party
divisions.

In the Old Dominion, during the rise of tobacco planting, men
of small means were unable to maintain themselves as land holders
in the fertile valleys of the tidewater, in competition with the
wealthy,[2] and found it necessary to retreat either to the more
barren upland between the river courses, or towards their sources,
for on the outskirts of settlement lands were to be had as bounties
for defence of the frontier.[3] A distinct sectionalism appeared within the colony even before the close of the seventeenth century, and
furnishes the true clue to Bacon's Rebellion.[4] A few men of the
upper social class, like Captain William Byrd, of more adventurous nature than most of their kind, interested themselves in frontier lands, but the great majority of the inhabitants of the back
settlements were poor men struggling to gain a foothold by dint
of their own labor. Throughout the colonial period, in fact, most
of Virginia's brilliant society, as well as her wealth and political power, centered in the slaveholding plantations of the tide-

---

[2] See Bruce, P. A., *Economic History of Virginia in the Seventeenth Century*, I, 527 *et seq.*,
on the tendency towards large holidngs. We can only conjecture the process by which en-
grossment affected the small farmers, but *cf.* the displacement, two centuries later, of the
small farmer in the Gulf region by the cotton planter: Phillips, U. B., "Origin and Growth of
the Southern Black Belts," in *Amer. Hist. Rev.*, XI, 798-816. See also *below*, 114 and *f. n.* 101.

[3] Bruce, *Economic History*, I, 510 *et seq.* The practice of "squatting" must have appeared early also. See Ford, A., *Colonial Precedents of our National Land System*, 113.

[4] Osgood, H. A., *The American Colonies in the Seventeenth Century*, III, 243-247.

water.[5] The Anglican establishment, like the economic system, tended to drive certain elements of the population from the coast regions. In the days of intolerance, the exclusion of non-Anglicans resulted in an overland migration from the James River to Albemarle Sound, making North Carolina for a time virtually a frontier of Virginia, but the tempered ecclesiasticism of the eighteenth century permitted the settlement of dissenters in the interior, thus adding another element of contrast with the coast. Although somewhat later in making themselves felt, similar forces came into play in North Carolina with the rise of the plantation system there, and with similar results.[6]

As the social order of the coast plain crystallized, the outlet to the frontier for those whom the system hampered impeded the formation of social strata, but stratification after the European fashion proceeded apace wherever the outlet was stopped. Such was the case for a time in South Carolina, where access to the interior was difficult because of the broad belt of "pine barrens," which ran parallel with the coast and isolated the piedmont. Substantially all of the good lands lying east of this barrier had been engrossed by the planters before population began to move into the district in its rear. Hemmed in on the coast the whites tended to divide into two classes: the planters and merchants who composed the aristocracy and were bent on such an organization of industry and government as would promote their own interests, and a proletariat which would probably have become a negligible political force. Foreign commerce, the professions, and planting were considered to be the only respectable vocations, and there was little room in the economy of the plantation save for the planter and the slave.[7] Farther north, New York affords another example of the tendency to stratification. Here expansion was retarded by the Catskills and the Iroquois Confederacy of the Mohawk Valley, while the system of large land grants in vogue from the days of the Dutch patroons enabled the landlords to lay claim to available lands far in advance of settlement. A legal system of small grants gave a measure of protection to poor settlers who would fight for their rights, but under the circumstances many preferred lands in

---

[5] Speculative land owning in the Virginia piedmont became common in the eighteenth century, but most of the population continued to consist of poor farmers with small holdings. Cf. Turner, "Old West," 205.

[6] Ibid., 207-209.

[7] Schaper, "Sectionalism," 274, 304.

other colonies where fee simple titles could be had more easily and safely. Vast tracts claimed by proprietors therefore remained unoccupied, while to a greater extent than in any other colony white cultivators of the soil sank to the status of semi-feudal tenants.[8]

The rise of an interest strong enough to compete with the coastal aristocracy was due to the settlement of the interior, and its story is a part of the history of the coming of the German and Scotch-Irish immigrants.[9] Into New York came, about 1710, Germans whom Governor Hunter planned to colonize in Livingston Manor. Dissatisfied with their treatment, the colonists "trekked" to the valley of the Schoharie, only to find that the lands on which they had settled were claimed by the avaricious landlords. Once more, therefore, they dispersed, many going northward to the Mohawk, where they formed pioneer communities of independent, democratic farmer folk.[10] Pennsylvania, however, received the chief influx of foreign immigrants, and from there they spread to the colonies farther south. By 1725 thousands of German redemptioners and Scotch-Irish were pouring into the colony every year. The search for unappropriated lands carried them into the interior, where some of them bought while the rest "squatted," declaring that "it was against the laws of God and nature that so much land should lie idle while so many christians wanted it to work on and to raise their bread."[11] Encountering the mountain ranges, the later comers, each wave advancing beyond its predecessors, turned southward, crossed Maryland, invaded Virginia on both sides of the Blue Ridge, and occupied the piedmont of the Carolinas by the middle of the century. Swelled in volume by streams entering by way of Baltimore and the coast of Virginia and the Carolinas, this German and Scotch-Irish population with a minority of English intermingled placed itself in possession of the belt of country between the fall line and the Alleghanies, from the Mohawk to the Savannah, by the time of the outbreak of the French and Indian

---

[8] Turner, "Old West," 195-196; Ballagh, J. C., "The Land System in the South," in Amer. Hist. Assn. *Report* for 1897, 110.

[9] Germans from the Rhine Valley had played a considerable part in the colonization of Pennsylvania in the early days of Penn's experiment, but the similarity between their religious views and those of the Quakers, together with the broad tolerance of the proprietor's government, had made for a ready assimilation. Faust, A. B., *German Element in the United States*, I, 30-52.

[10] *Ibid.*, I, 73 *et seq.*

[11] Ballagh, "Land System in the South," 112; Turner, "Old West," 216.

War.[12] Throughout this region the mean annual temperature is about the same, owing to the increasing elevation as one goes southward. Soil conditions are also similar, so that the whole belt constitutes a single physiographic province suitable throughout for grain farming and stock raising.[13] Here the settlers formed a primitive agricultural society, whose isolated farmers cultivated small tracts instead of plantations, aided by their sons and women folk instead of slaves, with subsistence in view at first rather than production for a market.[14]

Of all the colonies those in New England felt these differentiating influences least. Apart from a few Scotch-Irish settlers the non-English immigration touched this section but slightly, and the supervision of town planting by the theocratic governments carried along the Puritan social organization with the expanding population in a greater degree than was true of the coastal institutions of any of the colonies south of the Hudson.[15] Yet the regulations which the Massachusetts Bay Company found necessary in 1631, governing the admission of freemen with the right of voting, give evidence that from the very beginning of that colony there were among the immigrants many discordant spirits whose presence furnished the elements of social cleavage.[16] As in the case of Virginia, the story of the expansion of New England is the story of the geographical segregation of these inharmonious elements. The exodus to the Connecticut Valley was the first fruit of dissatisfaction with the Massachusetts order. In this case, because of the minor character of the differences, the migration merely divided the Puritan population into parts which remained essentially alike. But the religious controversies which led to the expulsion of Williams and Hutchinson gave birth to a community on Narragansett Bay of so different a type from those of Boston and Hartford as to cause its exclusion from the New England Confedera-

[12] Faust, German Element, I, chaps. 5-8; Hanna, C. A., The Scotch-Irish, II, 60 et seq.; Greene, S. W., "Scotch-Irish in America," in American Antiquarian Society Proceedings, X, 32-70; Kercheval, S., A History of the Valley of Virginia, 45-55; Ford, H. J., The Scotch-Irish in America, 378-400.

[13] Merriam, Life Zones and Crop Zones of the United States, United States Dept. of Agriculture, Division of Biological Survey, Bulletin No. 10, 20-24, 30-36.

[14] For a fuller description of life in the back settlements, see Schaper, "Sectionalism," 317 et seq.; Bassett, "Regulators," 144-148; Roosevelt, Th., Winning of the West, I, 101-133; Ambler, Sectionalism, 13-16.

[15] Osgood, American Colonies, I, 429. Cf. regulation of parish organization in South Carolina, below, 19.

[16] Ibid., I, 153-155.

tion.[17] Even with the more discordant elements driven beyond her bounds, Massachusetts exhibited a movement parallel to that in Virginia, by which the frontier became the goal of that part of her people who found themselves to be out of adjustment with the life of the older parts. In a general way the impelling forces behind the movement are discernible. The relative difficulty of obtaining land, the disfranchisement of the man without property after the abolition of the religious test, and the privileged position of the Congregational Church, alike invited the ambitious and aggrieved to try their fortunes on a stage where the action was freer.[18] Especially was this true after the General Court, in the second quarter of the eighteenth century, relaxed its supervision over the establishment of new towns, and even offered lands for sale to the highest bidder instead of restricting grants to groups of approved character, as in the earlier days. By these processes New England, like the southern colonies, was slowly divided into two parts, "the one coastal, and dominated by commercial interests and the established Congregational churches; the other a primitive agricultural area, democratic in principle, and with various sects." [19]

Antagonism was the natural result of the existence side by side of two societies so diverse as those the formation of which has been described.[20] There were marked differences between the Puritan commonwealths of New England and the "Cavalier" society

---

[17] Admission of the Rhode Island settlements was refused in 1644 and again in 1648 unless they would consent to annexation by Massachusetts or Plymouth. It would seem that the ground on which Maine was excluded was equally applicable to the settlements on Narragansett Bay—"because they ran a different course from us both in their ministry and civil administration." *Ibid.*, I, 399. Rhode Island was thus a part of the Massachusetts frontier, holding much the same relation to the Bay Colony that early North Carolina held to Virginia. In the matter of religious toleration Rhode Island remained essentially "frontier," but in time it developed a commercial aristocracy, while its political system imposed the usual disabilities upon the masses, besides some which were not to be found elsewhere. In short, Rhode Island developed a social class corresponding to the dominant class in other coast regions. But its democratic element remained strong and active, as is shown by the paper money legislation of the Confederation. Dorr's Rebellion of 1842 was due to the determination of the people to endure the remnants of the old aristocratic order no longer.

[18] *Ibid.*, I, 464-466. The struggles of commoners and non-commoners over undivided town lands seem to be connected with the planting of new towns on the frontier by the discontented. *Cf.* Turner, "Old West," 191-192.

[19] *Ibid.*, 194.

[20] "In general this took these forms: contests between the property-holding class of the coast and the debtor class of the interior, where specie was lacking, and where paper money and a readjustment of the basis of taxation were demanded; contests over defective or unjust local government in the administration of taxes, fees, lands, and the courts; contests over unfair apportionment in the legislature, whereby the coast was able to dominate, even when its population was in the minority; contests to secure the complete separation of church and state; and, later, contests over slavery, internal improvements, and party politics in general." *Ibid.*, 221-222.

of Old Virginia and her neighbors; and these differences have become the commonplaces of historians. But it is doubtful whether the contrast between the maritime and planting colonies is any sharper than that which distinguished the seaboard from Maine to Georgia from the interior along the whole frontier line. In England Congregationalism and Episcopacy had represented polities sufficiently diverse to cause civil war; yet they had this in common in America, that both embodied the principle of union of church and state. In the interior, on the other hand, scores of sects flourished side by side on a plane of equality, tolerating one another if for no other reason than that they could not do otherwise, but making common cause against the establishments.[21] Between the Anglican and Congregational colonies moreover there was a positive economic bond, for planting and maritime commerce were natural allies. The New England skippers found no inconsiderable portion of their cargoes in the staples of the South, dependent as the latter were upon the European market. The alliance of these interests dates back at least to the Navigation Acts of the Restoration era, and appears in many a political contest down to the period of tariff controversy in the nineteenth century.[22] The tendency of both ship-owners and planters was to depend upon foreign sources for supplies, devoting their energies to the production and marketing of the great staple crops. The joint interest of these coastal groups was quite different from that of the interior population. As the output of the farms increased beyond the needs of the occupants, the tendency was to convert the surplus into forms which could be readily marketed nearby, rather than to seek the foreign market required by the large-scale operations of the planter. So the back-country settlers became "manufacturers" in the contemporary sense of the word, supplying the coast towns with homespun cloth, smoked meats, and other products of household industry to such an extent as to affect the carrying trade. The imports of the interior were slight, while in South Carolina, for illustration, the do-

---

[21] The struggle for separation of church and state lasted about half a century, beginning in Virginia on the eve of the Revolution and culminating in Connecticut in 1818. On Virginia see James, C. F., *Documentary History of the Struggle for Religious Liberty in Virginia*. The struggle in Connecticut is an excellent illustration of the alliance of sects for the common purpose. There the Episcopalians, Baptists, and others united in the Democratic party, demanding a new constitution and complete equality of denominations. Johnston, Alexander, *Connecticut*, 352-355; Hart, Samuel, *et al.*, eds., *Connecticut as a Colony and as a State*, 105-119.

[22] *Cf.* votes on tariff bills in 1820 and 1824, on which the representatives of the planting and commercial regions joined in voting *nay*.

mestic supply of bread-stuffs and meat afforded by the opening of the piedmont farms relieved the colony of dependence upon external trade with a consequent decline in its volume and injury to the shipping interest.[23]

The lack of sympathy between the coast and interior is well shown by the history of currency legislation. The interior where specie was scarce had much more need of a paper circulation on a credit basis than was felt by the more developed coast region, but the legislation of the latter showed little regard for the views and needs of the frontier. During the French and Indian Wars the legislatures provided for paper issues to be retired later. The contraction of the volume of the circulating medium which accompanied retirement was distasteful to the remote part of the population, as it interfered with the course of trade and affected the debtor class adversely.[24] Throughout the second half of the eighteenth century, the pioneer belt was the region of paper money agitation, and Shay's Rebellion is the classic illustration of the explosive quality of the discontent engendered by the denial of relief legislation.[25] To the distress which contraction caused in itself was sometimes added injustice in the means employed in redeeming the issues and in the collection of taxes. Thus in North Carolina the wealthy planters who controlled law-making threw an unfair burden in the retirement of the issues of 1760 and 1761 upon the poor farmers by laying a poll tax for the purpose.[26] Other taxes were payable in specie, which the back settlers could not obtain without delays which enabled grasping officials to distrain on property and sell it for personal gain, through collusion with friends.[27]

The system of government everywhere was such as to keep the interior democracies in subordination to the coastal minorities. The settlement of the back country was welcomed by the coast as

---

[23] Schaper, "Sectionalism," 319. Wherever the surplus production of a farming area became great enough to create a pressure for a foreign market, the agricultural interest came into a degree of harmony with the maritime. *Cf.* the support of the constitution by the chief areas of surplus production. The development of the market for food-stuffs in the planting areas created a similar bond between the farmer and the planter. Neither bond was as constant as that which united the planter and ship-owner.

[24] Bassett, "Regulators," 154-155.

[25] Wildman, M. S., *Money Inflation in the United States*, 47-66.

[26] Bassett, "Regulators," 150, 152.

[27] *Ibid.*, 151.

a protection against the Indians,[28] but as the population increased those who were in possession of power were not inclined to risk their vested interests by recognizing the right of the inland majority to rule. The nearest approach to equality was to be found in New England. Yet even there the inland population was made up largely of those elements which had been unable to hold office or even to vote in the communities from which they had come, and in colonies where under the system of town meetings it became customary for a few influential men to hold a caucus to prearrange matters for the mass of the voters,[29] it would be surprising to find full recognition of the equality of rights of the frontier communities. By 1776, at any rate, some of the frontier towns were complaining of their grievances, as is shown by petitions from the New Hampshire towns in the Connecticut River Valley objecting to the lack of a fair system of representation, and to the property qualifications required of members of the council.[30] Farther south the new settlements were much worse off. The Carolina planters who had established their dominion east of the pine belt dared not share power with the non-slaveholding population to the westward. The same was true of the other planting colonies, and everywhere the fear of being taxed by the "Have-nots" was a bugbear to the wealthy. In Pennsylvania the great influx of foreigners, unfamiliar with English speech and governmental institutions, threatened to engulf the original stock.[31] The dominant classes therefore took pains to perpetuate their control. In England the growth of new centers of population and the decline of old ones unaccompanied by reapportionment of representation in parliament, was producing the glaring inequities of the "rotten borough" system, and playing into the hands of the landed and mercantile aristocracy which composed the governing class. The aristocracies of the New World shaped their political affairs in accord with old-world habit, if not in conscious imitation. The ease of acquiring land in the interior

---

[28] Cf. the Massachusetts laws forbidding inhabitants of frontier towns to abandon them during the early Indian wars. Turner, F. J., "The First Official Frontier of the Massachusetts Bay," in Colonial Society of Mass. Publications, XVII, 250, et seq.

[29] Ostrogorski, M., Democracy and the Organization of Political Parties, II, 3-4.

[30] Libby, O. G., The Geographical Distribution of the Vote of the Thirteen States on the Federal Constitution, 1787-8, 9.

[31] James Logan, the Governor of Pennsylvania, himself a Scotch-Irishman, exclaimed in 1725: "It looks as if Ireland were to send all her inhabitants hither; if they will continue to come, they will make themselves proprietors of the province." Quoted in Greene, "Scotch-Irish," 47. Cf. Franklin's apprehensions concerning the German immigrants: Bigelow, John, The Complete Works of Benjamin Franklin, II, 233-234, 296-299.

rendered ineffectual as a barrier against the frontier folk those property qualifications on the right of suffrage and office holding by which the mass of the population had from the beginning, in all of the colonies, been excluded from participation in government, and control had been retained in the hands of an aristocracy of the well-to-do.[32] Several new devices were therefore invented to insure the continuation of minority rule as the center of population moved westward. In Pennsylvania, where the county was the unit of representation in the assembly (as was the case generally outside of New England), the new communities were but tardily given county organization and then allowed only from one to four representatives each, while the old counties—Philadelphia, Bucks, and Chester—the home of the "Quaker" aristocracy, enjoyed eight each. To obtain this result it was necessary to fix the apportionment arbitrarily, instead of basing it either on population or taxable wealth. In 1760, on the basis of population, the city and the western counties had fourteen members less than their proportion, as compared with Philadelphia County; while on the basis of taxation Bucks and Chester had six members more than they should have had and the city and western counties twelve less than their due.[33] Virginia safeguarded minority rule equally well by a somewhat different plan. Although her counties were quite uniformly allowed two delegates each in the lower house, the new ones in the West were made so large that the two members represented a much more numerous constituency than did the delegates from the tidewater counties.[34] Add to this the practice of filling county offices by appointment of the governor and council, themselves holding by royal appointment,[35] and it becomes evident that the political influence of the people of the interior was very small in comparison with their numbers. In South Carolina the western boundaries of the parishes (the units of representation) were for a long time left

---

[32] At the close of the colonial period a freehold qualification prevailed in seven colonies; in the other six personal property was an alternative qualification. Typical requirements were a freehold of fifty acres or yielding an income of forty shillings per annum, or personal property valued at forty or fifty pounds. McKinley, A. E., *The Suffrage Franchise in the Thirteen English Colonies in America*, 480. In Massachusetts and Connecticut perhaps sixteen per cent. of the population were qualified electors; in Virginia and Rhode Island, nine per cent.; in New York City, eight per cent.; in rural Pennsylvania, eight per cent.; but in Philadelphia only two per cent. *Ibid.*, 487-488.

[33] Lincoln, *Revolutionary Movement*, 44-51.

[34] Turner, "Old West," 224.

[35] "Queries from ye Lds of Trade to Sr Wm. Gooch Govr of Virginia & his Answers Abridged," in *Virginia Magazine of History*, III, 114 *et seq.*

undetermined, and the inhabitants of the up-country were thus constructively represented by the members chosen on the coast.[36] When they took the pains to present themselves at the polling places in the eastern ends of the parishes, however, they were generally refused the right to vote.[37] Provision was made in 1730 by the crown for a group of new settlements in the middle portion of the colony, among the inducements offered to settlers being parish organization with representation whenever the settlement attained a population of one hundred families. In fact, however, the dominant class was able to delay parish organization until the people agreed to support a parish church of the Anglican type, and thus representation and the dominant social organization advanced *pari passu*.[38] The settled portion of the middle region had been provided for after this fashion before the Revolution, but the up-country had no separate representation previous to the meeting of the provincial congress of 1775. The demand for local government, meantime, was met by extending the machinery of the central government through commissions appointed by the legislature, and, finally, in 1769, by the creation of a few judicial districts each with its appointed sheriff. All writs, however, originated in and were returnable to the Charleston courts. Such as it was, this constituted the system of local government in the back settlements down to the Revolution.[39] Conditions in North Carolina were especially grievous. In general her scheme of governing the western settlements was like that of Virginia, but it was worse in operation because of the corruption of the county officials who exacted extortionate fees, were suspected of collecting heavier taxes than were warranted by the law, and undoubtedly failed to make honest returns to the public treasury.[40]

Delays and defects in the organization of local government in the new settlements left the inhabitants without adequate government protection against the acts of the lawless. Complaints to the court at Charleston were of little avail against horse stealing in the piedmont—a common crime in the days of disorder following the French and Indian War. Owing to the large size of the coun-

[36] Schaper, "Sectionalism," 335.

[37] *Ibid.*, 335, 348.

[38] *Ibid.*, 329.

[39] *Ibid.*, 331, 338.

[40] Bassett, "Regulators," 148, 152-154. See also "Documents concerning the origin of the Regulation movement," in *Amer. Hist. Rev.*, XXI, 320-332.

ties, inhabitants of Virginia sometimes lived thirty or forty miles from the parish church or county court house.[41] Conditions in Pennsylvania were similar. For the payment of taxes, the transaction of business connected with land titles, or the prosecution of suits, long and difficult journeys were the customary fortune of the people of the interior.

The population which found itself burdened with so many disabilities was not of a type to accept an inferior status meekly. The Calvinism of the Scotch-Irish Presbyterians and of many of the German sects tended towards political equality, as had been shown in earlier times. Even under the weight of a political system which had the rigidity of many centuries' growth, the democracy inherent in creeds which taught the equality of men before God and the ecclesiastical supremacy of the organized group of believers had produced an abortive "Commonwealth" in seventeenth century England. A long stride was taken towards modern democracy when the Puritans transplanted their religion to New England, where it enjoyed right of way unhampered by the established polity of an old country.[42] But the "Bible Commonwealth" of Massachusetts developed a rigidity all its own, which showed that it was still akin to the old-world system, and democracy first worked itself free from the incubus of European tradition upon the frontier. Indeed, the frontier was the natural birthplace of democracy. The actual equality of men under primitive conditions of life inevitably begot the ideal of political equality. Like castaways upon a desert island, the backwoodsmen forgot those artificial distinctions which had no correspondence with the facts of their life. While weary France was hearing the first faint prophecy of revolution in the back-to-nature call of the philosophers of the *ancien régime*, the American frontier was making a reality of Rousseau's dream.[43] The new settlements hardly needed to be taught the philosophy of the rights of man which was about to play so great a part in revolutions on both sides of the Atlantic. During the contest with the mother country the united colonies not only adapted

---

[41] Turner, "Old West," 224. *Cf.* conditions in South Carolina as presented in the petition of the Calhouns and others: Schaper, "Sectionalism," 335.

[42] Borgeaud, Charles, *The Rise of Modern Democracy.*

[43] Rousseau's *Discours sur les arts et les sciences* was published in 1749. It lauded the "state of nature" as the happiest state of man. It was this essay which Voltaire said made him wish to go upon "all-fours." The *Contrat Social*, which followed after a dozen years, and was the work which most influenced the French Revolution, stressed the absolute and inalienable sovereignty of the people.

Locke's philosophy to their own purposes in the declaration of independence, but the frontier offered its own elaboration of the Englishman's thought in the "squatter sovereignty" doctrine of Jefferson: the free inhabitants of the British dominions who colonized America "possessed a right which nature has given to all men, of departing from the country in which chance, not choice, has placed them; of going in quest of new habitations, and of there establishing new societies, under such laws and regulations as to them shall seem most likely to promote public happiness."[44]

Men of such ideals would not brook the unfair control of the coast. And yet this control was in most respects merely nominal. Although deprived of local government in the legal sense and allowed but little participation in general legislation in their respective provinces, the frontiersmen none the less regulated the greater part of the concerns of their everyday lives. This liberty and self-reliance made them the more impatient at the shortcomings and injustices of the legal authorities. Bacon's Rebellion has already been alluded to as an evidence of the early discontent of the Virginia frontier, the trouble being started in that historic episode by Bacon's taking matters into his own hands and proceeding against the Indians without the commission of the authorities. After the French and Indian War, the dissatisfaction of the interior found expression in numerous petitions complaining of the lack of adequate local government, of the remoteness of the courts and churches, and of the inequities in the systems of taxation and representation.[45] But, characteristically, the aggrieved men did not await the slow and uncertain action of government in matters which they could deal with themselves, and where the machinery of government proved ineffectual to check lawlessness, as in South Carolina, organized bands of "regulators" dealt summarily with the offenders. Such initiative was mistaken by the eastern gentry for mob violence, and served to heighten the mutual distrust of the

---

[44] Jefferson, T., *A Summary View of the rights of British America*, reprinted in *American History Leaflet*, No. 11. Revised form in Ford, P. L., *Writings of Thomas Jefferson*, I, 427.

[45] The South Carolinians repeatedly petitioned for local government and representation between 1752 and 1770. Notable among these petitions was one of 1768, signed by the Calhouns and others, asking for proper division of the parishes, for courts, schools, churches, and the rights of British subjects. They complained that they were 200 miles from the parish church. The memorial was referred to a committee, which reported that three-fourths of the white population of the colony was in the back settlements, and recommended the organization of new parishes with representation. No action followed. Schaper, "Sectionalism," 335. In 1764 the Pennsylvania frontiersmen made similar demands, including an equitable adjustment of apportionment. Hanna, *Scotch-Irish*, I, 63. For Virginia see Ambler, *Sectionalism*, 4-5.

upland and tidewater.[46] In North Carolina the regulation movement took the form of an attack upon the abuses in the tax and fee systems, and brought the democracy into a contest with the governing class which ended in armed conflict.[47] In Virginia the democracy found its leaders in men of some social standing but of western birth, under whom it began to undermine the foundations of the aristocracy by its attacks upon the church establishment and the system of primogeniture and entail.[48]

2. THE REVOLUTIONARY PERIOD

Thus at the opening of the Revolutionary era a well-defined contest was in progress between the coast and the interior, the former representing the minority who wished to maintain the *status quo* in industry and government, and the latter the cause of the people. In its early stages this contest was a struggle of the back settlers of each colony against the dominant class—a series of isolated contests, for it was a time when intercolonial relations were still slight. But the common characteristics of the frontier throughout its extent and the similarity of the grievances complained of by the frontiersmen everywhere were a prophecy of cleavage on a continental scale in the days of national unification. The Revolution, indeed, afforded occasion for the first interprovincial alignment—Whigs and Loyalists—but the issues arising from British relations served to obscure somewhat the workings of the older antagonisms, although the revolutionary movement is itself a phase of the contest which we are tracing.[49] The essays written in defence of colonial rights were filled with a philosophy of popular government which was equally hostile to the British system of administration and to the domination of the provincial aristocracies. The Whig philosophy fell in exactly with the ideals of the frontier democracy, and the Revolution and the democratic movement be-

---

[46] Schaper, "Sectionalism," 334-336. It was the regulation movement which led to the division of the up-country into judicial districts. *Above*, 19.

[47] Bassett, "Regulators."

[48] Ambler, *Sectionalism*, 5, 32-41; Hunt, in Amer. Hist. Assn. *Report* for 1901, I, 163-171; James, *Documentary Hist.*

[49] To some extent the former antagonists made common cause in the Revolution, yet where popular leaders headed the movement against England, as in Pennsylvania, the aristocrats tended towards Toryism, while the reverse was true where the aristocrats led, as in North Carolina; there many of the Regulators became Loyalists. These facts in themselves indicate that the old antagonism cut deeper than the issue between the colonies and England.

came identified in no small measure.[50] The frontier farmers found allies in the hitherto disfranchised classes in the coast towns, who suddenly became of political weight through the frequent resort to mass meetings and other extra-legal organs representing the whole people.[51] The latitude of the Continental Congress in admitting state delegates appointed by such irregular bodies, and in recommending the "assemblies and conventions" in states "where no government sufficient to the exigencies of their affairs hath been hitherto established, to adopt such government as shall, in the opinion of the representatives of the people, best conduce to the happiness and safety of their constituents," gave aid and comfort to the cause of democracy.[52] New leaders arose who relied upon the people in carrying forward the patriot cause; aristocrats ceased to attend meetings where they were "sure to be outvoted by men of the lowest order;" while the Pendletons and Randolphs and Galloways doubted whether insurgent radicalism were not a graver danger than British rule.[53] In Pennsylvania the reluctance of the moderates like Dickinson, Morris, and Wilson, to resort to extreme measures against England served to throw control into the hands of the radicals who led the Scotch-Irish and German democracy of the inland counties and the Philadelphia proletariat, and to deprive the moderates of influence in framing the first state constitution. The result was a most democratic scheme of government, drawn up by the radicals with the support of solid delegations from the western counties.[54] In South Carolina the revolutionary movement was inaugurated in Charleston by means of

---

[50] "With the intense preaching of majority rule and the emphasis placed on the individual . . . . the arguments which had been used against English misrule were turned against minority control and misgovernment . . . . and a colonial revolution accompanied and supported the international movement." Lincoln, *Revolutionary Movement*, 13-14. What was true of Pennsylvania was true in a measure throughout the colonies.

[51] Beard treats the proletariat of the towns as politically non-existent in the period of the framing of the constitution. *Economic Interpretation of the Constitution*, 24-26. The fact shows how the popular cause miscarried in the Revolution, for their influence was marked in the earlier period. See Lincoln, *Revolutionary Movement*, 159-180 *et passim;* Schaper, "Sectionalism," 357; Becker, *Political Parties*, 275 *et passim*. In a contest for equal political rights the working class of the towns was the natural ally of the farmer, but the dependent position of the employes tended to tie them to their employers. *Cf.* the support of the constitution by the Boston mechanics, whose economic welfare was involved in the prosperity of shipping. Bradford, A., *History of Massachusetts*, III, 22.

[52] Resolution of May 15, 1776. *Journals of the Continental Congress* (L. C. edn.), IV, 342, 358. *Cf.* resolution of Nov. 4, 1775: "That if the Convention of South Carolina shall find it necessary to establish a form of government in that colony, it be recommended to that Convention to call a *full and free representation of the people.*" [Italics mine.] *Id.*, III, 326.

[53] Becker, C. L., *Beginnings of the American People*, 243-245; Ambler, *Sectionalism*, 17-27.

[54] Lincoln, *Revolutionary Movement*, 277 *et seq.*

mass meetings in which the popular element controlled. A general committee chosen by the mass meeting summoned the Provincial Congress of 1775, because it felt the need of the support of a body representing the entire colony. In this body the back settlements as such were for the first time allowed representation.[55] In New York likewise and probably elsewhere the influence of the unfranchised was considerable in the early stages of the Revolution, while extra-legal machinery was being made use of to perfect the Whig organization.[56]

But the promise of a great forward movement towards democracy in government and equal rights for the inland population was hardly fulfilled by the outcome of the Revolution. The forces of conservatism were too strongly entrenched and too many of the Whig leaders were conservatives. "The liberty for which they had fought . . . was the sober, intelligent, fearless liberty of our English ancestors," not the rule of "King Numbers."[57] The advance towards popular government which the period brought may be measured by comparing the provisions of the state constitutions adopted during the war with the arrangements obtaining in the several provinces immediately preceding the struggle. The acceptance of democratic theory is notable. But bills of rights, declarations that the people are sovereign, and expositions of the compact theory do not hide the fact that the chief change in practice is the substitution of the authority of the assembly for that of the crown, while the assembly represents a constituency not much changed, taking the country as a whole, by extensions of the franchise or reforms in the apportionment of representation. For example, the Virginia constitution of 1776 was a compromise in which the bill of rights, drawn by Mason, the leader of the interior, represented the frontier contribution. Its principles "were those which Henry had instilled into the minds of the frontier people; they were the principles which had mastered the minds of Jefferson and Madison."[58] But in the working provisions of the instrument the conservatives triumphed. While the upper house became elective, the right of suffrage in the election of members of both houses re-

---

[55] Schaper, "Sectionalism," 357-359.

[56] Becker, *Political Parties*, 275 *et passim*.

[57] Lodge, H. C., *Life of George Cabot*, 421. "Families like the Otises who joined the patriot cause abandoned none of their conservative principles. They fought for independence from Great Britain, not independence from government and social restraint."—Morison, S. E., *Life of Harrison Gray Otis*, I, 49.

[58] Ambler, *Sectionalism*, 28.

mained as before, and there was no provision for uniformity in the size of the county units of representation, for reapportionment, for extension of the suffrage, for election of local officials, or even for amendment.[59] Jefferson, in his *Notes on Virginia*, written a few years later, pointed out that under the apportionment of 1780 nineteen thousand men living below the falls of the rivers "give law to upwards of thirty thousand living in" other parts of the state, "and appoint all their chief officers, executive and judiciary." [60] In New Jersey the right to vote had been limited to freeholders before the Revolution, while the new constitution granted it to all inhabitants who were "worth fifty pounds proclamation money." [61] In South Carolina, where the recognition of the interior in the provincial congress of 1775 gave some promise of redress of grievances, only forty members in a total of 184 were allowed to the up-country, although it had the majority of the white population; and the planters manipulated the elections so skilfully that "influential gentlemen" of English blood were chosen in every instance, no Scotch-Irish or German name appearing on the list of delegates.[62] The temporary constitution of 1776 allowed eighteen additional members to the upland, but the suffrage requirement remained unchanged, except for the additional qualification that the requisite amount of property must be possessed debt-free. Two years later the property restrictions were slightly reduced, and, probably under the influence of current political philosophy, a fair promise was given that a new apportionment should be made periodically, "according to the particular and comparative strength and taxable property of the different parts"—a promise the fulfillment of which was long delayed.[63]

The political philosophy of the Revolution is nowhere better set forth than in the Massachusetts constitution of 1780: "The body politic is formed by a voluntary association of individuals: it is a social compact, by which the whole people covenants with each citizen, and each with the whole people, that all shall be gov-

[59] Poore, B. P., *The Federal and State Constitutions, Colonial Charters, and other Organic Laws of the United States*, II, 1910-1912; Ambler, *Sectionalism*, 30. *Cf.* the democratic provisions of Jefferson's draft constitution of this year, covering inheritance, land holding, suffrage, apportionment, amendment of the constitution, and religious liberty; Ford, *Writings of Jefferson*, II, 7. See discussion of this draft by Ford in the *Nation* for August 7, 1890, and by D. R. Anderson in *Amer. Hist. Rev.*, XXI, 750-754.

[60] Ford, *Writings of T. J.*, III, 223.

[61] Art. IV. Poore, *Constitutions*, II, 1311.

[62] Schaper, "Sectionalism," 357-359.

[63] *Ibid.*, 365, 367-369.

erned by certain laws for the common good." [64] "The people alone
have an incontestible, unalienable, and indefeasible right to insti-
tute government, and to reform, alter, or totally change the same,
when their protection, safety, prosperity, and happiness require
it."[65] Yet the clause covering suffrage restricts the right to vote
to owners of a freehold of the annual value of three pounds, or
other estate worth sixty pounds.[66] The New York constitution,
drafted by John Jay, "was a special adaptation of the provincial
government, with as few modifications as the circumstances required." [67] The preamble recited that "All power-whatever [in the
state] hath reverted to the people thereof," from whom alone, according to section one, authority is derived;[68] but the freehold
qualifications for voting and office-holding were retained,[69] for it
was "a favorite maxim with Mr. Jay, that those who own the country ought to govern it." [70] There was no provision for amendment,
and Jay congratulated himself that the conservatives had succeeded
in providing a "measurably centralized and measurably aristocratic" government.[71] Even in Pennsylvania, following the democratic triumph of 1776, the conservatives carried on a campaign
for constitutional revision so successfully that a modified constitution was adopted in 1790 "after a decade of personal and party

---

[64] Preamble, Poore, *Constitutions*, I, 956-957.

[65] Part I, Art. VII. *Ibid.*, I, 958.

[66] Part II, Chap. I, Sec. 2, Art. II; Sec. 3, Art. IV. *Ibid.* The draft constitution of 1778
had been rejected by the voters in town meetings chiefly because of the lack of a bill of rights
which should "describe the Natural Rights of Man as he inherits them from the Great Parents
of Nature, distinguishing those, the Controul of which he may part with to Society for Social
Benefits from those he cannot;" for lack of any mode of amendment; and for inequalities in
the apportionment of representation. (*Cf.* grievances of back country of New England, *above*,
14.) Cushing, H. A. *History of the Transition from Provincial to Commonwealth Government
in Massachusetts*, 216, 219 (in Columbia University *Studies*, VII). The best critique of the
draft of 1778 was the so-called "Essex Result," which set forth the principles of government
on which the constitution of 1780 was later based. It was an admirable statement of the
political philosophy of the Revolutionary period, yet it held that the law-making majority
should include those "who possess a major part of the property in the state." *Ibid.*, 223-224.
In framing the constitution of 1780, the draft, including the bill of rights, was made by John
Adams. In the committee of which he was a member he was supported by Bowdoin, Cushing,
Parsons, and others, but opposed at some points by "divers members . . . . who wished for
what was termed a more popular government"—probably a reference to Samuel Adams. *Ibid.*,
235, and *f. n.* On John Adams, see *below*, 35, *f. n.* 103.

[67] Pellew, G., *John Jay*, 69.

[68] Poore, *Constitutions*, II, 1332.

[69] Sec. VII; *ibid.*, 1334.

[70] Jay, William, *The Life of John Jay*, I, 70.

[71] Becker, *Political Parties*, 275, 276, *et passim*. The phrase is Becker's.

struggles hardly equalled for intensity and bitterness in any period of our national or local history." [72]

In brief, in the contest between aristocracy and democracy, the coast and the interior, in the Revolutionary period, the old order held its own. The peace with England rather intensified than healed the domestic discord, by eliminating questions which had confused the main issue, and the people of the interior continued their contest for equal rights under the government of the United States. By 1784 the upland party in South Carolina was pressing for a reapportionment as promised by the constitution of 1778. They succeeded in bringing about the meeting of a convention in which they urged the doctrines of Locke and the French philosophers in support of the demand for equal representation; but the low country was represented on the same basis as that which prevailed in the existing legislature, and thus was able to prevent any real reform in the constitution of 1790.[73] Not until 1808, when the expansion of the plantation economy foreshadowed the extinction of the old sectionalism within the state, did the low country party agree to surrender control of the lower house to the up-country majority, now no longer dangerous.[74] A solution was not so easily reached in Virginia; in fact, the discordant eastern and western portions of that state remained unequally yoked together until the Civil War. In New York, Massachusetts, and elsewhere, the advent of manhood suffrage was delayed until well along in the nineteenth century.[75]

But the further history of sectional struggles within the states does not concern us, for our purpose has been to show that the two rival societies which had developed in the several colonies formed the basis of the first party divisions on a continental scale.

3. RISE OF THE FEDERALIST AND REPUBLICAN PARTIES

The period of the Confederation saw a renewal of the demand for paper money issues. The small farmers had suffered greatly from the war, and at its close found themselves a debtor class at a time when the drainage of specie in payment of foreign trade

---

[72] Lincoln, *Revolutionary Movement*, 287. See Cushing, 247 *et seq.*, foot notes, for extracts from state constitutions relative to compact theory, etc.

[73] Schaper, "Sectionalism," 369-379.

[74] *Ibid.*, 407-437.

[75] See sketch of the progress of constitutional revision by states in McMaster, J. B., *History of the People of the United States*, V, 373-394.

balances caused sharp alterations in the value of money and the burdens of debt. The paper money party was especially strong in the interior, as usual, where specie was always scarce, and where the people identified their creditors with the class which had so long dominated in government—the coastal merchants, planters, and money-lenders, with their friends the lawyers and judges. Along with the contest for political rights, therefore, went a struggle for relief laws, the denial of which embittered the farmer of the Berkshires towards his oppressors as much as unjust apportionment did his southern brother. The excesses of the paper money party were sporadic and it was without interstate organization, but the outbreaks were symptoms of a popular disregard for property rights, which, in a time of relaxed respect for authority, due to the war and the philosophy by which it was justified, was to the conservatives one of the most alarming aspects of that critical period.[76] The prevalent "excess of democracy" was one of the important factors, therefore, in shaping opinion in favor of a "more perfect union;" the movement for the constitution was the work of conservative reactionaries. "Their creed," wrote Henry Knox to Washington, speaking of the Shays rebels, "is, that the property of the United States has been protected from the confiscation of Britain by the joint exertions of *all;* and therefore ought to be the *common property of all;* and he that attempts opposition to this creed, is an enemy to equity and justice, and ought to be swept from off the face of the earth." "They are determined to annihilate all debts, public and private, and have agrarian laws, which are easily affected by the means of unfunded paper money, which shall be a tender in all cases whatever." [77] At which Washington exclaimed: "What stronger evidence can be given of the want of energy in our government, than these disorders? If there is not power in it to check them, what security has a man for life, liberty, or property? . . . . The consequences of a lax or inefficient government are too obvious to be dwelt upon. Thirteen sovereignties pulling against each other, and all tugging at the federal head, will soon bring ruin on the whole; whereas a liberal and energetic constitution, well guarded and closely watched to prevent encroachments, might restore us to that degree of respectability and consequence, to which

---

[76] See the discussion by McLaughlin, A. C., *The Confederation and the Constitution,* 138-167.

[77] Quoted by Washington in letter to Madison, Nov. 5, 1786. Ford, W. C., *Writings of George Washington,* XI, 81.

we had a fair claim and the brightest prospect of attaining." [78] Washington desired a new government, moreover, in order that the national character might be retrieved through just provisions for the public creditors.

The paths which led from the Articles to the Constitution were doubtless several. There was, indeed, the influence of those great and unselfish minds who regarded the fact that the honor and safety of all were endangered by the weakness of the union; but very potent also was the growing conviction of the ruling class that the protection of commerce, the payment of the public debt, and the enforcement of the obligation of contracts, in all of which its interests were peculiarly great, could be secured only by the establishment of a government vested with plenary power over commerce and revenue, and able, through limitations on the powers of states, to impose checks upon the license of the radicals. "I conceive," said Fisher Ames, in the light of his experience in the Massachusetts ratifying convention, "that the present Constitution was dictated by commercial necessity more than any other cause." [79] Hamilton attributed much to the influence of the holders of the public paper. "The public creditors, who consisted of various descriptions of men, a large proportion of them very meritorious and very influential," he declared after the establishment of the new government, "had had a considerable agency in promoting the adoption of the new Constitution, for this peculiar reason, among the many weighty reasons which were common to them as citizens and proprietors, that it exhibited the prospect of a government able to do justice to their claims." [80] And of the conservative class in general he adds: "There was also another class of men, and a very weighty one, who had had great share in the establishment of the Constitution, who though not personally interested in the debt, considered maxims of public credit as of the essence of good government, as intimately connected by the analogy and sympathy of principles with the security of property in general, and as forming an inseparable portion of the great system of political order." [81]

The convention which framed the Constitution was composed almost wholly of friends of the movement, chosen by legislatures

---

[78] *Ibid.*
[79] Quoted by Beard, C. A., *Economic Origins of Jeffersonian Democracy*, 7.
[80] *Ibid.*, 5-6.
[81] *Ibid.*

which represented property owners. The issue of a convention had not been before the voters in the legislative elections, and the intelligence and influence of the promoters procured the selection of delegates almost exclusively representative of the planting, mercantile, professional, and other wealthy groups of the seaboard.[82] "Not one member represented in his immediate personal economic interests the small farming or mechanic classes." [83] Naturally a body so constituted provided for a national government similar to those which their class had already set up in the states. One would not expect to find that in such a body any proposal was made to give a share in the new government to portions of the population not already enfranchised in the separate states. A few members, notably Wilson and Madison, would have extended the functions of the voters so far as to include the election of president and senators, as well as members of the lower house,[84] but the prevailing sentiment favored limitations upon the mass of voters such as were already in effect in the states. The provisions for the election of senators by state legislatures and of the president by an electoral college are familiar illustrations of the aristocratic temper of the fathers of the constitution. Even Mason, who as leader of the interior democracy had framed the Virginia bill of rights a few years before, joined in approval of these devices. He believed that "one important object in constituting the senate was to secure the rights of property," and supported a term of six years and a property qualification to give the members of the upper branch due weight.[85] "He conceived it would be as unnatural to refer the choice of a proper character for Chief Magistrate to the people, as it would, to refer a trial of colors to a blind man." [86] Some of the members considered popular choice even of the lower house as too democratic. Thus Sherman insisted that "the people should have as little to do as may be about the government immediately.

---

[82] Beard, *Economic Interpretation*, 71-72. *Cf.* the contemporary interpretation of the movement for the constitution, in letter of the French Minister Otto to Vergennes, Oct. 10, 1786: Bancroft, G., *History of the Formation of the Constitution of the United States*, II, App., 399-401; reprinted in Hart, A. B., *American History told by Contemporaries*, III, 185-187.

[83] Beard, *Economic Interpretation*, 149.

[84] Farrand, Max, *Records of the Federal Convention of 1787*, I, 68, 154; II, 56, 111.

[85] *Ibid.*, I, 428. *Cf.* Madison, 421-423.

[86] *Ibid.*, II, 31.

They want information and are constantly liable to be misled." [87]
Gerry, Charles Pinckney, and others expressed similar views.[88]

This distrust of the people was not expressed with reference to the disfranchised class, but to the farmers and other owners of small properties who belonged to the voting class. The more liberal members believed that the qualified electorate was a sufficient safeguard of the public interest,[89] but many desired to impose qualifications upon office holders as well. The convention voted in favor of the principle but was unable to agree upon a statement of the provision.[90] However, the choice of senators by state legislatures was felt to be an indirect guaranty of an upper house composed of men of wealth, which was the general desire;[91] while the adoption of the electoral system provided assurance of conservative action in the choice of the executive.[92] In providing for a

---

[87] *Ibid.*, I, 48.

[88] *Ibid.*, I, 48, 137. *Cf.* Mercer, 205, 216. Antagonism to the agrarian class appears in Pinckney's utterance: "An election of either branch by the people scattered as they are in many States, particularly in S. Carolina was totally impracticable. He differed from gentlemen who thought that a choice by the people wd. be a better guard agst. bad measures, than by the Legislatures. A majority of the people in S. Carolina were notoriously for paper money as a legal tender; the Legislature had refused to make it a legal tender. The reason was that the latter had some sense of character."

[89] *Cf.* Dickinson's objection to property qualifications for office holding: "The best defence lay in the freeholders who were to elect the Legislature. Whilst this Source should remain pure, the public interest would be safe. . . . . It seemed improper that any man of merit should be subjected to disabilities in a Republic where merit was understood to form the great title to public trust, honors & rewards." *Ibid.*, II, 123.

[90] On July 26 Mason moved "that the Committee of detail be instructed to receive a clause requiring certain qualifications of landed property & citizenship in members of the Legislature." *Ibid.*, II, 121. Mr. Pinckney seconded the motion. Mr. Pinckney and General Pinckney moved to insert the words "Judiciary & Executive so as to extend the qualifications to those departments which was agreed to nem con." *Ibid.*, II, 122. A discussion followed concerning the propriety of requiring landed property, and the word "landed" was stricken out by a vote of ten states to one. 124. Mason's motion as amended was then carried, Ayes 8, noes 3. 125. The Committee encountered difficulties (249), and in Art. VI, Sec. 2 of its report left the whole matter with Congress: "The Legislature of the United States shall have authority to establish such uniform qualifications of the members of each House, with regard to property as to the said Legislature shall seem expedient." 179. This proved unsatisfactory to the convention, but efforts to improve upon it failed, and the whole section was lost by a vote of 3 to 7. 251.

[91] *Cf., e. g.*, Dickinson, *ibid.*, I, 150; Gerry, 152; Mason, 428.

[92] Many thought that there should be specific provision to insure that judges and executive should be men of property. *Cf.* note 90, motion of the Pinckney's. Mr. Pinckney thought the president should possess an unencumbered estate of not less than one hundred thousand dollars value, and each judge not less than half as much, and moved that each official should be required to swear that he possessed such an estate as might be provided in the constitution for his office. The motion was opposed by Ellsworth because of the impropriety of fixed and uniform requirements, and by Franklin on the liberal ground that riches do not guarantee character, and that the constitution ought not to betray a great partiality to the rich. *Ibid.*, II, 246-251. Which argument was the more effective cause of the loss of the motion can only be conjectured.

"popular" lower branch of the legislature, the usual limitations on the suffrage were imposed indirectly by the provision that "the electors in each state shall have the qualifications requisite for electors of the most numerous branch of the state legislature." [93] Gouverneur Morris voiced a common opinion in the convention when he said that "property was the main object of society," [94] and it would appear that even the provision for representation in the lower house in proportion to population was in the minds of some acceptable chiefly because population seemed to be the most convenient measure of the relative wealth of states.[95] On this principle of basing apportionment upon wealth rather than people an influential minority wished to have a scheme adopted which would give the original states a permanent preponderance over the new states of the interior, after the model of the practice of the old seaboard aristocracies.[96]

As in the state constitutions, however, members were willing to grant some recognition to democratic theory, as appears in the provision for ratification of the constitution in popular conventions; that is, conventions representative of the voters. Declaring that the legislatures had no power to ratify, Mason asked: "Whither, then, must we resort?" and answered his own question by saying: "To the people, with whom all power remains that has

---

[93] Constitution, Art. I, Sec. 2. In discussing the report of the Committee of Detail, G. Morris proposed a restriction of the suffrage to freeholders. The fact that owners of other kinds of property enjoyed the franchise in some states, and regard for the prerogative of states in regulating the suffrage, defeated the proposal. *Ibid.*, II, 201-206. Mason opposed the motion on the ground that the predilection for the freehold qualification was a British tradition. "We all feel too strongly the remains of ancient prejudices, and view things too much through a British Medium. . . . . Does no other kind of property but land evidence a common interest in the proprietor?" *Ibid.*, 203. Note the tendency of the western leader to desire an American order.

[94] *Ibid.*, I, 533.

[95] *Cf.* Mason's statement *below*, 48. See the discussion of the basis of apportionment on July 12, especially statement of Wilson: "Less umbrage would perhaps be taken agst. an admission of slaves into the Rule of representation, if it should be so expressed as to make them indirectly only an ingredient in the rule, by saying that they should enter into the rule of taxation: and as representation was to be *according to taxation* [italics mine], the end would be equally attained." *Ibid.*, I, 595. This suggestion paved the way for the "three-fifths compromise;" *i. e.*, population, including three-fifths of the slaves, was accepted as the measure of the relative wealth and tax-paying ability of the states, and representation was to be allowed in the lower house in proportion to wealth and tax contributions. This was in harmony with the original proposal in the Virginia plan, Resolution 2: "The rights of suffrage in the National Legislature ought to be proportioned to the Quotas of Contribution, or to the number of free inhabitants." *Ibid.*, I, 20. With the addition of the slaves the compromise met both alternatives.

[96] See *below*, 46 *et seq.*

not been given up in the constitutions derived from them." [97] Madison also held that only ratification by the people could give the new system validity.[98] But there is no ground for the view that by "the people" any member had in mind any one except the voters; and the contention of Republican writers a few years later, based on such recognition of the sovereignty of the people as has been mentioned, that the constitution was intended to be a democratic instrument of government, was a case of the loose application to that document of terms which properly implied political doctrines very different from those which it embodied.

It may now be perceived that the opening of the constitutional era found the train well laid for political divisions coinciding in the main with the old economic and geographical divergences. The friends of the constitution were the owners of public securities, of shops and ships, of interest-bearing investments of all kinds, of plantations and farms producing crops which depended upon commerce for a market, and of personalty in slaves. They dwelt mostly near the seaboard, composed the class which had long dominated politically, and still clung to aristocratic theories of government. The vast majority of the antifederalists were small farmers, who composed the bulk of the democratic debtor class, dwelt inland, and, for both political and economic reasons, regarded the seaboard aristocrats with jealousy and distrust. The contest over the framing and adoption of the constitution was, then, an episode in the conflict between the two opposing groups the formation of which we have traced, and the effect of its adoption was to secure for the old governing class, on the scale of the nation (so long as it could control the administration of the government) much the same sort of dominance which it had so long enjoyed in the states. Of the continuity of the Federalist and Republican parties with the old divisions little need be said. That they were not identical

---

[97] *Ibid.*, II, 88. The practical problem of framing an instrument which would be likely to win the approving vote of constituent bodies in which the agrarian interest would possess considerable strength confronted the convention constantly, and tended to tone down the aristocracy of its provisions. *Cf.* the necessity of making a second effort at constitution framing in Massachusetts, largely for lack of "popular" features in the draft of 1778. *Above*, 26, *f. n* 66. The sincerity of Adams, Mason, Madison, and others, in their profession of the compact theory and belief in the sovereignty of the people is hardly to be doubted. *Cf.* the declaration of Adams: "The right of the people to establish such a government as they please, will ever be defended by me, whether they choose wisely or foolishly." Letter to Francis Dana, Aug. 16, 1776, quoted by Cushing, *Transition*, 199. But it was the work of practical statesmanship to secure the popular acceptance of instruments of government which would also embody the views of the conservatives. At this the constitution makers of the period were astonishingly successful.

[98] Farrand, *Records*, II, 92-93, 476.

in every respect is readily conceded, but the political philosophy and practical programs of the leaders of the respective parties were those of the seaboard interest on the one hand and the interior agrarian population on the other.[99]

For our purpose, sufficient insight into Hamilton's philosophy of government is given by his speech in the constitutional convention on June 18. "All communities divide themselves," he said, "into the few and the many. The first are the rich and well born, the other the mass of the people. The voice of the people has been said to be the voice of God; and however generally this maxim has been quoted and believed, it is not true in fact. The people are turbulent and changing; they seldom judge or determine right. Give therefore to the first class a distinct, permanent share in the government. They will check the unsteadiness of the second, and as they cannot receive any advantage by a change, they therefore will ever maintain good government. Can a democratic assembly who annually revolve in the mass of the people, be supposed steadily to pursue the public good? Nothing but a permanent body can check the imprudence of democracy." [100] While thus betraying his lack of confidence in the people at large, Hamilton did not advocate their exclusion from government and its monopolization by the "rich and well born." "Give all power to the many, they will oppress the few. Give all power to the few, they will oppress the many. Both, therefore, ought to have the power, that each may defend itself against the other." [101] "In his private opinion . . . . the British Government was the best in the world; and he doubted much whether anything short of it would do in America." [102] While entertaining no hope of the adoption of his ideas, he believed that a proper government should provide for a senate and executive holding during good behavior and chosen by the electoral system instead of by the voters directly. His measures spoke even more loudly than his words. As secretary of the treasury under Wash-

---

[99] Cf. Libby, *Geographical Distribution*, and Beard, *Economic Interpretation*. The degree of continuity between the parties of the constitutional period and the friends and opponents respectively of the constitution, is studied in Beard, *Origins*, with perhaps undue emphasis on the continuity. Beard also stresses the economic conflict and neglects the geographical aspects with which the present writer is especially concerned. For criticism of Beard's position see review by Libby in the *Mississippi Valley Historical Review*, III, 99. Libby minimizes the continuity. For fuller statement of Libby's view, see "A Sketch of the Early Political Parties in the United States," in *Quarterly Journal of the University of North Dakota*, II, 205-242.

[100] Farrand, *Records*, I, 299, *et seq.*

[101] *Ibid.*, I, 282-293.

[102] *Ibid.*

ington, and the leading spirit in the administration, his whole scheme of practical politics centered in his fiscal system, which favored the moneyed interests and allied the government with the financiers, merchants, manufacturers, and speculators. These were an influential portion of the party which had established the constitution, and Hamilton's creed embraced no hope of successful government apart from their active support. They were the rich and well born whose influence was essential to check the unsteadiness of the mass of the people. Under his guiding genius, therefore, the Federalist party became the party of the great majority of the old ruling class, especially in the North.

Hamilton was eminently a practical rather than a philosophical statesman. It was John Adams, his chief rival within the party, who essayed the role of political philosopher. With wearisome refinement of detail he worked out the theory which the Federalist leaders agreed, with minor variations, in holding. Society invariably divides into classes, of which the rich, well born, and able constitute a natural aristocracy. As the classes invariably contend for dominance, the desideratum in government is such a representation of classes as will establish a balance. As the aristocratic element represents stability and the other classes the more turbulent factor, the poor as well as the rich would be best off under a system by which substantial control remained in the hands of the propertied few. The benefits of order and security would then be diffused throughout the whole. "Give the property and liberty of the rich a security in the senate, against the encroachments of the poor in a popular assembly," and erect an independent executive with a long term to mediate between them, with an independent judiciary, removable only by joint consent of senate and assembly, to check both legislature and executive. The nearest approach to the ideal government Adams finds, like Hamilton, in the English constitution. "The English constitution is the only one which has considered and provided for all cases that are known to have generally, indeed to have always, happened in the progress of every nation; it is, therefore, the only scientific government." The Federalists showed small faith that America would succeed in improving greatly upon European models.[103]

---

[103] See Beard, *Economic Origins*, Chap. 11, for a sketch of the political economy of John Adams. A fuller study of Adams's opinions is made in Walsh, C. M., *The Political Science of John Adams*. For views of other Federalists and discussion of their debt to the thought of Adams, especially in the period of the Federal Convention, see *ibid.*, 304 *et seq.*; also 285 *et. seq.*

The unification of the Federalist party during the discussion of Hamilton's financial system precipitated a like movement among those who opposed his measures. These found their prophet and organizer in Jefferson. If Hamilton incarnated the spirit of that coastal order which derived its political creed from the Old World, Jefferson personified no less the spirit of that New World which contemned European tradition and had faith in an American order. Born himself on the Virginian frontier, his philosophy of the state was permanently influenced by his boyhood environment. The tendencies thus early imparted to his thought must have coincided remarkably with the impressions received from his later studies in political philosophy, and his residence in France during the early

---

and *f. n.* Contrasting the views of Adams and Hamilton Beard remarks: "The former feared the rich almost as much as the poor, believing that they were as prone to use the government in spoliation as the latter. Hamilton does not seem to have regarded the rich as a danger to the state. On the contrary, he viewed the rich and well born as the safest depositaries of public power, although he advocated the admission of the propertyless to a speaking voice in the government. Adams did not view the conflict as a struggle between personalty and real property owners but between the rich and poor, although in his classification most of the farmers and petty tradesmen were placed in the latter category. Hamilton was essentially the spokesman of the commercial and financial classes. Contrary to contemporary misrepresentation, it would appear that Adams' property was in land rather than stock and bonds. In fact his biographer says that 'in Mr. Adams's vocabulary, the word property meant land. He had no confidence in the permanence of anything else.' Such a man was not temperamentally fitted to become the leader of a party founded principally upon capitalistic as opposed to landed interests. Hamilton believed that his fiscal and commercial policy was advantageous to the beneficiaries and the nation at large; he wanted positive action in support of those policies, not 'mediation' between contending factions. Under the circumstances it is not surprising that Adams had about as much sympathy for Jefferson as for Hamilton." *Economic Origins*, 318-319. In reducing the principle of cleavage between Federalists and Republicans to the struggle between personalty and real property, Beard makes the issue too simple, and overlooks the geographical distribution of interests. Wealth in personalty was practically confined to the coast, hence the secret of the adhesion of one influential group to the Federalist party. But the party included the landed aristocracy in New England throughout its existence, because their interests and ideals were those of the coastal order,

Adams held liberal views in the Revolutionary period (see *above*, 26, *f. n.* 66) which yielded as time passed to those opinions which caused him to be regarded as an aristocrat. The equality of man, the social compact, and the consent of the governed were dogmas which he held in common with other "fathers of the Revolution." His rather humble origin places him fairly among the popular leaders of that era. His belief in restricting the suffrage to freeholders, joined with his advocacy of measures to facilitate subdivision of land ownership, remind us of Jefferson (*below*, 38). At the same time he aspired, before the Revolution, to become one of the influential class which "had succeeded in bringing into existence distant imitations of the English type of society and government" (Walsh, 228); and while he insisted upon the right of the people to adopt such government as they chose, whether good or bad, in the formation of state constitutions he "hoped our people would be wise enough . . . . to preserve the English constitution in its spirit and substance, so far as the circumstances of this country required and would admit," omitting only the hereditary features which had not existed in America and would not be tolerated. (*Ibid.*) Besides a property qualification for both electors and elected, "higher for the latter, and . . . . rising in gradation with the importance of the office," he desired a religious test confirming certain offices to Christians. (*Ibid.*, 11). Although his views became distinctly less liberal from about 1786 (*ibid.*, 258-259, 281 *et seq.*), his later opinions appear to have been the natural development of his early ones.

days of the Revolution brought him into contact with theories which confirmed his own conclusions concerning the conditions which conduce to human welfare and happiness. Conclusions which Rousseau and his compeers arrived at by dint of abstract reasoning, Jefferson held as naturally as if he had breathed them in with the air of the Virginia piedmont. It was fitting that the man who formulated the philosophical justification of revolution which the western part of the British world hurled against the eastern in the Declaration of Independence, should later become the leader of the inland farming democracy in its contest with the American heirs of British tradition. Jefferson's political creed was, indeed, the reflex of his philosophy of society. He believed that a simple agricultural economy afforded the best basis for a free state, since it fostered individualism and equality. Such a society America had done much to produce, and made possible in future, with its "immensity of land courting the industry of the husbandman." A complex industrialism with workshops and wage labor he wished to discourage, as tending to destroy self-reliance and equality of condition among men, and to introduce the class antagonisms which had led to the oppression and debasement of the people in the Old World. Commerce he admitted in his order as the means of exchanging the surplus of an agricultural country for the manufactures of the overcrowded countries of Europe, and hence as a means of keeping manufactures with their corrupting influences away from our shores. The ships of commerce, with their protecting navies, he preferred to let the European nations supply. In such an Arcadian society the functions of government would be at a minimum, the need of taxation slight, and individual freedom and initiative at their best.[104]

The relation of this conception of society and government to Jefferson's early surroundings and to the life of the class whose

---

[104] "Those who labor in the earth are the chosen people of God, if ever He had a chosen people, whose breasts He has made His peculiar deposit for substantial and genuine virtue. It is the focus in which he keeps alive that sacred fire, which otherwise might escape from the face of the earth. Corruption of morals in the mass of cultivators is a phenomenon of which no age nor nation has furnished an example. It is the mark set on those, who, not looking up to heaven, to their own soil and industry, as does the husbandman, for their subsistence, depend for it on casualties and caprice of customers. Dependence begets subservience and venality, suffocates the germ of virtue, and prepares fit tools for the designs of ambition. This, the natural progress and consequence of the arts, has sometimes perhaps been retarded by accidental circumstances; but, generally speaking, the proportion which the aggregate of other classes of citizens bears in any State to that of its husbandmen, is the proportion of its unsound to its healthy parts, and is a good enough barometer whereby to measure its degree of corruption. While we have land to labor, then, let us never wish to see our citizens occupied

spokesman he was, is obvious. Very appropriately he has been called a "backwoods statesman," for this set of theories, born of frontier conditions, affected his policies throughout his public career.

While Jefferson thus identified the cause of good government with the dominance of the agricultural class, as opposed to the capitalistic interests which formed the nucleus of the Federalist party, his democracy was not without limitations. He declared in 1800 that he had always been in favor of a "general suffrage." [105] It does not appear that he was ready to insist upon manhood suffrage, however, for in the draft constitution prepared for the use of friends in the Virginia convention of 1776 he provided a small freehold qualification for the exercise of the franchise.[106] If the whole of his plan be considered, however, this qualification becomes almost equivalent to manhood suffrage, for, in harmony with his faith in agriculture as the best foundation for a state, he would have had estates granted to all males, from the public lands.[107] His theory of democracy did not embrace all orders of society, for he could not overcome his distrust of the working class of cities. His hope of an American order was bound up with the continued preponderance of agriculture, for he believed that "when we get piled upon one another in large cities, as in Europe, we shall become corrupt as in Europe, and go to eating one another as they do there." [108] Thus he appears not so much as the apostle of a complete democracy, as he does the champion of an Arcadian form of society as the one best calculated to promote the happiness of mankind. Hence in contrast with Hamilton his program was

---

at a workbench, or twirling a distaff. Carpenters, masons, smiths, are wanting in husbandry; but, for the general operations of manufacture, let our workshops remain in Europe. It is better to carry provisions and materials to workmen there, than to bring them to the provisions and materials, and with them their manners and principles. The loss by the transportation of commodities across the Atlantic will be made up in happiness and permanence of government. The mobs of great cities add just so much to the support of pure government as sores do to the strength of the human body." "Notes on Virginia," written in the winter of 1781-1782. Ford, *Writings of Jefferson*, III, 268-269.

To this description of the ideal economic basis for a free state may be added the statement of the ideal of government given in the inaugural address of 1801: "A wise and frugal government, which shall restrain men from injuring one another, shall leave them otherwise free to regulate their own pursuits of industry and improvement, and shall not take from the mouth of labour the bread it has earned." *Ibid.*, VIII, 4. See Beard's summary of Jefferson's views, in *Origins*, Chap. 14.

[105] *Ibid.*, 461.

[106] See *above*, 25, *f. n.* 59, and text of draft in Ford, *Writings*, II, 7.

[107] See discussion in Beard, *Economic Origins*, 457-463, and Anderson, in *Amer. Hist. Rev.*, XXI, 750-754.

[108] Letter to Madison, Dec. 20, 1787. Ford, *Writings of Jefferson*, IV, 479.

largely negative, or *laissez faire*, and he appears in national politics as the opponent of changes conceived in the interest of the capitalist class; the preserver of the social and political *status quo*, rather than as the leader of further democratic advance.[109]

While it is true that the Federalist and Republican parties separated in the main along the old lines of cleavage, one notable exception must be mentioned. As a class the planters had constituted one of the groups of the dominant order which had joined in the movement for the formation of a stronger government. Within a few years, however, most of them had accepted the leadership of Jefferson. The causes of this defection lie partly in specific issues. Many planters, especially in Virginia, stood in somewhat the same relation to their British creditors that the interior farmers did to the merchants of the coast region. Desire to escape from their obligations has been charged as one cause of their Whiggism during the Revolution, and fear that the claims would be enforced by the federal courts may have been a factor in the opposition which some of them showed to the new constitution.[110] Jay's treaty, with its provision for a joint commission to adjudicate the debts due British merchants, was a further cause of alienation.[111] Hamilton's assumption scheme laid a burden upon Virginia, which had paid its debt, for the benefit chiefly of northern security holders;[112] and in most of the planting states lack of fluid capital deprived even the wealthy of opportunity of profit

[109] This is true during the Federalist regime. His program of social reform fell within his conception of the sphere of state rather than federal action. His program of federal action became more positive when he reached the presidency.

Cf. Madison's reasons for joining the opposition to Hamilton which developed into the Republican party: "I deserted Colonel Hamilton, or, rather, he deserted me; in a word, the divergence between us took place from his wishing to . . . . adminster the government into what he thought it ought to be; while on my part, I endeavored to make it conform to the constitution as understood by the convention that produced and recommended it, and particularly by the state conventions that adopted it." Rives, *Life of Madison*, III, 177, quoted by Gordy, J. P., *Political History of the United States*, I, 140. In this desire of Madison, shared by Jefferson, to hold the constitution to their conception of its original meaning we have the origin of the Republican doctrine of strict construction.

[110] Oliver Wolcott, quoted by Beard, *Economic Origins*, 297.

[111] *Ibid.*, Chap. 10.

[112] The Republican view of the tendencies of Hamilton's measures can be summed up by quoting a single sentence: "In an agricultural country like this . . . . to erect, and concentrate and perpetuate a large monied interest, is a measure which your memorialists apprehend must in the course of human events produce one or other of two evils, the prostration of agriculture at the feet of commerce, or a change in the present form of federal government, fatal to the existence of American liberty." Resolutions of the General Assembly of Virginia on the Assumption Act of 1790, reprinted in Ames, H. V., *State Documents on Federal Relations*, 5. *Cf.* discussion of Hamilton's fiscal system in Beard, *Economic Origins*, Chaps. 5, 6.

through subscribing for stock of the United States Bank.[113] For reasons of this nature, although many planters remained true to the Federalist party as late as the election of 1800, there was a pretty steady drift to the ranks of the opposition.[114] Through community of opposition to measures which advanced the interest of a class of fluid capital owners, located chiefly in the northern states, the two classes of agriculturists which had been so long in conflict in the southern states, came together in the national party known as Jeffersonian Republicanism. It must be recognized, too, that the aristocratic faction, through the privileged position which it enjoyed in the states, was able to dominate this alliance, so that southern republicanism became a party consisting largely of small farmers led and represented by planters. This union was brought about the more readily because of the absence of a positive democratic propagandism on Jefferson's part, which might have alienated the planters.

---

[113] *Ibid.*, 153.

[114] Phillips, "The South Carolina Federalists," in *Amer. Hist. Rev.*, XIV, 529-543; 731-743, gives some insight into the motives of the planters who adhered to the Federalist party during the nineties, as well as the motives of those who espoused Republicanism.

CHAPTER II

THE TRIUMPH OF THE PRINCIPLE OF WESTERN EQUALITY

In the foregoing chapter an attempt has been made to show that the first parties in our national history grew out of antagonisms in the region between the Alleghany Mountains and the Atlantic Ocean, and that these antagonisms were to a considerable degree geographical, the more aristocratic group occupying the coast regions and the more democratic the interior. It has also been shown that in the conflict of the two the coastal order held its ground well. Indeed, it may be questioned whether, on the original arena, the popular cause would ever have triumphed. The population of the hinterland could hardly have gained sufficient weight to break down the strongly entrenched peripheral social order. In the southern states, in fact, throughout the slavery era, the plantation system displayed the power to advance steadily at the expense of the area of small farms.[1] The back settlements could not have saved their social order by seceding and establishing independent communities, for want of an outlet save through the Atlantic ports. If there had been no other way of escape, it seems that nothing short of revolution could have prevented the independent farmers from sinking in time to the level of European peasants. The acquiescence in aristocratic leadership of the Republican party was ominous. The division of national parties would probably have been sharper along lines of latitude and less marked along those of longitude. Such was the tendency shown when planters and small farmers united in the Republican party. The fate of the northern masses is not so easily conjectured. They showed less tendency to accept the leadership of their former antagonists, and might have maintained themselves as an important political group or party.

But the fate of the farming democracy was not to be determined east of the Alleghanies. The geographical basis of parties

---

[1] *Cf.* advance of plantation system to piedmont in Virginia and Carolinas: Ambler, *Sectionalism*, 113; Schaper, "Sectionalism," 389 *et seq.* See also Phillips, in *Amer. Hist. Rev.*, XI, 798-816, and Smedes, *Memorials of a Southern Planter*, extracts in Callender, *Selections from the Economic History of the United States*, 641 *et seq.*

was to be greatly changed during the first generation under the constitution, with proportionally significant changes in their spirit and purposes. When Jay and Adams triumphed over the unfriendly diplomacy of Vergennes in the peace negotiations of 1782 and secured the Mississippi boundary for the United States, they unwittingly prepared the overthrow of the political order to which they were attached. A few years later the national domain was doubled by the acquisition of the vast province of Louisiana. Into the wilderness beyond the mountains the discontented poured again, when conditions became unsatisfactory in their former homes, just as the pioneers had come to the "Old West" east of the mountains. Here a type of society similar to that which first developed at the eastern base of the Alleghanies struck its roots more deeply than ever into the soil, and with its widened geographical basis in time made its influence dominant in the nation.

This result could not have followed had not liberal principles won one notable victory on the stage of action east of the mountains. The oppressed might, indeed, have found freedom in the western wilderness even under a foreign flag. Or, under pressure of injustice, they might here have established independent communities, as they could not do on the Atlantic slopes. But the determination that the western communities should in due time be formed into states which should be admitted into the Union on terms of equality with the original states, decided in advance that western interests and western ideals should one day play the chief part in shaping the policies of the government.

The origin of the idea of new settlements with liberal political rights goes well back into the colonial period. The probable necessity of new governments in the West was beginning to be perceived as early as the outbreak of the French and Indian War, the expected success in which would give the English control of the Ohio Valley.[2] A provision, for which Franklin was chiefly responsible, was therefore made in the Albany Plan of Intercolonial Union, vesting in the general government the power to make new settlements and to "make laws for regulating and governing" them "till the crown shall think fit to form them into particular governments."[3] Franklin's reflections upon the matter of new colonies led him to conclude that liberal government would be one of the essential in-

---

[2] Alden, G. H., *New Governments West of the Alleghanies before 1780.*
[3] Bigelow, *Works of Franklin*, II, 368.

ducements to settlers to incur the hazards of the wilderness; in his own words, they would have to be allowed "extraordinary privileges and liberties." [4] Indication of the nature of these extraordinary privileges is found in his suggestion that they should include the right of the settlers to choose their own governor, which suggests colonies of the self-governing, or corporate, type, rather than the royal type to which the crown was attempting in the eighteenth century to reduce all of the colonial establishments. [5]

The twenty years following the Albany Congress were filled with projects for new colonies, and the discussions of the period gave opportunity for the formation of a public opinion as to the most suitable type of government for transmontane settlements. [6] The British ministry also grappled with the problem, and Lord Hillsborough, the president of the Board of Trade, contended (despite the purpose implied in the Proclamation of 1763) that new colonies in the interior were undesirable because they would be too remote to be of benefit to British trade, or to be held in due subordination to British authority. [7] Hillsborough's view thus virtually recognized that the western pioneers would inevitably govern themselves in their own way, whatever forms might be imposed upon them. Franklin as agent for the Vandalia Company, which was seeking a grant in the West Virginia region, urged the necessity of the new government, declaring that the tract asked for already contained a population of 30,000 souls, who could not be governed effectively from Williamsburg. [8] This argument, based on the impracticability of remote governments, stressed one of the grievances of the settlers which we have seen was the cause of complaints and petitions from the back country of Pennsylvania and the Carolinas in this same period; [9] and, with other considerations urged by Franklin, won the Privy Council's approval of the Vandalia grant, with a scheme of government similar to those of the existing royal colonies. [10] The outbreak of the Revolution, however, prevented the consummation of the grant, and transferred the whole problem of new western governments to Congress. The question next became

---

[4] *Ibid.*, II, 474.
[5] *Ibid.*
[6] *Ibid.*, 12-48. Carter, C. E., *Great Britain and the Illinois Country*, 103-144..
[7] Bigelow, *Works of Franklin*, V, 4.
[8] *Ibid.*, V, 73, 74.
[9] *Above*, 21, *f. n.* 45.
[10] Alden, *New Governments*, 28-35.

involved in the dispute over the ownership of the western lands. As soon as it became evident that the struggle with the mother country would lead to a declaration of independence, the Virginia legislature reasserted the claim, long dormant, to all territory east of the Mississippi granted to that colony by the royal charter of 1609.[11] Other colonies revived similar claims. The validity of these claims was challenged by the small states, under the leadership of Maryland. The resolutions adopted by the legislature of the latter, in October, 1776, give probably the first clear and authoritative expression of what must have become, by that time, under the influence of experience and the revolutionary philosophy, a common opinion as to the proper policy to be pursued in providing for the government of settlements beyond the mountains—"such lands ought . . . . to be parcelled out at proper times into convenient, free and independent governments." [12]

This was the beginning of the struggle which ended in the land cessions of Virginia and the other "claimant" states. The refusal of Maryland to ratify the Articles of Confederation unless cessions were promised,[13] the desire of land companies for confirmation by Congress of grants which the British Government had been ready to make,[14] the necessity of concessions to secure the alliance of Spain,[15] the reluctance of the landless states to include a demand for the West in the terms of peace unless the territory were to be common property,[16] and the desire of the western settlers themselves for distinct governments,[17] are the more important factors in the complicated history of the cessions.

In order to procure the adoption of the Articles, which remained ineffective so long as a single state ratification was lacking, Congress repeatedly appealed to the claimant states for concessions. In the most notable of these appeals Congress committed itself to the policy of erecting new states in the western territory

---

[11] Hening, *Statutes*, IX, 118, reprinted in *Amer. Hist. Leaflet*, No. 22, 2.

[12] *Ibid.*, 3.

[13] Adams, H. B., "Maryland's Influence on the Land Cessions," in Johns Hopkins University *Studies*, III, 7-54.

[14] *Journals of the Continental Congress* (L. C. edn.), XV, 1063-1064.

[15] Phillips, P. C., *The West in the Diplomacy of the American Revolution*, 177-188.

[16] *Ibid.*

[17] Turner, "Western State Making in the Revolutionary Era," in *Amer. Hist. Rev.*, I, 70-87; 251-269.

with all the rights of the original states.[18] Virginia made this provision one of the conditions of her cession, and thus a guarantee of equal rights for the new West became embodied in a compact safeguarded by the obligations of good faith.[19]

This recognition of the rights of the West is the chief fruit of the democratic doctrines of the Revolutionary era. Much as the liberal ideals of the Puritans, though failing of realization in the mother country, found their opportunity in the northern colonies, the democracy of the Old West, though suppressed in the original states, because of the dominant position of the aristocratic class, was to find a freer stage in the communities beyond the mountains. The conservatives, moreover, who jealously guarded their favored status in the old states notwithstanding the implications of the revolutionary philosophy, were readier to give it free reign in the proposed new jurisdictions. The turbulence and discontent of the western portions of the old states lent practical force to the theoretical philosophy, and showed the impossibility of imposing unwelcome restraints upon peoples still more remote. The memorials of the inhabitants of the settlements in western Virginia (West Virginia and Kentucky) and North Carolina (Tennessee) spoke eloquently if uncouthly of the westerners' belief in their right of establishing governments to suit themselves.[20] But one conclusion was possible: the West would be either autonomous or independent.

Nevertheless the acts of cession did not place the status of the states-to-be beyond further controversy. The growth of the West was contemplated with apprehension in some quarters. Timothy Pickering among others opposed the plans to extinguish the Indian title to lands west of the Miami River, in 1785, on the ground that they would be occupied by "lawless emigrants." [21] Both North and South regarded with doubt the effect which the rise of new states might have upon the balance of political power, and this apprehension was one reason for reducing the number of states pro-

---

[18] "*Resolved*, That the . . . . lands . . . . shall . . . . be settled and formed into distinct republican states, which shall become members of the federal union, and have the same rights of sovereignty, freedom and independence, as the other states . . . . " *Am. Hist. Leaflet*, No. 22, 8. *Journals of Cont. Cong.*, XVIII, 915.

[19] *Am. Hist. Leaflet*, No. 22, 13.

[20] Turner, "Western State Making;" Roosevelt, *Winning of the West*, II, 398-399; Alden, "The State of Franklin," in *Amer. Hist. Rev.*, VIII, 271-289.

[21] Winsor, J., *The Westward Movement*. 270.

vided for in the Ordinance of 1784.[22] While the committee of Congress was drafting the Ordinance of 1785 for the sale of the ceded lands, certain eastern gentlemen showed uneasiness as to "the consequences which may result from the new states taking their position in the Confederacy," apparently wishing "that this event may be delayed as long as possible." [23] The feeling of the western people towards the East was no more cordial. Neglected by the impotent Confederation Congress, and both bullied and cajoled by the agents of Spain and Britain, the separation of the West from the Union seemed inevitable. The clash of its interests with those of the northern seaboard was revealed in the willingness of the latter to sacrifice the navigation of the Mississippi for the promotion of its own commercial relations with Spain, and many westerners were ready to risk the adventure of independence.[24] Unprincipled though he was, Wilkinson showed sagacity when he declared: "The Atlantic states of America must sink as the western settlements rise. Nature has interposed obstacles and established barriers between these regions which forbid their connection on principles of reciprocal interests. . . . . These local causes, irresistible in their nature, must produce a secession of the western settlements from the Atlantic states . . . ." [25]

The constitutional convention with its reactionary temper brought the contest against the equality of the new states to a head. The stress which was laid upon property interests as the main reason for political society raised a presumption against the equal rights of the poor western communities as members of the Union, which found vigorous expression during the debate on the basis of representation in the lower house.[26] Gouverneur Morris alluded to the method by which the eastern part of his state (Pennsylvania) had kept power out of the hands of the western portion, and advocated the adoption of a similar plan on a national scale. "The lower part of the State had ye. power in the first instance. They kept it in yr. own hands, and the country was ye. better for

---

[22] Barrett, J. A., *Evolution of the Ordinance of 1787*, 34, *f. n.* 3, 39, 40, and *f. n.* 2.

[23] William Grayson to Washington, April 15, 1785, quoted by Bancroft, *Hist. of the Const.*, I, 425. Grayson was a member of the committee. Rufus King was the Massachusetts member and may be the subject of the allusion, in view of the sentiments expressed by him in the constitutional convention. See *below*, 47.

[24] Roosevelt, *Winning of the West*, III, 89-202.

[25] Quoted by Turner, "The Diplomatic Contest for the Mississippi Valley," in *Atlantic Monthly*, XCIII, 679.

[26] Farrand, Max, "The Compromises of the Constitution," in *Amer. Hist. Rev.*, IX, 479 *et seq.*

it." [27] "The Busy haunts of men not the remote wilderness, was the proper School of political Talents. If the Western people get the power into their hands they will ruin the Atlantic interests. The Back members are always most averse to the best measures." [28] "Property was the main object of Society. . . . . He thought the rule of representation ought to be so fixed as to secure to the Atlantic States a prevalence in the National Councils. The new States will know less of the public interest than these, will have an interest in many respects different, in particular will be little scrupulous of involving the Community in wars the burdens & operations of which would fall chiefly on the maritime States. Provision ought therefore to be made to prevent the maritime States from being hereafter outvoted by them. He thought this might be easily done by irrevocably fixing the number of representatives which the Atlantic States should respectively have, and the number which each new State will have." [29] In words which echo the sectional conflict in South Carolina, Rutledge maintained that "Property was certainly the principal object of society. If numbers should be made the rule of representation, the Atlantic States would be subjected to the western." [30] The conservatism of Massachusetts spoke through King, Gorham, and Gerry. The first held that the "number of inhabitants was not the proper index of ability & wealth; that property was the primary object of Society; and that in fixing a ratio this ought not to be excluded from the estimate. . . . . [In the West] 10 new votes may be added without a greater addition of inhabitants than are represented by the single vote of Pena." [31] Gorham, supporting the report from his committee of a plan for representation in the first congress, suggested that "The Atlantic States, having Government in their own hands, may take care of their own interests, by dealing out the right of representation in safe proportions to the Western States." [32] Gerry soon afterwards moved that the representation of the new states should never exceed that of the old, and King seconded the motion. [33] Butler "con-

---

[27] Farrand, *Records*, I, 583.
[28] *Ibid.*
[29] *Ibid.*, I, 533-534.
[30] *Ibid.*, I, 534.
[31] *Ibid.*, I, 541. The Ordinance of 1784, not yet superseded by that of 1787, provided for the admission of each western state as soon as its population equalled that of the least populous of the original states, while the Articles of Confederation gave each state one vote.
[32] *Ibid.*, I, 560.
[33] *Ibid.*, II, 3.

curred with those who thought some balance was necessary between the old and the new States. He contended strenuously that property was the only just measure of representation." [34] While Williamson thought that it would be necessary to return to the rule of numbers in apportioning representation, he believed that the "western States stood on a different footing" until their property should be rated as high as that of the Atlantic states.[35] Madison and Mason, whose political careers in Virginia had stamped them as moderate leaders of the western section, although advocates of conservative provisions in the federal instrument of government, proved true to the cause of the West in this contest over equal rights. The former, although generally in accord with Morris in the convention, upbraided him for his inconsistency in the matter of representation. "At the same time that he recommended . . . . implicit confidence to the Southern States in the Northern majority, he was still more zealous in exhorting all to a jealousy of a western majority." "It must be imagined that he determined . . . . character . . . . by the . . . . compass." [36] Mason's remarks showed that he comprehended that the issue was beyond the power of the convention to settle by a constitutional provision. "If the Western States are to be admitted into the Union, as they arise, they must . . . . be treated as equals, and subjected to no degrading discriminations. They will have the same pride, and other passions, which we have; and will either not unite with, or will speedily revolt from, the Union, if they are not in all respects placed on an equal footing with their brethren. . . . . He did not know but that, in time, they would be both more numerous and more wealthy, than their Atlantic brethren. . . . . Numbers of inhabitants, though not always a precise standard of wealth, was sufficiently so for every substantial purpose." [37] More open in avowal of the right of the majority to rule, and even more convincing in logic, was the argument of Wilson: "The majority of the people, wherever found, ought in

---

[34] *Ibid.*, I, 542.

[35] *Ibid.*, I, 560.

[36] *Ibid.*, I, 584. "The case of Pena. had been mentioned where it was admitted that those who were possessed of the power in the original settlement, never admitted the new settlemnts. to a due share of it. England was a still more striking example. The power there had long been in the hands of the boroughs, of the minority; who had opposed & defeated every reform which had been attempted. Virga. was in a lesser degree another example. With regard to the Western States, he was clear & firm in opinion that no unfavorable distinctions were admissable either in point of justice or policy." Madison, *ibid.*

[37] *Ibid.*, I, 578-579.

all questions, to govern the minority. If the interior country should acquire this majority, it will not only have the right, but will avail itself of it, whether we will or no. This jealousy misled the policy of Great Britain with regard to America. . . . . Like consequences will result on the part of the interior settlements, if like jealousy and policy be pursued on ours. . . . . He could not agree that property was the sole or primary object of government and society. The cultivation and improvement of the human mind was the most noble object." [38]

There is no way of determining whether the real inclination of the majority in the convention was more toward the views of Morris or of Wilson. It is quite conceivable that a conviction that the West could not be kept in permanent subordination outweighed the desires of members. At any rate, Gerry's motion was rejected by a vote of four states to five.[39] But the matter was not yet disposed of. The Committee of Detail, governed, one may suppose, partly by the vote on Gerry's motion, and perhaps even more by knowledge of the pledge of Congress made in 1780 and the terms of the Virginia cession, reported a clause providing for the admission of new states on terms of equality with the original states.[40] The opponents of equality were not yet beaten, however, and secured the adoption of a substitute provision *permitting* Congress to admit new states, and omitting the phrase concerning equality. The acceptance of the substitute may indicate considerable sympathy with the views of Morris and his group.[41] He, at any rate, seems to have hoped that the phraseology adopted would leave a doubt as to the right of new states to equal rank in the Union, and so enable Congress, when admitting new members, to impose terms in behalf of the vested interests of the original states.[42] Contemporaneously with the deliberations of the conven-

[38] *Ibid.*, I, 605.

[39] *Ibid.*, II, 3.   *Cf.* Sherman on Gerry's motion: "We are providing for our posterity . . . . who would be as likely to be citizens of new Western States, as of the old States. On this consideration alone, we ought to make no such discrimination." To which Gerry replied: "There was a rage for emigration from the Eastern States to the Western Country and he did not wish those remaining behind to be at the mercy of the Emigrants. Besides foreigners are resorting to that Country, and it is uncertain what turn things may take there." *Ibid.*

[40] *Ibid.*, II, 188.

[41] *Ibid.*, II, 454-455. The motion to substitute was made by Morris, and the portion referred to was passed *nem. con.*

[42] In 1803 Morris declared his belief that Congress might acquire territory to be held in permanent dependence, but could not admit new states from such territory. "In wording the third section of the fourth article," he says, "I went as far as circumstances would

tion, however, the Confederation Congress was framing the Ordinance of 1787, in which was renewed the pledge of ultimate statehood on equal terms with the old states, for the divisions of the Northwest Territory. One of the early acts of Congress after the adoption of the constitution was the repassage of this ordinance, and almost at the same time the final cession of North Carolina bound Congress to a similar policy in dealing with the Tennessee area. Thus the cause of western liberty gained an impetus which boded ill for any Atlantic groups which might oppose expansion or whose interests should conflict with those of the new West in the day of its power.

---

permit to establish the exclusion." Sparks, J., *Life of Gouverneur Morris*, III, 192. It is not clear that he believed in a similar power over states erected within the original territory of the Union.

CHAPTER III

THE DECLINE OF FEDERALISM

The perpetuation in the Federalist party of many of the old views and policies of the coastal class foredoomed it to destruction through the growth of the West, which meant the growth of the agrarian interest and of the belief in the political equality of men. Federalism proved to be almost non-expansive, the new settlements being uncongenial soil for much that the party represented, and it became consciously opposed to western development. This opposition was foreshadowed, as our study should already have made clear, even before the elements of Federalism coalesced into a party. It was men who later on were members of that party who showed apprehension of the consequences of admitting new states, when that question was discussed in the Confederation congress and in the constitutional convention.[1] The leaders of Federalism were discerning men, and suffered from no illusions concerning the effects of the growth of the West. The character of the transmontane settlements when the constitution went into effect was well calculated to arouse their apprehensions, for the Kentucky and Tennessee frontiersmen came chiefly from that stock which had so long challenged the claims of the tidewater section, and had given birth to the American ideal of democracy. During the days when parties were forming on a national scale, the West tended naturally towards Republicanism. It cast, indeed, a few votes in favor of the constitution, but the test of Federalist policy soon proved the real affinity of the pseudo-federalism of Kentucky and Tennessee to be the party of Jefferson. The West found much more to condemn than to praise in the measures of the new government. Hamilton's financial system was generally disliked and the whisky tax was peculiarly odious. Even in those matters which were designed to promote western interests the policy of the gov-

---

[1] See *above*, 46-49. All of the men quoted as opposing the equality of the western states acted with the Federalist party during all or part of the last decade of the century. *Cf.* Beard, *Economic Origins*, Chap. 2. The views of Morris and his supporters were the natural views of the old seaboard governing class both North and South, but the union of planters and farmers in the Republican party in the South caused Federalism to stand out more and more as the "eastern" party.

Framingham State College
Framingham, Massachusetts

ernment did not conciliate. The ineffectiveness of the early efforts to pacify the Indians and to secure the navigation of the Mississippi and the surrender of the northwest posts persuaded the people that the federal government was indifferent to their interests.[2] South of the Ohio Federalism was never a force to be seriously reckoned with; the rare references to adherents of the party prove that it was almost non-existent, and as time passed it lost rather than gained in strength. The treaties of 1795 were made the text of an exhortation of the region by Washington in his farewell address, but whatever favorable disposition may have been excited thus was more than counterbalanced soon after by the passage of the Alien and Sedition Acts.[3] The Kentucky Resolutions of 1798 may be accepted as the public confirmation of the people of the Southwest in the Republican creed.[4]

----

[2] The feeling of the inhabitants of Kentucky on these matters is well described in Mc-Elroy, R. M., *Kentucky in the Nation's History*, Chap. 7.

[3] "The inhabitants of our western country have lately had a useful lesson on this head; they have seen, in the negotiation by the executive, and in the unanimous ratification by the Senate, of the treaty with Spain, and in the universal satisfaction at that event, throughout the United States, a decisive proof how unfounded were the suspicions propagated among them of a policy in the general government and in the Atlantic States unfriendly to their interests in regard to the Mississippi; they have been witnesses to the formation of two treaties, that with Great Britain, and that with Spain, which secure to them everything they could desire, in respect to our foreign relations, towards confirming their prosperity."—Richardson, J. D., *A Compilation of the Messages and Papers of the Presidents*, I, 217. The reference to the British treaty was unfortunate, as the people of the West did not consider it favorable to them. See next *note*.

[4] There seem to have been a few admirers of Hamilton's policies in Tennessee in the early nineties, and Genet's partisans, by their excesses, produced a mild reaction in Kentucky favorable to the administration. Phelan, J., *Tennessee*, 241-242; Shaler, N., *Kentucky*, 129. Senator Marshall, of Kentucky, was one of the leaders of the Federalist group. He saw advantages for the West in Jay's treaty and voted for its ratification, contributing, moreover, a series of essays in vindication of the treaty to the *Kentucky Gazette* during the winter of 1795-1796. But the vast preponderance of opinion remained unfavorable. McElroy, *Kentucky*, *loc. cit.* There were even two Federalists in the Lexington region who dared publicly to defend the policy of the administration in passing the Alien and Sedition Acts. The local aspects of this controversy are discussed, *ibid.*, Chap. 8. As late as the period of the Burr Conspiracy, "a Mr. Wood, of Richmond, Virginia, was invited to Kentucky and made editor of *The Western World*, a newspaper devoted to the interests of Federalism."—Ambler, C. H., *Thomas Ritchie*, 38.

Naturally, some of the early western officials holding their positions by presidential appointment were of the Federalist faith; *e. g.*, Governor Blount, of the Territory South of the Ohio River, and St. Clair, governor of the Northwest Territory, as well as minor officials. See *below*, 55, *f. n.* 15.

Michaux, returning from Tennessee in 1796, encountered one Mansko who may have been a Federalist, as he was "a declared enemy of the French because, he said, they have killed their King." Michaux would not accept his offer of supper, and was mortified because the inclement weather obliged him to spend the night in the house. "But I slept on my Deer skin and paid for the Maize he supplied me with." In 1802 Michaux declares concerning John Adams: "His memory is not held in great veneration in Upper Carolina and the Western States . . . . where nobody durst confess himself publicly attached to the federal party."—Michaux, F. A., *Travels to the Westward* (in Thwaites, R. G., *Early Western Travels*, III), 94.

Meantime Federalism had shown its disposition towards the admission of new states. The occasion was Tennessee's application for statehood in 1796. The people of the "Territory South of the Ohio River," as it was officially designated, acting under an ordinance of the territorial legislature, without authorization of Congress, had held a convention and adopted a constitution under which they claimed recognition.[5] Congress was pledged to grant eventual statehood, not only by the resolution of 1780,[6] but by the terms of North Carolina's cession which imposed the same conditions stiplated by the Ordinance of 1787 for the Northwest Territory. Not venturing to impugn these pledges openly, the Federalists professed friendship for the statehood aspirations of the people of the territory, and confined their objections to insistence upon safe precedent, since "in a few years, other States would be rising up in the Western wilderness, and claiming their right to admission," and "it was of considerable moment to the United States, that a proposition which admitted a new State to the equal rights in one important branch of government in the affairs of the nation should be seriously considered and grounded on clear constitutional right." [7] They maintained that action by Congress must precede the organization of a state government, and pointed out that it was quite within the power of Congress, by dividing the territory into two states, to "leave less than sixty thousand inhabitants in either, and consequently deprive them of any claim whatever to admission into the Union at this time." [8] In reality, the Federalists had no desire to increase the number of Republican states, as such a division would ultimately have done, and sought only the advantage which would accrue to their party through delay. They believed the eagerness of their opponents to grant recognition to be due to the aid which the electoral vote of the new state would give in the election of Jefferson,[9] and wished to delay

---

[5] Portions of the following pages follow closely an earlier study by the present writer entitled "Federalism and the West," in *Turner Essays in American History*, 113-135.

[6] *Above*, 45, *f. n.* 18.

[7] Speech of William Smith, a South Carolina Federalist. *Annals of Congress*, Fourth Cong., 1 sess., 1300-1304.

[8] *Ibid*.

[9] "No doubt this is but one twig of the electioneering cabal for Mr. Jefferson." Chauncey Goodrich to Oliver Wolcott, Sr., quoted by Phelan, *Tennessee*, 188. Jefferson called the Tennessee constitution the "least imperfect and the most republican of the state constitutions."—Caldwell, J. W., "John Ball of Tennessee," in *Amer. Hist. Rev.* IV, 652 *et seq.* The course of the Federalists in opposing the admission of the state "had the effect of confirming her Republicanism. The people were indignant on account of the opposition, and for many years no public man in Tennessee dared to admit that he entertained Federalist principles." *Ibid*.

recognition long enough to deprive the Republicans of three electoral votes in the presidential campaign then in progress. In the Senate, Rufus King presented a committee report which declared Tennessee, for want of action by Congress, not yet entitled to admission.[10] This report was adopted, and by a vote of 15 to 8 the Senate passed a bill reported later from King's committee for "laying out into one State the territory ceded by the State of North Carolina." [11] Meantime, however, by a vote of 43 to 30, the House took action in favor of immediate recognition, and in the end the Senate passed the House bill.[12] On the whole, the Federalists went as far as they could, in the Tennessee affair, to show their antipathy for new western states; their conduct was what one would expect in the light of the antecedents of the party. They displayed a willingness to prolong the territorial status which was in marked contrast with the Republican view of it as a "degraded situation," lacking "a right essential to freemen—the right of being represented in Congress." [13]

South of the Ohio Federalism proved incapable of being grafted upon a democratic stock. North of the river it was subjected to a different kind of test. In that portion of the Northwest Territory which became the State of Ohio, it failed to hold its own as a colonizing force in competition with democracy of the type which settled Kentucky and Tennessee. Yet the Federalists were the first on the ground: the New England veterans who followed Putnam to Marietta found themselves, in the period of nascent parties, in sympathy with their eastern relatives.[14] In the settlements around Cincinnati, also, were many easterners who inclined to similar views, and the pioneers who came a little later to the Western Reserve and eastern Michigan were from the strongholds of Federalism. Arthur St. Clair, the territorial gov-

---

[10] *Annals*, Fourth Cong., 1 sess., 91-94.

[11] *Ibid.*, 97, 109.

[12] It is difficult to ascertain positively the politics of the less prominent congressmen of that period, and vote analysis on party lines is of doubtful value because of incompleteness. The House vote shows 17 Republicans for this bill and only one against; Federalists, two for and 12 against. Although less than half of those voting are accounted for in this division, the party alignment seems to be clear. The vote in the Senate was a tie, which was determined favorably by the ballot of acting-president Livermore. The chagrin of the Federalists at Livermore's action is manifest in the letter of Goodrich, cited *above*, note 9.

[13] Madison. *Ibid.*, 1308-1309.

[14] New England looked rather coldly upon the Ohio Company's project of colonization, fearing a rapid drainage of population. "Nathan Dane favored it, in part because he hoped that planting such a colony in the West might keep at least that part of it true to 'Eastern politics.' " Roosevelt, *Winning of the West*, III, 256-257.

ernor, Winthrop Sargent, the secretary, and Jacob Burnet, one of the judges, supported Federalism.[15] St. Clair entered the lists as a pamphleteer in defence of the Adams administration.[16] The sentiment of these early days is suggested by the fact that the legislature voted a complimentary address to President Adams in 1798 with but five dissenting voices.[17] These five votes, however, were ominous of approaching discord. Into the Cincinnati region and the Virginia military district had been pouring a tide of southern immigrants who were imbued with the feeling that the dependent territorial status was a "degraded situation," and with characteristic impatience at arbitrary power the leaders of this element soon clashed with St. Clair. The result was the firm conviction that they should never secure fair treatment under the territorial regime, and a demand for early statehood as a means of obtaining full self-government.[18] St. Clair, true to his Federalist instincts, distrusted the classes to whom he foresaw control would fall in that event. To him they seemed an indigent and ignorant people, ill qualified to form a government and constitution for themselves, and too remote from the seat of government to feel a wholesome respect for the federal power. "Fixed political principles they have none. . . . . Their government would most probably be democratic in form and oligarchic in its execution, and more troublesome and more opposed to the measures of the United States than even Kentucky." [19] Observing the preponderance of southerners among the newcomers in portions of the Territory, he fell back upon the time-honored devices of ruling minorities, and proposed to Timothy Pickering, the Secretary of State, a departure from the

---

[15] Sargent was of Massachusetts birth and a veteran of the Revolution. Becoming interested in the Ohio Company of Associates, he acted as surveyor for the Company in 1786. Upon the organization of the Territory, he was appointed secretary, holding the office until he was made governor of the new Mississippi Territory, in 1798. His Federalism made him so unpopular with his Republican neighbors in Mississippi that Jefferson removed him. Thwaites, *Early Western Travels*, IV, 323, *f. n.*

Burnet was a native of New Jersey, a Princeton graduate, and by profession a lawyer. In explanation of his Federalist principles he tells us "He had more confidence in the men who formed the Constitution than in their opponents, who had uniformly resisted its adoption and opposed its measures." Burnet, J., *Notes on the Early Settlement of the North-western Territory*, 297-298.

[16] Smith, W. H., *St. Clair Papers*, II, 442.

[17] *Ibid.*, I, 213; II, 484.

[18] "We shall never have fair play while Arthur and his Knights of the Round Table sit at the head." Extract from a letter of Judge Symmes, June 24, 1802, *ibid.*, I, 241. In the same letter Symmes says that one of his Cincinnati correspondents asserts that the papers there print everything for the "Aristocrats" and only now and then a piece for the "Democrats."

[19] St. Clair to James Ross, Dec., 1799. *Ibid.*, II, 481-483.

plan of division laid down in the Ordinance of 1787, "in such a manner as to make the upper or Eastern division surely Federal, and form a counterpoise . . . . to those who are unfriendly to the General Government." [20] Upon reflection he abandoned this project, perceiving that "the eastern division is too thinly inhabited, and the design would be too evident," and, as suggested in the Tennessee debate, proposed a line which, while leaving each portion "a sufficient number of inhabitants to continue in the present [second territorial] stage of government," would keep them in a colonial state for a good many years to come." [21]- Although one of the most violent of the Federalists in his antipathy towards the West, Pickering, for some reason, instead of lending himself to St. Clair's scheme, submitted the letter to William Henry Harrison, delegate to Congress from the Northwest Territory, on whose recommendation a division was made (May, 1800) in accordance with the Ordinance. Hoping to secure a reconsideration by Congress, St. Clair's partisans next (November, 1801) carried through the territorial legislature a boundary act assenting to a division which would promote the governor's plan, and Fearing, Harrison's successor as territorial delegate, was instructed to seek the approval of Congress. Meantime, the Jeffersonian regime had been inaugurated at Washington, and St. Clair's opponents met the issue by appealing to their friends at the national capital, not only to reject the boundary act, but to take steps favorable to the admission of the state.

The quarrel of the Federalists and Republicans in Ohio, now transferred to the larger arena of Congress, bade fair to become a national party issue. It was predicted that Federalists would oppose admission, because the increase of western and southern states accrued to the advantage of their opponents.[22] On the other hand, the Republicans were eager to add to their party strength three electoral votes which might be needed in the contest of 1804.

---

[20] This letter has been lost. St. Clair gives a summary in his communication to Ross, cited above.

[21] *Cf.* letter to Woodbridge: "I ventured to open to [Todd, of Trumbull County] my opinion that . . . . many advantages would flow to the upper eastern division . . . . by proposed lines . . . . Being settled entirely by the people from the eastward . . . . as they would forever have the preponderancy over the other parts of that district, it would be in their power to introduce those laws and customs, and fix them so as they *could never be overthrown* . . . ." [Italics mine]. *Ibid.*, 543-549.

[22] *Ibid.*, I, 238, quoting R. J. Meigs, Sr.: "The Federalists will oppose it, because a multiplication of western and southern States will multiply Republican Senators."

Approval of the boundary act was decisively refused on January 27, 1802, only five votes being recorded in its favor; and the next day the first steps towards a statehood bill were taken under a motion of the zealous Republican Giles of Virginia.[23] In the debate which ensued the expected Federalist opposition failed to appear. Roger Griswold, of Connecticut, was allowed, almost unsupported, to voice the protest of the minority. In the Tennessee debate, the Federalists held that an act of Congress must precede the formation of a state government by the people of a territory; now Griswold maintained that the passage of an act giving the assent of Congress to the formation of a constitution, upon the petition of individuals, and contrary to the wish of the legislature as implied in the boundary act, was an unwarranted interference with the concerns of the people of the territory.[24] The Republicans maintained, as in 1796, that territorial governments "were arbitrary at best, and ought not to exist longer than they could with propriety be dispensed with. They were opposed to the genius of the people of this country. . . . . The people resident in the Territory had emigrated from the different States in the Union, where they had been in the habit of enjoying the benefits of a free form of government; they no doubt looked forward to a very short period, at which they might again enjoy the same as pointed out by the Ordinance . . . . but if the doctrine now contended for in opposition, shall prevail in this House, all their hopes are blasted," for it was "not to be supposed that men who have power to nullify every act of the people, will ever sanction one to put an end to their own political existence." [25] In support of this contention the boundary act of the territorial legislature was cited.

---

[23] *Annals*, Seventh Cong., 1 sess., 465-6, 469.

[24] *Ibid.*, 1104-1105. Goddard, also of Connecticut, seconded Griswold's argument. *Ibid.*, 1116.

[25] Speech of R. Williams, of North Carolina. *Ibid.*, 1107-1110. The Ordinance of 1787 pledged the admission of the parts into which it provided that the Northwest Territory should be divided, whenever the population of any part reached 60,000. Ohio had not yet reached this population, and the speech of Williams indicates the danger of delay involved in the proposal of the territorial legislature. Of course, if no change in boundaries were made, statehood would soon be due under the provisions of the Ordinance, and Williams's argument would hardly be applicable.

Griswold's plea was not consistent with the Federalist contention of 1796. Then it was asserted that the action of the territorial legislature should not be taken as conclusive evidence of the wish of the people of Tennessee, since many were known to oppose statehood; while now Griswold maintained that the action of the legislature was the only evidence of the sentiments of the inhabitants of a territory which Congress should notice. In both cases the argument was evidently shaped by the desire to restrain the growth of an adverse interest. The final vote on the Ohio statehood bill shows more clearly than the debate the partisan na-

The Ohio statehood bill as passed gave further offence to the Federalists by separating what is now eastern Michigan from the new state. This they believed to have been done from the fear that that district, where Federalists were numerous, would, if included, give a majority against statehood or carry the new state into the Federalist column. While the matter was under consideration in committee of the whole, Bayard objected to cutting off the Michigan portion of the territory about to be admitted, after the inhabitants had been advanced to the self-governing stage. To this Giles replied that the northern portion of the territory could not be a permanent part of the new state, and that it would be unjust to allow its inhabitants a voice in forming a constitution for the people of the southern portion. By being attached to Indiana Territory, moreover, it would not revert to the first stage.[26] The people of Detroit and vicinity remonstrated against the action of Congress, claiming the right to be included in the new state, but were reconciled by the prospect of a territorial government seated at Detroit, with offices to be distributed among local men.[27] It is significant of the extent to which Federalism had invaded the West that a gerrymander of this sort was necessary to insure Republican ascendancy in the first state created in the old Northwest.

But the passage of the enabling act was the beginning of disaster for the Ohio Federalists. Their delegates in the constitutional convention were outnumbered nearly three to one.[28] St. Clair was dismissed by Jefferson with scant courtesy before the expiration of his term, for criticising the action of Congress in a speech before the convention.[29] The convention, true to the current creed of democracy, and mindful of the conflicts with the late governor,

---

ture of the issue. The vote of those whose politics have been ascertained shows the Republicans 14 to 1 in favor of it, with 7 Federalists opposed. *Ibid.*, 1161-1162.

[26] *Ibid.*, 1120-1122. "The inhabitants of that part of the Territory with scarcely one exception, were also decidedly opposed in politics to the party which had just possessed themselves of the administration of the general government. They were also numerous. . . . . It was, therefore, almost certain, that if they were united with the opposers of the proposed constitution, in the Southern part of the district, they would reject the law of Congress, and prevent the formation of a State government. But if this should not be the case, still they would become citizens of the new State, which, with the aid of their numbers and influence, would most probably be placed in the ranks of opposition to the administration of the general government, by the men then in power." Burnet, *Notes*, 337.

[27] *Ibid.*

[28] An account of the convention, with source material, is given in Smith, *St. Clair Papers*, I, Chap. 9; II, 586 *et seq.*

[29] Charges against St. Clair had been presented to the President by his enemies early in the year 1802, but at that time Jefferson had been satisfied by the defence offered. *Ibid.*, I, 244-245; II, 592-601.

framed a constitution which entrusted large powers to the legislature, but reduced the governor to a figurehead. In the first election the Republicans carried even Marietta by a large majority, most of the disheartened Federalists casting blank ballots in view of the certainty of defeat.[30] The rout of the party by these occurrences was so complete that it soon ceased to act as a political organization. Among the politicians of the early days were many men from New England, and especially Connecticut, but they either found that their Federalism barred the way to political preferment in the social and political atmosphere of the West, or had imbibed the principles of democracy in their earlier homes. At all events the politically ambitious, whether Virginian, New Yorker, Yankee, Scotch-Irishman, Irishman, or Englishman, was speedily drawn into the party of democracy. All of these stocks were represented in the governor's chair within a quarter-century, but few men who bore the party title of Federalist attained important office until about 1820, by which time that designation had lost all real significance both East and West.[31]

Yet the story of Ohio Federalism after 1803 is not one of sudden disappearance, but of gradual decline and fusion with Republicanism. Members of the party seem to have been active locally in those parts of the state where they were numerous or party lines not too rigidly drawn.[32] But never did they put forward their own candidate for the governorship. In 1809 an anonymous correspondent of the *Supporter* asserted that "The federalists of Ohio not being ignorant that their opponents outnumber them, I think I may say five to one, never have made any general effort against

[30] The Federalists considered plans for rallying their forces and making a fight for the election of St. Clair, but he refused to allow his name to be used, and apparently no other name afforded even a fighting chance of success. *Ibid.*, I, 247.

[31] Hockett, "Federalism and the West," in *Turner Essays*, 128, *f. n.*, gives antecedents of early Ohio politicians. Judge Burnet declared: "My political influence and that of my associates sank into a common grave. We were proscribed, and as soon as the plan of our competitors was consummated, we submitted to our destiny with good grace and withdrew from all participation." Burnet, *Notes*. Twenty years later Burnet was elevated to the supreme bench by a Republican legislature.

[32] William McMillan ran as the party candidate for Congress in 1803, and received 1960 votes out of a total of 7518. (Randall & Ryan, *History of Ohio*, III, 146). In the presidential campaign of 1804 the electoral ticket of the party polled 364 votes in the state. (*Ibid.*, 145). Levin Belt, a Federalist, was chosen one of the supreme court justices in 1807, by joint ballot of the two houses (*Supporter*, Aug. 11, 1810), and was afterwards for several years mayor of Chillicothe, where he made the address of welcome upon the occasion of Monroe's visit in 1817. (*Ibid.*, Sept. 2, 1817.) George Nashee, also a Federalist, was a member of the town council of Chillicothe. (*Ibid.*, Jan. 12, 1814). These instances are chosen at random.

their enemy." [33] Nevertheless they were not without influence in gubernatorial elections. It is significant that in the contest between Return Jonathan Meigs, Jr., and Nathaniel Massie, in 1806-1807, the former's majority was furnished by those portions of northern and eastern Ohio where settlers from New England were most numerous.[34] Still more notable was the part taken by the Federalists in the controversy which grew out of a decision rendered by the supreme court in 1807, in which an act relating to the jurisdiction of the justices of the peace was held to be unconstitutional.[35] Leading Republicans attacked the judges who rendered this decision, one of them being a Federalist, Levin Belt, much as Jefferson and his friends had attacked John Marshall for his decision in the case of Marbury vs. Madison, and the Ohio Democracy divided on the issue. It became a factor in the three-sided contest of 1808, in which Huntington, Worthington, and Kirker were candidates for governor. This question of the functions of the judiciary involved the dogmas of Federalism as had no other issue arising in the politics of the state. One of their writers explained: "The federalists, lawyers and all, believe that the courts possess the power of declaring the legislative acts unconstitutional. They consider, that without this power in the judiciary, a written constitution is of no real or essential value.— Hence they cling to this principle as to the vital stream of life." [36] Their support was given to Huntington and he was elected.[37] In

---

[33] Issue of Dec. 16. The *Supporter* was a Federalist newspaper, founded at Chillicothe in the autumn of 1808, but it does not appear to have been any part of its purpose to foster hopes of partisan success. Its comment on state politics is rare; it echoes, by reprinting, the strictures of the party papers to the eastward on the foreign policy of the administration.

[34] Massie, D. M., *Nathaniel Massie*, 93-94. After defeating Massie, Meigs was adjudged ineligible for lack of the residence qualification, having been absent from the state for a considerable period within the four years preceding his election, and the vacancy was filled by Kirker as acting-governor. Meigs was of Connecticut birth. He was one of the settlers of Marietta, in 1788, where he practiced law. *Congressional Biographical Directory.* His political conduct in early life was so moderate that he is variously described as a conservative Democrat (Taylor, *Ohio in Congress*, 40) and as "originally a Federalist and supporter of St. Clair" (Massie, *N. Massie*, 93, 94).

[35] An account of this decision may be found in Randall & Ryan, *History of Ohio*, III, 155 *et seq.*

[36] "A Federal Lawyer," in *Supporter*, Aug. 11, 1810.

[37] Samuel Huntington was the adopted heir of his uncle of the same name, the signer of the Declaration of Independence and governor of Connecticut. He came to Youngstown, Ohio, in 1801, and afterwards removed to Cleveland. While belonging to the moderate Republicans, he had the confidence both of the Federalists and the extreme Republicans. St. Clair appointed him lieutenant colonel of Trumbull County. He served as delegate to the state constitutional convention, and was afterwards speaker, senator from Trumbull, and judge of the state supreme court. Whittlesey, Charles, *Early History of Cleveland*, 382-384.

the campaign of 1810 the claim was made that their action had controlled the result, and the friends of Worthington were warned that ill treatment of the Federalists would again jeopardize his election.[38] Some effort was made to rally the Federalists to the support of Meigs, now again a candidate, and considerable insight into political conditions is afforded by the arguments adduced in his behalf.[39] Meigs was elected, and thus for the third time that candidate succeeded whose moderation won the favor of the Federalist voters. To say, however, that they acted as a consistent group would be to go too far. The editor of the *Supporter* doubtless spoke for many of the apathetic when he wrote: "We conceive that *Federalists* have no interest in the present rupture between the two parties styling themselves *Republicans*. Federalists have nothing to expect from either—they have no hopes of emolument— no ambitious views to gratify. . . . . Should federalists join the ranks of either, they would reap nothing but discomfiture and disgrace. Under these impressions we have decided to remain neutral during the present electioneering campaign." [40]

The Federalist support of Meigs is, indeed, not so much evidence of a tendency to maintain a distinct party holding the balance of power between the Republican factions, as of a tendency to merge into Republicanism because all real differences of opinion were dissolving. Even on the judiciary question a large part of the Republicans were coming to the Federalist view, while the approximation of western Federalism to views held also by Republicans is well shown by the words of the same writer who urged the support of Meigs: "You [Federalists] have been in the habit of thinking there is no good among democrats, that the whole mass

---

[38] "A Federal Lawyer," in *Supporter,* cited *above:* "It was the federalists that made HUNTINGTON governor; but the 'federal lawyers' never supposed or represented him to be a federalist. . . . . They supported him, because Gen. Worthington and his friends placed the controversy upon such grounds as left them no alternative. The same game seems likely to be played over again, and I warn you in time to beware of a similar result."

[39] "Federalists, you are not uninterested in the scenes passing in review. Your language is, 'Let the democrats fight it out among themselves.' . . . . Federalists come forward. . . . . Unite with moderate Republicans. Unite with all honest men in the election of Judge Meigs. . . . . The destruction of federalism is the whole burden of their song [Worthington's supporters.] Will you aid in the election of such a man? Will you sharpen a knife to cut your own throats? . . . . If you refuse to vote for Judge Meigs, you, in effect, do the same. . . . . Turn out to a man and vote for Judge Meigs. He is the least evil of the two. He is a moderate Republican. His rival charges him with being friendly to federalism.—We believe he considers them as men entitled to civil usage and the rights of citizens . . . . but we declare again, that he is no federalist. Would to heaven he were, and not only he, but all the people of the land."—"Timothy Trowell," "a humble mechanic," in *Supporter,* Sept. 22, 1810.

[40] *Supporter,* June 29, 1811.

of democracy is a polluted lump. Whereas, the great body of the people, among them, are well meaning, patriotic citizens, and would always do right were they rightly informed. It is some of their leaders you ought to oppose. . . . . The *name* I am not tenacious of. Throw it away. Give us genuine federal principles. Let the constitution be our polar star. Give us equal and righteous laws. Place honest and able men in public offices. Let them be *Americans,* in contradiction to Englishmen and Frenchmen. Let canals and roads chequer this goodly land. Encourage commerce, but more particularly domestic manufactures. These are federal principles. Pursue these and we shall have another golden age." [41] These principles are hardly distinguishable from those of western Republicans. They make clear that by the era of the second British war the chief obstacle to the amalgamation of parties in Ohio was prejudice.[42]

The bit of Ohio history which we have traced shows that Federalism was carried westward by the migrating New England stock, and that Republicanism prevailed in some frontier regions only after a struggle. Nevertheless, Federalism was not able to withstand frontier influences long even in those regions where the settlers were exclusively of New England stock. This fact appears from the study of the fate which befell it in middle and western

---

[41] "Timothy Trowell," in *Supporter,* Sept. 22, 1810.

[42] In this *rapprochement* of the two parties doubtless lies the real explanation of the infrequency of the *Supporter's* comment on state politics. It was absorbed by the contest in progress to the eastward. But on the eve of the War of 1812 it ceased to echo the opposition of New England Federalism to the policy of the administration. Instead the editor wrote, on receipt of the news of the declaration of war: "It appears that congress have at last, taken a firm and decided stand—they have *declared war,* and however we may differ in political sentiments it now becomes the duty of every citizen to cling to his country and rise or fall with it." (Issue of July 4, 1812). The persistence of the paper in its traditional faith is shown by its comment on the success of the Federalists in Maryland in the autumn of 1812, after twelve years of Democratic rule, as affording "a happy presage of the returning good sense of the people of the United States." (Issue of Oct. 24, 1812). A week later like news from New Jersey elicited the remark "thus are the good old times returning." (Issue of Oct. 31).

The Clintonian movement of 1812 found some support in Ohio. An electoral ticket headed by Calvin Pease, one of the judges who had joined in the decision setting aside the act of legislation in 1807, was placed before the voters of the state, and one man on this ticket, William W. Irwin, of Fairfield County, received 3301 votes. The vote for the Republican electors varied from 5738 to 7420. (*Supporter,* Nov. 14, 1812). But it may be questioned whether Clinton's support in Ohio was due to sympathy with the Peace Party movement, which made him the candidate of the commercial class of New England and New York, or to the belief that he would prosecute the war with greater vigor than Madison. Although sometimes regarded as the Federalist candidate in 1812, Clinton, in fact, received support from Republicans also under the impulse of a variety of motives. See Hammond, J. D., *History of Political Parties in the State of New York,* I, 298 *et seq.* Already, too, Clinton's fame as the chief advocate of a canal connecting the lakes with the Hudson had won him friends in Ohio, where public interest responded quickly to the project of a waterway to the Atlantic.

New York. In the period of ratification of the constitution, the favorable vote in that state was cast by delegates from the commercial regions of the lower Hudson; the patroon aristocracy and their tenants on the upper river, and the German population of the Mohawk Valley were strongly opposed to the new plan of government. If New York had been among the first states to pass upon the constitution, the antifederalists would doubtless have prevailed, but her geographical position made rejection impracticable in the face of the action which the other states had taken before her convention met. But while the Federalist cause was strengthened somewhat by this initial victory, and later aided by the use made of the patronage within the state, they could hardly have prevailed over the democracy led by George Clinton without the augmentation of voting strength which resulted from the immigration of New Englanders. To this immigration chiefly must be attributed the capture of the state by the Federalists in 1794. The influx of New Englanders during the nineties affected most the very regions which had been antifederal, and the frontiers. The opening of cheap lands in New York drew swarms of farmers from Connecticut and Massachusetts, while the establishment of new counties attracted to the county towns young lawyers and merchants of Federalist proclivities, whose political talents provided leadership for the rural settlers.[43] In the apportionment of 1791, the population of the Western District entitled it to five of the twenty-four state senators.[44] The rapid increase of freeholders, due chiefly to the immigration from New England, necessitated a reapportionment four years later, when, of the twenty additional senators for the whole state, twelve fell to the Western District.[45] During the nineties, this district was the most safely Federalist area in the state, electing candidates of that party almost without opposition. By 1798, however, Republican gains gave warning of the early passing of Federalist control in the state at large, and in the election of 1800, which restored the Republicans to power, the Federalists

---

[43] "The great influx of population from New England between 1790 and 1800 had changed the political aspect of the county. . . . . While the eastern population seated within Oneida county, almost unanimously acted with the federalist party, the immigration to Herkimer seems to have been more equally balanced, although a considerable majority of the population which settled in this county adhered to their New England proclivities." "A republican lawyer or a republican merchant was seldom to be found in the country villages or at the county seats in this part of the state."—Benton, N. S., *A History of Herkimer County, Including the Upper Mohawk Valley*, 259-260.

[44] Hammond, *Political Parties*, I, 52.

[45] *Ibid.*, 99.

were defeated even in the Western District, which now became as regularly Republican as it had been Federalist.[46]

This change in the political complexion of western New York points to the actual conversion of Federalist voters to Republican-ism, and suggests that the Federalism of the New England-New York frontiersman was conventional rather than vital. As always, the appeal of the wilderness was strongest with the younger and less prosperous men—the very class least steeped in the orthodoxy of their native communities. Transplanted from its original en-vironment, Federalism of this type easily yielded to the strong solvents of the frontier and blended with Republicanism. The ac-tual process may be traced in some cases which seem typical. Dur-ing the two or three years preceding 1800, there were in the as-sembly eight or ten members who had been chosen as Federalists, but who were beginning to lose faith in the tenets of that party and to act with the Republicans.[47] Among them was Jedediah Peck, an uneducated immigrant from Connecticut, who plied the trade of surveyor in behalf of his fellows who during the nineties redeemed Otsego County from the wilderness. "He would survey your farm in the daytime, exhort and pray in your family at night, and talk on politics the rest part of the time."[48] From the character of the man chosen by the settlers to represent them in the councils of the state some inference may be drawn as to the character of the con-stituents. The Old World traditions of Federalism, which became manifest in the legislation of 1798, alienated people of this type. Peck circulated a petition for the repeal of the Sedition Law, and for this Judge Cooper, the novelist's father, an ardent Federalist, caused him to be arrested and taken, in the spring of 1800, two hundred miles to New York for trial. The effect of such a spec-tacle upon a population already disaffected, on the eve of a state and national election, is easily imagined. "A hundred missionaries in the cause of democracy, stationed between New York and Cooperstown, could not have done so much for the Republican cause as this journey of Jedediah Peck from Otsego to the capital

---

[46] 1801 was an exception, the Federalists carrying the district because, as Hammond says, of "some local cause with which we are at present unacquainted. Perhaps the republican candidates, or some of them, were personally unpopular." *Ibid.*, 164.

[47] *Ibid.*, 123.

[48] *Ibid.*, 124.

of the State." [49] Meantime other influences had been working in the same direction. Of a type similar to Peck was Obadiah German, member from the neighboring county of Chenango.[50] To these waverers Aaron Burr had been paying court, conscious that their espousal of Republicanism would be an important factor in the winning of the West. Falling in as it did with the events narrated, Burr's efforts were successful, and in the decisive campaign of 1800 these counties followed their converted leaders into the Republican ranks.[51] Herkimer, another of this group of western counties, was won by similar means, disaffection caused by the policies of the Adams administration coinciding with the coming of a Republican lawyer sent to organize the democratic movement.[52]

In its new garb the Western District speedily became dominant in state politics. In 1805, German was the recognized leader of the Republicans in the assembly;[53] in 1809 western New York dictated the choice of United States senator, German being elected over several prominent competitors.[54] In 1810 the gubernatorial campaign was admittedly determined by the same section. In the hope of carrying this stronghold of the enemy, the Federalists nominated Jonas Platt, a pioneer of Whitesborough, who had retained his popularity in this part of the state in spite of the revolution in political sentiment; but the Federalists failed to carry the state, or even the Western District.[55] Never after 1796 did New

---

[49] *Ibid.*, 132. The petition was written by John Armstrong, author of the "Newburgh Addresses," who was, until 1798, a Federalist. Alexander, D. S., *Political History of New York*, I, 89. Armstrong was elected to the United States Senate in 1800 almost unanimously. Hammond thinks the Federalists supported him as the least objectionable Republican, as they could not elect a Federalist. *Hist. of Pol. Parties*, I, 154. The conversion of Ambrose Spencer, who later became a famous "boss," dates from about this time, a conjectural cause being that he foresaw the decline of the Federalist party. Alexander, *Polit. Hist.*, I, 87.

[50] Hammond characterizes German as uneducated, but distinguished for strong and vigorous intellectual powers. *Ibid.*, 276. [51] *Ibid.*, 124, 134.

[52] Benton, *History of Herkimer County*, 261-262. "An up-state writer frankly avowed that Jefferson was the friend of the farmers and the enemy of the financiers. This partisan publicist . . . . declared of the party leader: 'He has on all occasions shown himself the friend and patron of agriculture. You then whose lives are devoted to agricultural pursuits cannot surely approve of those who unjustly asperse his well-earned reputation. Hear him on the subject which must be nearest to your hearts, since it is most intimately connected with your interests.' Here the writer quoted at length from the *Notes on Virginia* the passages to the effect that those who labor in the earth are God's chosen people and the mercantile and laboring element of the towns the measure of a nation's decay."—Beard, *Economic Origins*, 367.

[53] Hammond, *Pol. Parties*, I, 218.

[54] *Ibid.*, 276.

[55] For outcome of Platt's campaign see Hammond, *Pol. Parties*, I, 279. Hammond gives the following explanation of the downfall of the Federalists: "They did not properly appreciate the intelligence and good sense of the mass of the community. . . . . It was this unjust estimate . . . . which carried them into a course of reasoning and action which resulted in . . . . utter overthrow." *Ibid.*, 162.

York cast a Federalist electoral vote,[56] and the party gradually sank to the position of a faction acting with one or other of the Republican groups according to the dictates of local interest.

The fate of Federalism on the Pennsylvania frontier is in harmony with the conclusions reached from the study of Ohio and New York. New England contributed largely to the settlement of a belt of territory stretching across northern Pennsylvania from the Delaware River to the Ohio line. Connecticut, especially, had been interested in the lands of this region, to which she laid claim under the terms of her charter from Charles II; and notwithstanding the adverse outcome of the controversy with Pennsylvania which resulted, she made the largest contribution to the early settlement of the counties on the upper Susquehanna. From the rest of New England, sometimes by way of New York, came most of the immigrants who filled in the northern tier of counties, to Erie, in the extreme northwest corner of the state.[57] "Erie County became more like New York than Pennsylvania." [58] As in New York, the New England stock brought with it the traditional political faith. Luzerne County (which included also the present Bradford, Susquehanna, Wyoming, and Lackawanna) was a "veritable hot-bed of Federalism."[59] Scotch-Irish settlers were intermingled with the New Englanders, however, and a detailed study is not needed to reveal the fact that Federalism fought a losing fight.[60] In Erie County, in 1807, Snyder, the Republican candidate for governor, defeated James Ross, the Federalist, by a vote of 345 out of a total of 589.[61] The early settlements near the forks of the Ohio

---

[56] The vote for De Witt Clinton, in 1812, might be regarded as an exception to the statement in the text, since Federalists helped the Clinton faction carry the state. The decline of the Federalist party in New York was steady until the period of international controversy beginning with the embargo, when there was a partial recovery as in other states. In 1804 Hamilton's opposition to combination with the Burr faction led to the ill-fated quarrel and duel in which he lost his life. Many Federalists abandoned the party on this occasion, considering it ruined. Hamilton's death and Jay's retirement also left it without first rate leadership. In 1806 most Federalists supported Lewis against Clinton, but this campaign again led many disgusted Federalists to forswear the party from that time forth. The support of Federalists gave Tompkins the victory over Lewis in 1807. *Ibid.*, 209, 235, 246.

[57] Mathews, L. K., *Expansion of New England*, 151-152.

[58] *Ibid.*

[59] *Ibid.* Also *History of Lackawanna, Luzerne, and Wyoming Counties*, 58.

[60] In 1807, Lycoming County gave 894 votes to the Republican candidate for the legislature, and 441 to the Federalist. The Republican candidate for sheriff won a victory over his opponent by the narrow margin of 702 to 694, but the Republican commissioner was elected by a vote of 751, his rival polling only 588.—Meginness, *Official Report of Proceedings of the Centennial Anniversary of Lycoming County*, 24. Lycoming County in this early period included the whole of north central Pennsylvania.

[61] Sanford, L. G., *History of Erie County*, 97.

were preponderantly Scotch-Irish and intensely democratic from the beginning. Although beyond the mountains, they had, as part of Pennsylvania, escaped the probationary period which accorded so well with the Federalist idea of government for the western settlements.[62] In lieu of this, Hamilton sought to imbue them with a proper regard for the power and authority of the federal government by means of the excise law.[63] The Whiskey Rebellion followed, and in the trial of its leaders a prominent part was taken by Judge Alexander Addison, the "first law judge in Western Pennsylvania," and one of the few prominent Federalists of that region.[64] The suppression of the insurrection undoubtedly inspired respect for the government, as Hamilton planned it should, but it was little calculated to win western votes for his party. As early as 1798, therefore, there was no such thing as a Federalist party in Westmoreland County, although James Ross believed that a permanent, sensible leader might have won a small following. A small group of that party had maintained itself in Fayette County, but was powerless in congressional elections for lack of support from Westmoreland.[65] Four years later the enmity against Judge Addison brought about his impeachment and removal. While his primary offence was doubtless his conduct during the Whiskey Rebellion, his Federalist principles rendered him, it seems, "perhaps too impatient in his temper," and "not sufficiently courteous to his demagogical colleague," although there was no doubt as to his learning or integrity.[66]

Another straw which shows which way the wind blew in western Pennsylvania is the case of Major Isaac Craig. He was one of the earliest citizens of Pittsburg, a Federalist, and a man of some note in the region. He had served during the Revolution, and in 1780 had commanded at Pittsburg. From the time of

---

[62] Referring to the two stages of territorial government provided for by the Ordinance of 1787.

[63] The whole history of the Whiskey Insurrection is an interesting chapter in the story of the division between the seaboard and interior. Comments of the easterners are typical of their attitude towards the interior. Fisher Ames, referring to the rebel manifesto, said that these views "had tainted a vast extent of country beside Pennsylvania." (Winsor, *Westward Movement*, 485). Wolcott referred to the rebels as "the wild men of the back country," but predicted that they would not have the perseverance to oppose the steady pressure of law and must finally submit. (*Ibid.*) *Cf.* Washington's view that the rebellion was the fruit of the democratic societies.

[64] Thwaites, *Early Western Travels*, III, 363, *f. n.*

[65] Ross to St. Clair, July 5, 1798. *St. Clair Papers*, II, 422-423. St. Clair was inquiring into the probability of success as a candidate for Congress.

[66] Craig, N. B., *History of Pittsburgh*, 286-287.

Wayne's Indian campaigns he was in charge of the military stores at Pittsburg until deprived of the office by Jefferson, in 1802, because of his political views.[67] Thus through adverse public opinion and administration influence Federalists lost their hold on official positions in the West. Yet, as in Ohio, some clung tenaciously to the Federalist name in the face of defeat, and party feeling ran high at times. Cuming, while on his tour through the region in 1807, was amazed at the bitterness shown. "They nickname each other *Aristocrats* and *Democrats,* and it is astonishing to what a height their mutual animosity is carried. . . . . The most illiberal opinions are adopted by each party, and it is sufficient with a federalist that another man is a republican, to pronounce him capable of every crime, while the republican takes care not to allow the federalist the smallest of the attributes of virtue." [68] He adds that their opinions "are argued with more warmth and are productive of more rancour and violence in Pittsburg than in any other part of America." [69]

The change in the political complexion of western New York swung the twelve electoral votes of the state to Jefferson in 1800 and was a decisive factor in the election.[70] Yet narrow as was the victory, an acute analyst of political forces and tendencies might even then have read *finis* for Federalism in the light of its first defeat. Many southern members of the party, assured of satisfactory political adjustments at home, were sufficiently content with Jefferson's policies in national affairs to become apathetic, lacking an issue worth fighting for.[71] From this period Federalism retained vitality nowhere except in New England, where it had always found its chief support.[72] Even there Jefferson's measures met with popular approval, as was shown by the result of the

---

[67] Thwaites, *Early Western Travels,* IV, 96, *f. n.*

[68] Cuming, F., *Tour to the Western Country,* in Thwaites, *Early Western Travels,* IV, 70-72.

[69] *Ibid.,* 85. The editor of the first edition of the *Tour,* a Pittsburg printer, inserts at this point a note explaining that Cuming visited Pittsburg at a time when party feeling was unusually high, but that "at the present [1810] rancour has subsided."

[70] If Hamilton's proposal to choose electors by districts (Lodge, H. C., *Works of Hamilton,* VIII, 549 *et seq.*) had been adopted and had saved five New York electors for Adams, he would have defeated Jefferson by a vote of 70 to 68.

[71] Phillips, "The South Carolina Federalists," in *Amer. Hist. Rev.,* XIV, 529-543; 731-743, traces the causes of the collapse of the state organization which followed the election of Jefferson. The article is suggestive of the fate of the party elsewhere in the South. *Cf.* Beard, *Economic Origins,* Chap. 13.

[72] "In New England, Federalism had always found its chief support; and there alone, after the downfall of the party in 1800, did it retain any real vitality." Lodge, *Cabot,* 419.

election of 1804, in which he carried every state in that section except Connecticut.[73] Federalists might, indeed, have indulged hope of recovering lost ground in the Atlantic states, but it was plain that the growth of the West accrued to the benefit of the rival party, and it was also plain that the West would continue to grow. During the nineties Kentucky had sent two members to Congress; under the apportionment based on the census of 1800 she sent six and enjoyed a doubled allotment of presidential electors. The admission of Ohio added three more Republican electors, destined to swell to eight under the next apportionment. That the fate of the party was involved in this western growth was perceived by some of its chief men.[74] "In thirty years," wailed Timothy Pickering in 1804, "the white population on the Western waters will equal that of the thirteen States when they declared themselves independent of Great Britain." [75] As if the menace involved in the settlement of the original western territory of the Union were not enough, the acquisition of Louisiana added a vast new world certain to hold Republican views and in time to swell the number of Republican states. The obligation to grant statehood sooner or later to the communities which arose within the original territory had hampered the Federalists hitherto and forced them to be content with dilatory tactics. No such pledges impeded the expression of their views concerning the future of Louisiana. Although professing skepticism as to the value of the province and objecting to the purchase on the ground that it was not expedient, it was the belief that the treaty involved the obligation to confer statehood that filled them with alarm and caused their chief opposition to its ratification.[76] They did not deny the constitutionality of territorial

[73] The Massachusetts legislature abandoned the choice of electors by districts in 1804 and substituted a general ticket, confident that the state would return a Federalist majority. Bradford, *Hist. of Mass.*, III, 87.

[74] *Cf.* 63-65, *above.*

[75] Letter to Rufus King, March 4. Adams, Henry, *New England Federalism*, 352. *Cf.* actual situation as described *below*, 83-84.

[76] "Our party though with numerous exceptions, opposed it; for one reason, that it cost money the greater part of which we to the northward must pay, and it gains territory which will, in their apprehension, by giving strength to the Southern representation, diminish the Eastern influence in our councils."—Gouverneur Morris to R. L. Livingston, Nov. 28, 1803: Morris, A. C., *The Diary and Letters of Gouverneur Morris,* II, 444. *Cf.* speech of Tracy of Connecticut in Senate in which he declared that the relative strength which "admission gives to a Southern and Western interest is contradictory to the principles of our original union." *Annals*, Eighth Cong., 1 sess., 56. Rufus King and John Quincy Adams "agreed, and lamented that one inevitable consequence of the annexation of Louisiana to the Union would be to

acquisitions, but combated the right of Congress to admit acquired territories to statehood; insisting that they must be held as dependent provinces.[77]

Thus through the growth of the West the ruin of the Atlantic interest, predicted by Morris in 1787, seemed drawing near; the

diminish the relative weight and influence of the northern section." Adams, *New England Federalism*, 148.

"They did not fear the measure of acquiring Louisiana *per se*, but the supremacy of Democracy, which was its meaning to them. They saw in it the assurance of a perpetuation of Jefferson's power and of his maxims."—Lodge, *Cabot*, 435-436.

[77] See, *e. g.*, speech of Timothy Pickering: "He had never doubted the right of the United States to acquire new territory, either by purchase or by conquest, and to govern the territory so acquired as a dependent province." But he denied that such territory could be given statehood by treaty, or Congress, or even an amendment, unless assented to by every state. *Annals*, Eighth Cong., 1 sess., 45. Griswold of Connecticut maintained likewise that acquired territory could not be incorporated either by conquest or purchase, but "must remain in the condition of colonies and be governed accordingly." *Ibid. Cf.* view of G. Morris, in letter to H. W. Livingston: "I always thought that, when we should acquire Canada and Louisiana it would be proper to govern them as provinces, and allow them no voice in our councils." Sparks, J., *Life of Gouverneur Morris*, III, 192.

Morris was ready to acquiesce in the purchase of Louisiana. "I like well your treaty with France," he wrote to Livingston. Morris, *Morris*, II, 444. He had, indeed, felt grave apprehensions lest Jefferson's laxity should permit France to take possession of it. "Si notre administration permet aux Français de s'y nicher, on n'en sera quitte que par des guerres et des convulsions affreuses. Nous avons actuellement le malheur d'être gouverné par l'esprit de vertige que, dans le siécle ridicule où nous sommes, on est convenu de nommer philosophe," he wrote to M. Necker shortly before the purchase. *Ibid.*, 433-434. He therefore regarded Livingston's treaty as having "saved" Jefferson's administration, and thought this was one reason for the Federalist's dislike of it. *Ibid.*, 444. He anticipated some benefits even for New England. "From the moment when the citizens of Louisiana were made members of our Union, they became the natural and political allies of the Northern and Eastern States. We have with them no competition of interest; on the contrary, our shipping and mercantile capital are essential to their wealth and prosperity, and equally indifferent is it to us whether the produce of our skill and industry be vended to those who speak English or to those who gabble the provincial dialects of France and Spain." *Ibid.*, 454. Morris thus stands in contrast with the more extreme Federalists like Pickering, in foreseeing the possibility of advantageous economic relations with this new West, but he must have used the word "political" in the above passage in a very loose sense, as he could hardly have anticipated a party alliance between New England and Louisiana. One is tempted to conclude, upon the whole, that Morris was trying to make the best of a situation which he thought rather bad, for on January 7, 1804, in a letter to Jonathan Dayton, while still expressing his approval of the cession, he pointed out objectionable features of the treaty. Especially, he says, "the stipulation to admit the inhabitants into our Union will, I believe, prove injurious to this country." *Ibid.*, 453. Only three days before writing to Livingston approving the treaty, he betrayed the temper of the anti-expansionist in a letter to another correspondent: "I am very certain that I had it not in contemplation to insert a decree *de crescendo imperio* in the Constitution of America, without examining whether a limitation of territory be or be not essential to the preservation of republican government. I am certain that the country between the Mississippi and the Atlantic exceeds by far the limits which prudence would assign if, in effect, any limitation be required. . . . . I knew as well then as I do now that all North America must at length be annexed to us—happy, indeed, if the lust of dominion stop there. It would therefore have been perfectly utopian to oppose a paper restriction to the violence of popular sentiment in a popular government." *Ibid.*, 442.

Cf. views of King and Adams: "The alternative to acquisition of Louisiana was,— Louisiana and the mouths of the Mississippi in the possession of France, under Napoleon Bonaparte. The loss of sectional influence, we hoped and believed, would be more than compensated by the extension of national power and security." Adams, *New England Federalism*, 148.

friends of commerce, of conservative government and good order seemed destined to permanent subjection by the party of "incongruous materials, all tending to mischief." [78] Under these circumstances some of the ultra Federalists began to feel that the Union had failed to secure their dearest interests, and to consider the feasibility of a northern confederation.[79] "The people of the East," wrote Pickering to George Cabot, "cannot reconcile their habits, views, and interests with those of the South and West. The latter are beginning to rule with a rod of iron. . . . . I do not believe in the practicability of a long-continued union. A northern confederacy would unite congenial characters." [80]

But the desperate situation of the Federalists was not to be relieved by secession. Separation might free them from the iron rod of western and southern democracy, but could not protect them from the rising democracy within New England itself. Only such a reactionary policy as was impracticable could afford a remedy. If Federalism could have turned back to the aristocratic regime of colonial days—"if," as Cabot expressed it, "no man in New England could vote for legislators who was not possessed in his own right of two thousand dollars' value in land," then, as he added, it might be possible to "do something better." [81] But Federalism could not save itself either by secession or by turning back,[82] and

---

[78] Hamilton's characterization of the Republican party, in letter to Jay, 1800. Lodge, *Works of Hamilton*, VIII, 550.

[79] Pickering was a leader of the Essex Junto, "composed chiefly of hard-headed merchants and lawyers of Essex County, where mercantile and maritime interests were even stronger than in Boston. Stephen Higginson, George Cabot, and Theophilus Parsons were its earliest leaders . . . . a few Boston Federalists, such as Fisher Ames, Timothy Bigelow, Christopher Gore, and John Lowell, Jr., afterwards became identified with the group. This Essex Junto, the ultra-conservative and ultra-sectional wing of the party, refused all compromise with democracy . . . . failed entirely to sympathise with the South and West, and, in short, was blind to the fact that the world had moved forward since 1775 and 1789." Morison, *Otis*, I, 48. *Cf.* Morse, A. E., *Federalist Party in Massachusetts*, 17, *f. n.* See *above*, 30, *note 66*, for connection of the Essex leaders with constitution making in Massachusetts.

[80] January 29, 1804. Adams, *New England Federalism*, 339.

[81] To Pickering, February 14, 1804. *Ibid.*, 346-349. Federalist control in the old states was doubtless prolonged by the emigration which drained off many who would have been Republicans if they had remained. It has been estimated that Massachusetts alone lost 180,000 souls between 1800 and 1810, through the westward movement. Haight, in *Milwaukee Sentinel*, Nov. 25, 1900.

[82] "I greatly fear that a separation would be no remedy, because the source [of the evils] is in the political theories of our country and in ourselves. . . . . *We are democratic altogether;* and I hold democracy, in its natural operation, to be the *government of the worst.*" Cabot to Pickering, Feb. 14, 1804: Adams, *New England Federalism*, 346-349. *Cf.* the advice of Hamilton: "Dismemberment of our empire will be a clear sacrifice of great positive advantages, without any counterbalancing good; administering no relief to our real disease, which is *Democracy;* the poison of which by a subdivision will only be the more concentrated in **each part,** and consequently the more virulent." *Ibid.*, 365. John Quincy Adams and Rufus

nothing but the unpopular foreign policy pursued by the Republicans themselves, after 1807, prevented the speedy dissolution which the election of 1804 portended. The popular approval which Jefferson had won in New England and New York by the moderate measures of his first term, he lost again through the embargo. The system of commercial restriction and the war which followed fell with crushing weight upon the maritime class and all of its dependents, driving many of the newly-made Republicans back to the Federalist party as the means of voicing their protest, and galvanizing the dying party into the semblancē of returning life where there was no enduring source of vitality. The elections of 1807 had for the first time placed the Republicans in control of both houses and the executive in Massachusetts, much to the satisfaction of the Washington government; but the prompt reaction due to the embargo restored Federalist power in the legislature the next year.[83] In New York also the Federalists made considerable gains, but not enough to shake the dominance of the Republicans.[84] Even in Virginia, where also Federalism had shown a marked decline since 1800, the party received an accession of strength because of the effect of the restrictions on commerce. Not only did the tidewater counties poll heavy anti-administration votes, but portions of the piedmont and Shenandoah Valley, deprived of their market for wheat, recurred to Federalism.[85] Monroe's friends, the Quids, sought aid of the Federalists in their efforts to defeat Madison as the successor to Jefferson's place and policies, and joined forces with them in advocating the recharter of the First United States Bank and in opposing the war and measures of prep-

King "considered a severance of the Union as a remedy more desperate than any possible disease." *Ibid.*, 148.

Those who shared Pickering's views were Griswold and Tracy, of Connecticut, and Plumer of New Hampshire. Other Federalists in Congress, for example, Hillhouse of Connecticut, sympathized to a degree. Pickering sounded King, Ames, Cabot, and Parsons, also, but received no encouragement from the Massachusetts Federalists, even of the Essex Junto. Lodge, *Cabot*, 438-439. For Plumer's views see Adams, *New England Federalism*, 144-145.

[83] Bradford, *Hist. of Mass.*, III, 99, 100: "The embargo law was so injurious to the prosperity of the State . . . . that the people withdrew their confidence and support from candidates for public offices, who were friends to the embargo, and to the general policy and measures of the national government." It was at this time that John Quincy Adams resigned his seat in the United States Senate, and was read out of the Federalist party, on account of his support of the embargo.

[84] Hammond, *Political Parties*, I, 265.

[85] Ambler, *Sectionalism*, 87, 90. The Valley had been one of the few Federalist areas in the West in 1788. See also Ambler, *Ritchie*, 47, 48, 56, *et passim*.

The gains of the Federalists were not limited to the regions mentioned in the text. Maryland was recovered in 1812, etc., etc.

aration for it.[86] The Quids disappeared as a distinct opposition
group after the restoration of harmony between their leader and
Madison, but the re-election of Virginia Federalists to Congress
during the war period suggests that many of them were less easily
reconciled than Monroe.[87] The leader of the Virginia Federalists
during these years was Daniel Sheffey, of Augusta County; and
through their representatives both in Congress and in the State
Assembly, the interior counties of Virginia showed an "opposition to the War of 1812 excelled only by that of the New England
Federalists." [88]

These facts signify merely a temporary revival of Federalism
in some of the old centers. Strong undercurrents had already
undermined its foundations. With the adjustment of foreign relations interest would recur to questions of domestic development
and westward expansion, and the final collapse would come. Indeed, even while the issues arising from our foreign difficulties
were uppermost, the antipathy of Federalism for the West was
strikingly manifested. One occasion was afforded by the bill for
the admission of the state of Louisiana, the first to be formed within the territory purchased from France—the first fruit of that
policy which the Federalists had anticipated with so much dread
in 1803. The speech of Josiah Quincy, of Massachusetts, in the
House of Representatives, in opposition to this bill, has long been
famous for its open threat of secession in the event of the bill's
passage. The ground of objection, however, rather than the threat,
deserves our attention. "The debates of that [convention] period,"
said he, "will show that the effect of the slave votes, upon the political influence of this part of the country, and the anticipated
variation of the weight of power to the West, were subjects of
great jealousy to some of the best patriots in the Northern and
Eastern States. Suppose, then, that it had been distinctly foreseen, that, in addition to the effect of this weight, the whole population of a world beyond the Mississippi was to be brought into this
and the other branch of the Legislature, to form our laws, control
our rights, and decide our destiny. Sir, can it be pretended that
the patriots of that day would for one moment have listened to it?
They were not madmen. . . . . It is impossible such a power could

---

[86] Ambler, *Sectionalism*, 88, 91, 92.
[87] *Ibid.*, 93.
[88] *Ibid.*, 92.

be granted. It was not for these men that our fathers fought. You have no authority to throw the rights and liberties, and property of this people, into a 'hotch pot' with the wild men on the Missouri, nor with the mixed, though more respectable race of Anglo-Hispano-Gallo Americans, who bask on the sands, in the mouth of the Mississippi." [89] Wheaton, of the same state, echoed in striking language the arguments of 1803 against the constitutionality of admitting new states created from acquired territory. "Who can tell where will be our ultimate bounds, or what number of States we may have in the Union? . . . . Then what will become of the Old United States, who first entered into the compact contained in the Constitution, and for whose benefit alone that instrument was made and executed. Instead of these new states being annexed to us, we shall be annexed to them, lose our independence, and become altogether subject to their control." [90] While New England voiced the opposition most vigorously she was not left without support from other sections. In fact, Sheffey spoke before either Quincy or Wheaton, but in moderate terms, counselling delay. "He was not, he said, directly hostile to the admission of this Territory into the Union." But he asked "Would gentlemen favor this French population at the expense of their own interests and rights [by premature admission]? . . . . Under the fostering hand of the General Government, let them become accustomed to our Government, before those were permitted to govern themselves who had so lately emerged from despotism." [91] This was a mild course, but the Republicans would have none of it. As in previous debates over the admission of states, they regarded territorial government as odious because not free, and desired the briefest possible apprenticeship.[92]

The extravagant language of Quincy was not inaptly referred to by Poindexter as "the ebullitions of political drunkenness," for in their frenzy the New Englanders were blind to the simple fact

---

[89] *Annals of Cong.*, Eleventh Cong., 3 sess., 537.

[90] *Ibid.*, 493-495.

[91] *Ibid.*, 484-485.

[92] "He would treat these people as he would the people of every other Territory. They were a part of the nation, and so ought to be considered. There ought to be no question as to what stock they sprung from. . . . . They had already served a sufficient apprenticeship to the United States, but not under a free Government, for the Territorial governments were not free. . . . . Wished to treat this Territory as well as the others and no better; he would not treat one as a daughter and the other as a step-daughter. He was as willing now to make Orleans a State as he had been to make Ohio a State." Speech of Nathaniel Macon. *Ibid.*, 484-485.

that much of the West would be peopled by emigrants from their own section. This the speaker just quoted tried to bring to their attention. "The people of the Eastern States will never give their assent to a dissolution of the Union. They are bound to the Western country by inseparable ties of nature and of interest. The hardy and adventurous sons of New England will, in a short time, compose a large proportion of the population on the waters of the Mississippi, and I undertake to assure the gentleman from Massachusetts, that they will never return to 'break into his house . . . .' " [93] But the Federalists would not be reassured, and of the 36 nays in the final vote 26 at least may be traced to them.

Following this defeat on the floor Quincy declined re-election to Congress, but entered the Massachusetts senate where he continued the agitation against expansion. In 1813 he drew up a report accompanied by a series of resolutions, denouncing as unconstitutional the admission of states created in territories not within the original limits of the Union, and especially the admission of Louisiana, and instructing the senators and requesting the representatives of the state to use their utmost endeavors to obtain a repeal of the act admitting her.[94] Thenceforth in the statements of the grievances of New England against the general government, commercial restrictions and the western policy are frequently united. Thus, in the resolutions which the Massachusetts legislature passed early in 1814, on account of the embargo act of the preceding December, occurs a recital of the woes of New England. Referring to the memorials sent up by the towns throughout the state, the report which precedes the resolutions says: "The people, in their numerous memorials from all quarters of the common-

---

[93] *Ibid.*, 569. The Massachusetts "blue bloods" were unable to persuade themselves that their own western emigrants were people of worth. When the traveller Faux visited the Federalist merchant Lyman, in Boston, in 1818, he records not only that "my host seems to regret that his freehold and other large estates give to him no more power than that of the humblest citizen," but that when the conversation turned to the plans of Birkbeck for an English settlement in Illinois, Lyman exclaimed: "If Mr. Birkbeck and others must emigrate why should they go into our wilderness, far from society, or at best mixing up with the refuse of our population, with men of stained names, thieves, and insolvents, who go thither to hide themselves; voluntary exiles, of whom society is well rid, because unable to endure them." Faux, W., *Memorable Days in America*, in Thwaites, *Early Western Travels*, XI, 57. *Cf.* View of Timothy Dwight, in his *Travels*, published a few years later—II, 458-463.

"The people in the Atlantic states have not yet recovered from the horror, inspired by the term 'backwoodsman.' This prejudice is particularly strong in New England, and is more or less felt from Maine to Georgia."—Flint, Timothy, *Recollections of the Last Ten Years*, 174. (Published in 1826).

[94] *Niles Register*, IV, 285-287. Reprinted in Ames, H. V., *State Documents on Federal Relations*, II, 25-31.

wealth, appear to despair of obtaining redress from that government, which was established 'TO PROMOTE THE GENERAL WELFARE.' They see that the voice of the New England States, whose interests are common, is lost in the national Councils, and that the spirit of accommodation and regard for mutual safety and advantage, which produced the constitution and governed its early administration, have been sacrificed to the bitterness of party, and to the aggrandizement of one section of the union, at the expense of another . . . ." The fundamental cause of these evils is found in the growth of the West. "They have seen a power grow up in the southern and western sections of the Union, by the admission and multiplication of states, not contemplated by the parties to the constitution, and not warranted by its principles; and they foresee an almost indefinite progression in this system of creation, which threatens eventually to reduce the voice of New England, once powerful and effectual in the national councils, to the feeble expression of colonial complaints, unattended to and disregarded." [95] The Hartford Convention, which brought this chapter of dissent and protest to its close, did not fail to include among its proposed amendments to the constitution one which was designed to afford at least a partial remedy for this grievance, in the provision that "No new State shall be admitted into the union by Congress in virtue of the power granted by the Constitution, without the concurrence of two-thirds of both Houses." That the moderate party controlled the Convention may be inferred from the mildness of this proposal in comparison with the demands of the radicals who framed the previous utterances.

Thus in all of the clamor of disaffected New England during the period of war there sounds this note of dislike and dread of the growing West. The quieter tones were in accord. From 1812 to 1815 Pickering busied himself, as in 1804, in correspondence with Federalist leaders as far south as Virginia, and seems to have been in touch with kindred spirits. [96] Once more he suggested

---

[95] *Niles Register*, VI, 4-8. Reprinted in Ames, *State Docs.*, II, 25-31.

[96] Adams, *New England Federalism*, 405. A. C. Hanson wrote to Pickering from Baltimore: "I am rejoiced to see Quincy making such a noble stand in the House of Representatives. . . . . He ought to be supported, and no doubt will . . . ." Considering the administration's foreign policy "and the creation of so many new States,—I shall become heartily sick of the Union. For my part, I say without reserve that *the Union was long ago dissolved;* and I never thought it criminal to compass a dismemberment of the States, although we have been educated in that belief. But I should prefer producing such an event by quiet means. I should like conventions to be called in the several States so disposed, and to proceed with calmness and dignified firmness. . . . . I think, if the question was barely *stirred*

secession as a remedy, although in guarded language. "To my ears there is no magic in the sound of Union. If the great objects of union are utterly abandoned,—much more, if they are wantonly, corruptly, and treacherously sacrificed by the Southern and Western States,—let the Union be severed. Such a severance presents no terrors to me." [97] The desirability of secession, in the thought of Pickering, lay, however, not so much in the fact that it would rid the East of southern control, as that it would free it from the pernicious connection with the West. It was the democratic West which he abhorred; for the aristocratic Republicanism of the old South he recognized the affinity of Federalism. He inclined to the belief that the southern States, if separated from the North, would seek a reunion, and that "the only permanent severance" would " be of the Western from the Atlantic States." [98] This he thought "would be a real blessing to the 'good old thirteen states,' as John Randolph once called them." [99] The British attack on New Orleans aroused the hope that such a separation might be the fortunate result of the war. In January, 1815, he wrote: "By taking and holding New Orleans, and consequently commanding the whole Western country, she will break the Union. . . . . The Atlantic States remaining united will in due time acquire a force sufficient to guard them from insult and injury, but short of that which would tempt ambition to involve them in destructive wars with children of our common ancestors. This view of things presents an additional reason to repress solicitude, where it exists, among any Atlantic citizens to recover New Orleans, should it fall into the hands of the British. Domestic or internal motives have excited in many a willingness, and in some a wish, that the Western States might go off and leave the Atlantic States free from their mischievous control,—a control every day becoming more powerful and dangerous." [100]

---

in New England, some States would drop off from the Union like fruit, *rotten ripe*. . . . . Virginia, with the other Southern States, and all Louisiana, and the Floridas in her rear, would then be left to govern her black population as she lists." *Ibid.*, 382.

[97] To Edward Pennington, July 12, 1812. *Ibid.*, 390.

[98] *Ibid.*

[99] To George Logan, July 4, 1813. *Ibid.*, 391.

[100] To Lowell. *Ibid.*, 425-426. Pickering vacillated somewhat in his opinions, but the above quotations seem to represent those which dominated him most of the time. He saw advantages and disadvantages both in union with the West and in separation. He feared separation would leave the old states saddled with the whole of the war debt and deprived of the public lands, which would be seized by the states within which they lay. *Ibid.*, 391. He did not fear the physical might of the West, believing that a single frigate could blockade the Mis-

At the date of this letter the war was over: the British had been repulsed at New Orleans, and the treaty of peace was a month old. The control of the United States over the Mississippi Valley had been threatened for the last time, and the expansion of the Republic was ensured. An unprecedented westward movement of population followed the return of peace, and a half-dozen states entered the Union within as many years. Such an increment of western power would have destroyed Federalism had it survived the war. But with the election of 1816 it ceased to maintain a national organization. Here and there in the old states groups of men clung to the party name for many years.[101] Occasionally they exerted some influence even in national politics. But even in its old strongholds Federalism was making its last fight against the reflux of the tide of democracy which had swept the West, and the adoption by the northeastern states of new constitutions or amendments granting manhood suffrage drove it from its last entrenchments and left its members no alternative except to join forces with the new party movements of the twenties. The history of parties for a decade following the war might detail the dissolution of the fragments of Federalism in the several states. Such a study would recount the activities in New England, the middle states, and even in the upper South, which resulted in mixed delegations to Congress, and discuss the attitude and influence of Federalists on the measures of Congress during the period. The part played by them in states where the dominant party was divided into factions might be included to show how they sometimes elected a governor or con-

---

sissippi and bring the inhabitants to terms by cutting them off from market. *Ibid.*, 390. He also saw the possibilities for the New England carrying trade in connection with the products of the Mississippi Valley. *Ibid.*, 407. The fear that the old Atlantic states would become insignificant politically as new states were multiplied, clung to him, however, and was the weightiest factor in determining his convictions. *Ibid.*, 407. At the least he hoped the demands of the Hartford Convention might result in restricted power in Congress to admit new states. He saw in the severance of the Atlantic coast and Mississippi Valley, which might result from the success of the British campaign, a condition which would force the Atlantic states into the close union which he believed desirable. "Should the severance . . . . take place," he wrote to Hillhouse, Dec. 16, 1814, "from that moment the necessity of Union among the Atlantic States will strike every man who thinks, as forcibly as during our Revolution; and the feebleness of the States south of the Potomac will urge them to cling to those of the North, as the Connecticut vine to the tree which supports it. The terms of a new compact will be adapted to this new state of things." *Ibid.,* 418. Can it be that the New England extremists desired to bring about secession through the Hartford Convention, as a means to reunion with the South on better terms, and with the West excluded?

[101] *E. g.*, Federalists cast 16,000 of the 40,000 votes in the Maryland state election of 1820. *Niles Register*, XIX, 111. In New Hampshire a Federalist electoral ticket received 1600 votes in that year, the Republican electors polling about 9,000. *New Hampshire Patriot*, January, 1821.

trolled a legislature. The influence of the undying hatred of the Essex Junto toward John Adams upon the fortunes of his son is typical of another class of data which might be collected. Of broader interest would be the story of such contests as that by which the Baptist-Methodist-Episcopalian alliance under the banner of Republicanism overturned the Congregationalist-Federalist regime in Connecticut and established a more liberal constitution in 1818. But to fix attention upon such details would be to follow eddies instead of the main current, since Federalism as the national rival of Republicanism came to an end in 1816.

Prior to the election of 1816 it was felt that the outcome of that campaign would decide the fate of the party. "If we cannot make any impression upon the presidential election, this time, I see no hope for the future," wrote T. Dwight to Rufus King in February.[102] For such an impression success in New York was a prerequisite, and as the best hope of carrying that state King was nominated for governor and his acceptance urged by the most influential Federalists.[103] The efforts in New York had, however, no other effect than to unite the Republicans who easily carried the election. Thereupon King abandoned hope for the party, and wrote to Gore of Massachusetts: "I presume that the failure will, as I think it should, discourage the Federalists from maintaining a fruitless struggle. It has probably become the real interest and policy of the country, that the Democracy should pursue its own natural course. Federalists of our age must be content with the past." [104] To his son Edward he confided his conviction that "so effectually prostrate is Federalism, that I have no kind of Expectation that [it] can be again in Favor." The only remaining course, in his opinion, was to support the "least wicked Section of the Republicans" in case of division among them.[105]

Already some correspondence had passed among the leaders concerning the most suitable candidate for the presidency. R. Morris believed "that if Howard of Maryland were started against Monroe, he would stand a tolerable chance. . . . . Should James Ross of Pennsylvania be held up also as Vice President, it would

---

[102] King, C. R., Life and Correspondence of Rufus King, V, 502.

[103] J. R. Van Rensselaer wrote, Feb. 16: "I most sincerely believe the existence of the federal party in this State depends on the decision you shall make." Others who wrote in similar vein were James Kent, Jacob Morris, W. A. Duer, T. Dwight, T. J. Oakley, D. B. Ogden, S. Rensselaer, et al. Ibid., 506.

[104] May 15, 1816. Ibid., 535.

[105] May 21. Ibid., 537.

conduce to the Union of one Party and contribute to distract the other. Howard has good Sense, Honor, Courage, and Integrity. Ross is a man of the highest order of Talents." [106] King himself seemed inclined to favor Ross.[107] In view of the discouraging defeat in New York, however, no formal steps were taken to unite upon a leader or to rally the party; the few Federalist electors cast their votes for King, and we may well accept his words quoted above as a fitting close to the history of the party.

So perished Federalism. Its aristocratic temper, its identification with the moneyed and commercial class of the seaboard, were the primary causes of its unfitness for expansion into regions where society was of a primitive agricultural type. But the West and the Northeast were not destined to permanent antagonism. By the mid-twenties the older section had felt the influence of the democratic spirit, the Northwest was entering a maturer stage marked by the growth of towns as centers of trade and manufacturing, and improved facilities for communication were drawing the two sections together—all of which revealed a partial harmony of interest which found political expression. How this came about, however, is the story, not of the decline of Federalism, but of the rise of a new party.

---

[106] March 15. *Ibid.*, VI, 15.
[107] Nov. 22. *Ibid.*, 35.

CHAPTER IV

THE DISRUPTION OF THE REPUBLICAN PARTY

1. THE ERA OF NATIONALISM

The exit of the Federalist party left the Republicans in triumphant possession of the field, but the Republican party of 1815 was far different from that of 1793 or 1798. Once firmly established in power, Jefferson and his friends found their views of the limits of federal authority greatly altered by their new situation. The functions of government might well be reduced to the minimum when performed by "aristocrats" but the *raison d'être* for restrictions disappeared in large measure with the advent of the party of the people. The Republicans took up the task of administration in 1801 with a boldness which soon made their change of temper evident even to the Federalists. "By downright demonstration," wrote Gouverneur Morris, "it is shown that the republican party were not dissatisfied because the power of the Government was too great, but because it was not in their hands." [1]

The party which had been so transformed by possession of power was now to be disrupted by the forces of a new era. The usual characterization of the decade following the War of 1812 as an "era of good feeling" and personal politics but thinly veils the truth that deep-seated forces were working a revolution in the basis of parties. In later periods of party reorganization, the cause of realignment is found in social and economic changes. The rapidity of the nation's growth has brought forward new problems with each generation, and each generation has accordingly seen a reshaping of party lines. The dramatic history of the decade preceding the Civil War is the most striking example of this truth: despite the earnest efforts of all those who foresaw the disruption of the old parties if not of the Union, the slavery question then thrust itself irresistibly into politics, destroying the Whig organization, dividing the Democracy, and giving birth to the Republican party. Again, as the century drew to its close, the readjustment of national life to the scale of the great continent which had been

---

[1] To H. W. Livingston, Nov. 25, 1803. Morris, *Morris*, III, 443.

brought under the hand of man involved notable changes in national problems and in the spirit and program of parties, notwithstanding the persistence of old party names.

The connection of the dissolution of the old Federalist and Republican parties and the birth of the National Republican and Democratic organizations with social and economic forces has been less studied and is more difficult to trace. At later epochs new tendencies were perceived and conscious efforts were made to counteract them; party discipline, highly developed since the Jacksonian epoch, has ever shown itself fearful of new issues. At the earlier epoch, however, not only were party methods and machinery less highly developed, but discipline was slight, and there was less perception of the relations between parties as such and the problems of the day. The decline of the old organizations after 1815 was at that time rather welcomed than deplored.[2] The belief prevailed widely that parties were unnecessary and even undesirable agencies in carrying on government, and while much was said about sound principles, party loyalty was lightly esteemed and sometimes even denounced as the spirit of faction.[3] A belief in the permanence of non-party government is implied, too, in the various proposals of the early twenties to amend the constitution in such a way as to prevent the quadrennial choice of the President by the House.[4] But even while cherishing the belief that all might unite in support of the principles of true republican government, men were dividing into groups according to divergent interests, and, through the operation of unperceived forces, were moving directly towards the new party organizations of the later twenties.

The first parties, as we have seen, grew out of conditions as they existed at the beginning of the national period. In the in-

---

[2] A typical comment of the period is the following reference to Monroe's tour: "Everything like *party* seems entirely forgotten—Federalists and Democrats appear emulous who shall render him most honor. . . . . There is reason to believe that Mr. Monroe will be the President of the United States, and not the President of a party; if so, he will command the support and esteem of the wise and virtuous of all parties, and retire from office amidst the benedictions of a grateful and happy people." *Winchester Gazette,* quoted by *Supporter,* July 1, 1817.

[3] Perhaps the most famous expression of this kind is contained in Jackson's letter to Monroe, Nov. 12, 1816, just after the latter's election, in which he said: "Everything depends on the selection of your ministry. In every selection, party and party feeling should be avoided. Now is the time to exterminate that *monster* called *party spirit* . . . . the chief magistrate of a great and powerful nation should never indulge in party feelings . . . ." Parton, James, *Life of Andrew Jackson,* II, 357 *et seq.*

[4] Ames, H. V., *Proposed Amendments to the Constitution* (in Amer. Hist. Assn. *Report* for 1896, II), 106 *et seq.*

terval between the adoption of the constitution and the presidency of Jackson an empire arose beyond the frontier of 1790 which exceeded the whole settled region of the former date in both population and area. The inhabitants of the United States according to the first census numbered somewhat less than four millions, of which, by the most liberal estimate, the entire transmontane region contained not more than two hundred and seventy-five thousand.[5] Even under a regime of equal rights, this ratio of about one in fifteen would have been the measure of an almost negligible influence in the affairs of the nation. But the next generation saw a great change in the relative weight of the two sections separated by the Alleghanies. By 1830 Kentucky and Tennessee boasted nearly one million four hundred thousand people, the wilderness of western New York had become the home of nearly half as many, and transmontane Pennsylvania, Maryland, and Virginia contributed a like number to the total population of the West. Moreover, into the old Northwest, into the Gulf Plains, and even into the acquired territory beyond the Mississippi, had poured a flood of migration which had peopled these vast spaces with two and a half millions more. Thus it came to pass that the West of the Jacksonian era contained more than five million inhabitants, exceeding by more than one-fourth the population of the entire country at the epoch of the first census, while the area settled after 1790 exceeded that occupied before by two-thirds.[6] As in population and extent, so in

---

[5] This estimate is reached as follows: Kentucky, 73,677; Tennessee, 35,691 (Thirteenth Census, *Population*, I, 30); to which must be added figures for the population northwest of the Ohio River, and in the western counties of some of the old states. The first census did not include the Northwest Territory in the area of enumeration, but Governor St. Clair estimated the inhabitants at 4,000 (*Century of Population Growth*, 54). Jedediah Morse's estimate of 1792 was 7,820. (Cited *ibid.*) In New York, settlement had not yet passed the lake region, the whole western end of the state being embraced in Ontario County with about 1,000 inhabitants. (Twelfth Census, *Population*, I, 32. County maps of the states for 1790 are given in *Century of Population Growth*, 61-70.) The transalleghany portions of Pennsylvania, Maryland, and Virginia contributed about 160,000 to the total—Virginia counties now composing West Virginia, 55,873; Allegheny, Washington, Fayette, Westmoreland, Bedford, and Huntington Counties, Pa., as bounded in 1790, 84,211; Allegany and Washington Counties, Maryland, 20,631. As some of the population of counties included was intramontane rather than transmontane, the estimate of the text is generous, even without making allowance for Northumberland County, Pa., which lay beyond the mountains in part, but for which figures are not available. (Estimates based on statistics in Population volumes of Thirteenth Census, and maps in *Century of Population Growth*). Pitkin, T., *Statistical View*, 533, says: "In 1790, the whole population of this country . . . . was only two hundred and thirty-seven thousand and eighty-four."

[6] Kentucky, 687,917; Tennessee, 681,904; New York counties west of Syracuse, 625,452; Pennsylvania counties west of Bedford, 384,891; Washington and Allegany Counties, Maryland, 35,877; counties now composing West Virginia, 176,924. In Georgia, counties created west of the frontier of 1790 contained 281,612 persons in 1830. Adding the population of the

economic importance, the West of 1830 approached the whole United States of 1790. The value of the exports of 1790 is fairly matched by that of the surplus produce of the West forty years later, and the tonnage employed in export trade at the former epoch by that employed on the western waters at the latter.[7] Of course, this transformation of the wilderness was partially counterbalanced by the growth of the older region, which shows an increase in population between 1790 and 1830 of about four millions. But the change in relative weight is indicated by a sixfold increase in the ratio of transmontane population to the total, and a corresponding movement westward of the center of population and of economic and political power. New states carved from what was wilderness when Washington was inaugurated elected more than one-third of the members of the House of Representatives under Jackson—more than all of the South Atlantic States and nearly twice as many as the whole of New England.[8] The result was a disturbance of the former relations of economic groups. The weight of the commercial, manufacturing, agrarian, and planting interests was altered, and new adjustments, new combinations and alliances, necessitated. Politically the results were new issues, new sectional antagonisms

---

northwestern, southwestern, and transmississippi states and territories, the total for 1830 is 5,172,532. Pitkin's estimate (1835) was "between four and five millions." *Op. cit.*, 533.

In 1790 the settled area (at least two inhabitants to the square mile) measured 238,935 square miles; in 1830, 632,717. *Century of Population Growth*, 54.

[7] Value of all goods exported from the United States for year ending Sept. 30, 1790, $20,205,156. *American State Papers, Commerce and Navigation*, I, 34. "We hazard nothing in estimating the whole surplus production of what we have called the western country, in 1834, at from $28,000,000 to $30,000,000; being about fifty per cent. more than the whole exports of the United States in 1790." Pitkin, *Stat. View*, 534 et seq. If the Gulf region and lower Mississippi Valley were included in the estimate the total would be much larger.

Total tonnage, American and foreign, employed in export trade, 1789, 233,983. *Ibid.*, 352. Total tonnage employed on western waters, 1834, about 230,000. *Ibid.*, 536.

[8] Representation in the House, compiled from Thirteenth Census, *Population*, I, 37:

	Apportionment of 1790	Just before Apportionment of 1830	Just after Apportionment of 1830
New England	29	39	38
Middle States	29	67	75
South Atlantic	45	60	60
West	3*	47	67

The relative decline of the old states is shown even more strikingly by the loss and gain in the representation of individual states, as the ratio of representation rose. Thus Massachusetts, represented by 14 members under the first apportionment, rose to 17 under that of 1800, but fell to 13 in 1810 and to 12 in 1830. Connecticut likewise fell from 7 in 1790 to 6 in 1830. On the other hand, states with a "West" within their bounds gained; Georgia's increase was from 2 to 9; New York's from 10 to 40; Pennsylvania's, 13 to 28; Virginia's, 19 to 21. After 1830 even New York felt the drain of the newer West and lost representation through the higher ratio, its delegation falling to 34, 33, and 31 at successive census periods.

*Kentucky 2, after 1792; Tennessee 1, after 1796.

and affinities, and finally new party groupings. As the development of the West was a prime cause of the disturbance of the old order and the source of many of the new issues, so its growth in political power made it a leading factor in determining the readjustment.

With the close of the War of 1812 the energies of the United States, for a quarter-century so largely concerned with European relations, were released for the furtherance of domestic interests. The reorganization of finances and the currency, and the attempt to organize the nation's resources as a means of preparation against the contingency of future war, were fruits of the conflict just closed which were presently overshadowed by the problems arising from the wonderful internal development of the country.[9] The weight of these new problems fell upon that group of "Young Republicans" who had come forward with the war, and whose dominance had been foreshadowed by their success in forcing a war policy upon the pacifist president of the generation then passing from active life; and under the lead of Clay, Calhoun, Grundy, Cheves, and Porter this rising group approached its task overflowing with the spirit of a new nationalism which swept the country with the return of peace.

The experiences of the war period unmistakably taught the need of a larger exercise of federal power. The evils of irredeemable bank paper cried aloud for that remedy which had been denied in 1811 when the Republicans refused to recharter the United States Bank. The dependence of the country upon foreign sources of supply for manufactured goods of prime necessity, at a time when the enemy's ships patrolled the paths of ocean commerce, was a convincing argument in favor of that protection which Hamilton had advocated. The difficulty in handling troops and supplies in the frontier campaigns, because of the want of military roads, brought the question of internal improvements forward as one of the most pressing problems of the new day.

---

[9] "What will you do for news now that Napoleon is vanquished?" Thomas Ritchie, editor of the *Richmond Enquirer*, asked himself in order to answer: "Have the Americans no watercourses to clear? No canals to construct? no roads to form? no bridges to erect? . . . . " Ambler, *Thomas Ritchie*, 63. Contemporaries had a vague feeling that the close of the war would mark the beginning of a new era in politics. ". . . . The great commotions of the old world, the effects of which were felt in both periods [Federalist and Republican] of our governmental history, have just ceased, and of course, the next administration will be placed in a situation, in many respects, unlike that of all their predecessors." *Albany Daily Advocate*, quoted by *Supporter*, Oct. 29, 1816.

By the logic of such events even the Old School leaders were swept into the current of the new nationalism. In his "Notes on Virginia," in 1785, Jefferson had written: "For the general operations of manufacture, let our workshops remain in Europe. It is better to carry provisions and materials to workmen there, than to bring them to the provisions and materials, and with them their manners and principles." [10] But in 1816 he confessed to an altered opinion. "We have experienced what we did not then believe, that there exists both profligacy and power enough to exclude us from the field of interchange with other nations: that to be independent for the comforts of life we must fabricate them ourselves. We must now place the manufacturer by the side of the agriculturist. . . . . Shall we make our own comforts, or go without them, at the will of a foreign nation? He, therefore, who is now against domestic manufacture, must be for reducing us either to dependence on that foreign nation, or to be clothed in skins, and to live like wild beasts in dens and caverns." [11]

President Madison's message of 1815, frankly admitting that the doctrine of *laissez faire* was subject to exceptions, pled for such an adjustment of the tariff as would make for economic preparedness.[12] In the same message he called the attention of Congress to the "great importance of establishing throughout our country the roads and canals which can best be executed under the national authority," urging not only the economic value but "the political effect of these facilities for intercommunication in bringing and binding more closely together the various parts of our extended confederacy." A year later he recurred to the subject.[13] Monroe, like his two predecessors, favored encouragement of domestic manufactures, declaring in his inaugural that "we ought not to depend in the degree we have done on supplies from other countries. While we are thus dependent the sudden event of war, unsought and unexpected, can not fail to plunge us into the most serious difficulties." [14]

---

[10] See *above*, 37, *f. n.* 104.

[11] To Benjamin Austin, Ford, *Writings of Jefferson*, XIV, 389-393.

[12] "In selecting the branches more especially entitled to the public patronage, a preference is obviously claimed by such as will relieve the United States from a dependence on foreign supplies . . . . for articles necessary for the public defence or connected with the primary wants of individuals." Richardson, *Messages of the Presidents*, I, 567.

[13] *Ibid.*, 576.

[14] *Ibid.*, II, 8.

In these utterances the veterans were but following "with caution and good heed" the new leaders upon whom had devolved the real initiative. The preparedness program of the new school was set forth by Clay in a speech in opposition to the reduction of the direct tax imposed during the war. The unsatisfactory state of our relations with foreign countries, he urged, was a warning of the possibility of further wars which made it prudent to increase the standing army and to augment the navy. As part of the same system of national defence, he wished the construction of roads and canals to unite the extremes of the country, and the protection of manufactures, both to provide a source of supply for our wants when commerce should be interrupted by hostilities, and to create resources the taxation of which in war time would replace the import duties.[15] Clay's argument, vigorously seconded by Calhoun, was several times reiterated during the discussion of the tariff bill of 1816. "Whenever," said Calhoun, "we have the misfortune to be involved in a war with a nation dominant on the ocean . . . . the moneyed resources of the country to a great extent must fail. . . . . Commerce and agriculture, till lately almost the only, still constitute the principal, sources of our wealth. . . . . They both depend on foreign markets. . . . . Our commerce neither is nor can be protected by the present means of the country. What, then, are the effects of a war with a maritime power—with England? Our commerce annihilated, spreading individual misery and producing national poverty; our agriculture cut off from its accustomed markets. . . . . The failure of the wealth and resources of the nation necessarily involved in the ruin of its finances and its currency. . . . . When our manufactures are grown to a certain perfection, as they soon will be under the fostering care of Government, we will no longer experience these evils. The farmer will find a ready market for his surplus produce; and, what is almost of equal consequence, a certain and cheap supply of all his wants. . . . . The arm of Government will be nerved; and taxes in the hour of danger . . . . may be greatly increased. . . . . To give perfection to this state of things, it is necessary to add, as soon as possible, a system of internal improvements, and at least such an extension of our navy as will prevent the cutting off our coasting trade." [16]

---

[15] *Works of Clay* (Federal edition), VI, 83-99, esp. 98.
[16] Cralle, R. K., *Works of John C. Calhoun*, II, 164-168.

It is plain that the emphasis in these discussions is laid upon the safety of the nation in time of war. The force of the tariff argument was derived from the relation of economic independence to national preparedness, and protectionism was fairly free in this stage from the suspicion of seeking to favor the manufacturing interest to the disadvantage of commerce or planting. Both of the great leaders disavowed such motives. "It was the duty of this country, as a means of defence, to encourage the domestic industry of the country. . . . . I lay the claims of the manufacturers entirely out of view," said Calhoun.[17] It may have seemed probable that commerce and agriculture would resume with peace substantially their ante-bellum status, and the patriotic appeal of the nationalist argument explains the small part which sectionalism played in the discussion of this tariff.[18] Calhoun's explanation of his own attitude may be accepted as fairly typical of opinion in the non-manufacturing districts: "Coming, as he did, from the South, having, in common with his immediate constituents, no interest but in the cultivation of the soil, in selling its products high, and buying cheap the wants and conveniences of life, no motive could be attributed to him but such as were disinterested." [19] Incidentally there appeared during this debate, however, a view which was soon to overshadow that which dominated in 1816. Calhoun had declared that "When our manufactures are grown to a certain perfection . . . . the farmer will find a ready market for his surplus produce; and . . . . a certain and cheap supply of all his wants. . . . . To give perfection to this state of things, it will be necessary to add, as soon as possible, a system of internal improvements." In these words was foreshadowed a scheme of domestic development which would stress national self-sufficiency even more for the sake of economic prosperity than with the thought of safety in war time. This ideal appears now and then in the discussions, and was expounded with much force in the report of a committee of Congress, early in 1816, which predicted the beneficial results of protection in the following terms: "Different

---

[17] *Annals*, Fourteenth Cong., 1 sess., 837.

[18] See *below*, 117, for opposition to this bill.

[19] *Annals*, Fourteenth Cong., 1 sess., 1329. With the views of Clay and Calhoun contrast those of Ingham, of Pennsylvania, a member of the Ways and Means Committee, who urged that protection should not be confined to articles indispensable in time of war and of first necessity in time of peace. Stanwood, E., *American Tariff Controversies in the Nineteenth Century*, I, 142.

sections of the union will, according to their position, the climate, the population, the habits of the people, and the nature of the soil, strike into that line of industry which is best adapted to their interest and the good of the whole; and active and free intercourse, promoted and facilitated by roads and canals, will ensue. The states that are most disposed to manufactures, as regular occupations, will draw from the agricultural states all the raw materials which they want, and not an inconsiderable portion also of the necessaries of life; while the latter will, in addition to the benefits which they at present enjoy, always command in peace or in war, at moderate prices, every species of manufacture, that their wants may require. Should they be inclined to manufacture for themselves, they can do so with success, because they have all the means in their power to erect and to extend at pleasure manufacturing establishments. Our wants being supplied by our own ingenuity and industry, exportation of specie to pay for foreign manufactures will cease." [20]

Here, then, is an adaptation of Adam Smith's theory of free trade among nations in which the great sections of the Union take the place of nations, and Smith's ideal world economy is replaced by a theory of national self-sufficiency based upon the vastness and diversity of resources of the different parts; the sections, bound together by improved means of communication and transportation, should become reciprocally dependent but collectively independent of the rest of the world. This scheme of a national economy, destined to become known as the "American System," soon supplanted the preparedness program of the New Republicans. The phrase was due to Clay, with whose name the policy came to be most closely associated. When Calhoun withdrew from the congressional forum to accept the war portfolio in Monroe's cabinet, Clay become the central figure in the group, and it was he who

---

[20] *Annals,* Fourteenth Cong., 1 sess., 1665 *et seq. Cf.* P. B. Porter's recognition of the division of the United States into eastern and western sections by the mountains, with the agriculturists on the one side and the merchants and manufacturers on the other. This diversity, which it had been asserted would lead to separation, he believed, might be made the means of closer union: "It will be obviously for the interests of the interior States to exchange the great surplus products of their lands, and the raw materials of manufactures, for the merchandise and manufactured articles of the Eastern States, and on the other hand the interests of the merchants and manufacturers of the Atlantic will be equally promoted by this internal commerce; and it is by promoting this commerce by encouraging and facilitating this intercourse—it is by producing a mutual dependence of interests between these two great sections, and by these means only, that the United States can ever be kept together." *Annals,* Eleventh Cong., 1 and 2 sess., 1388.

gathered together the hints and suggestions of lesser men, harmonizing and systematizing them, and finally giving them their clearest and most convincing form of expression. The depression of all branches of industry during the early twenties, by centering attention upon the need of remedial measures, did much to crystallize the theory, which reached maturity about 1824.[21] "We have shaped our industry, our navigation, and our commerce, in reference to an extraordinary war in Europe, and to foreign markets which no longer exist," said Clay, in discussing the tariff bill of 1824.[22] "The consequence of the termination of the war of Europe has been the resumption of European commerce, European navigation, and the extension of European agriculture and European industry in all its branches. Europe, therefore, has no longer occasion, to anything like the same extent as that she had during her wars, for American commerce, American navigation, the produce of American industry." Continuing, he explained the relation of the market for the surplus produce of all forms of labor to the prosperity of society, and pointed out that the surplus produce of the United States was increasing much more rapidly than the consuming power of Europe. Besides, it was the policy of European states to reject the food products of America, in order to foster their own agriculture; receiving only those raw materials for their factories which they could not produce. "A genuine American policy," while cherishing the foreign market, would create also a home market for the products of our agriculture "in all its varieties, of planting, farming and grazing." "If we cannot sell, we cannot buy." European manufactures cannot be had by the American farmer who has nothing the foreigner will take in exchange. Nor, since the planter cannot purchase the entire surplus of the farmer, can his staple exports pay for the imports of both. The establishment of manufactures would create a home market for the planter

---

[21] The prominence of the West in the agitation for increased protection, while the Act of 1816 was still in force, is noteworthy. In Pittsburg, one of the earliest centers of manufactures beyond the mountains, it was found that the depression from which her factories suffered extended to the farmers, by curtailing the local market for their surplus. McMaster, *History of the People of the United States*, IV, 344. The mutual dependence of farm and factory was thus shown by an object lesson. Baldwin, of the Committee on Manufactures, who reported the tariff bill of 1820, represented the Pittsburg district. In reporting the bill he tried hard to meet the criticism of those who contended that protection favored particular interests at the expense of the nation as a whole. "If this bill . . . . cannot be supported on national principles, we are willing that it should fall, and that its fate shall be ours." *Annals*, Sixteenth Cong., 1 sess., II, 1916 *et seq.*

[22] *Works of Clay* (Federal edition), VI, 254-294. *Cf.* speech on bill of 1820, *ibid.*, 219-287.

and farmer, and a source of supply for their necessities by way of exchange. "The superiority of the home market results, first, from its steadiness and comparative certainty at all times; secondly, from the creation of reciprocal interest; thirdly, from its greater security; and, lastly, from an ultimate and not distant augmentation of consumption (and consequently of comfort) from increased quantity and reduced prices. But this home market, highly desirable as it is, can only be created and cherished by the protection of our own legislation against the inevitable prostration of our industry which must ensue from the action of foreign policy and legislation." [23]

2. DEVELOPMENT OF ECONOMIC LIFE AND THOUGHT OF THE WEST

Although they spoke in terms of nationalism, the Republican leaders voiced the demands of the rising western section of the Union. Whether he led or followed, Clay's opinions especially, except in the matter of the Second United States Bank,[24] show a remarkable correspondence with western sentiment. During the years 1815 to 1830, the western movement, swelled by many favoring influences, reached unprecedented volume. By 1815 the older transalleghany settlements were already well out of the pioneer stage, and the frontier line was advancing in form of a wedge the point of which was rapidly ascending the Missouri, while the irregular sides slanted back to the northeast and southeast, crossing Illinois and Indiana well south of the center, and following roughly the Tennessee boundary and the Oconee River on the South. The banks of the Mississippi bore scattered settlements, and the State of Louisiana formed a kind of island of population lying in advance of the main frontier. Within a few years after the signing of the Peace of Ghent, the acquisition of Florida and a series of treaties with the Indian tribes, now lacking the support of foreign influences, opened to white occupation vast tracts in the Northwest and Southwest. The land laws of 1820 and 1821 made easier than ever before the acquisition of land by the poor pioneer, while the vast extent of the frontier favored the squatter by diminishing the prob-

---

[23] Cf. nationalism of the speech of Martindale of New York on this bill. Annals, Eighteenth Cong., 1 sess., I, 1631.

[24] See below, 185, f. n. 32.

ability of government interference. The diversion of New England agriculture from grain raising to wool-growing and dairying, under stress of competition with the fresh lands of the West, displaced a portion of the population which, not taking kindly to labor in the rising factories, joined the westward-moving stream. The culture of short-staple cotton, made profitable by the gin, was invading the southern piedmont, displacing the small farm economy and converting the farmer into a planter or driving him to the frontier in Alabama or Illinois.[25]

Prior to 1840, most of New England's contribution to this migration was absorbed by western New York, that portion of it which reached the Northwestern states furnishing only a sprinkling in the total population.[26] For several years after 1815, indeed, the chief element in the settlement of both Northwest and Southwest was supplied by that "piedmontese" stock which had pioneered the way into the transalleghany country a generation before, and which now felt a new impulse in the push of the advancing plantation system. The spread of this stock from its original western centers and the addition of newcomers from its old seats bore fruit before 1820 in the four new states of Indiana, Illinois, Mississippi, and Alabama.[27] For a decade after the war, however, the Ohio Valley was the heart of the West, and this region, where society was in the making, was in this period coming rapidly to self-consciousness, and was not backward in voicing the demand that its interests be promptly and effectively provided for.

The significance of the rise of this new section has been indicated by a recent writer in the statement that the "improvement in the economic condition of the West which set in about the time of the second war with England, and which in a decade or two entirely changed the relation of that region to the rest of the country," is "the most important event in our economic history during the first half of the nineteenth century."[28] Contemporaries were not unaware that the star of economic and political empire was passing westward. The course of the Federalists for years is proof of this.

---

[25] Turner, F. J., *Rise of the New West*, Chaps. 1-6.

[26] Mathews, L. K., *Expansion of New England.*

[27] As late as 1850, one-third of the population of Indiana consisted of Carolinians and their children. Turner, F. J., "Dominant Forces in Western Life," in *Atlantic Monthly,* LXXIX.

[28] Callender, G. S., "Early Transportation and Banking Enterprises," in *Quarterly Journal of Economics,* XVII, 116 *et seq.*

Excepting in New York, Pennsylvania, Maine, and Georgia, which still included unsettled areas within their bounds, the population of the coast states had come almost to a standstill, and the exodus was so great as to cause grave concern to the authorities.[29] Inquiries were made under legislative authority, especially in the South, to discover what could be done to counteract the attractions of the West, and resulted in numerous schemes of internal improvements by states to facilitate the marketing of the produce of the interior farms.[30] Privately, far-sighted men were advising the younger generation to "Go West." Even King, the last presidential candidate of the Federalist party, held the opinion that "Unless the navigation and commerce of the United States become more extensive and prosperous, the Northern States will continue to lose their importance, and, with this, their population and wealth will be certain to suffer. If we are not to be commercial, but agricultural, and, if you please manufacturing, the Western country ought, and will be, the favored region in which both will prosper." [31]

The story of the economic development of the West during its first half-century is an epitome of the history of the evolution of modern industrial society. From the self-sufficing household it advanced to a local economy, then to a provincial, and before the mid-twenties was the advocate of a national economy.

The transalleghany pioneer had found himself cut off from the rest of the world by stretches of unpeopled wilderness and mountain. Thrown upon his own resources, his first productive efforts were consumed in securing the rudest necessities of existence. The scanty yield of his crude agriculture was supplemented by the use of the rifle, and his manner of life sank almost to the level of that of the savage. No division of labor was possible except within the household, which constituted a self-sufficient economic unit. Such was the economy which moved westward with the frontier, but the older settlements emerged from this primitive stage as the pro-

---

[29] The following is a typical press comment of the period: "That alarming disease denominated the *Ohio fever*, (says a New-Hampshire paper) continues to rage in many parts of New-England, by which vast numbers are *taken off*. In Connecticut it has spread to such a surprising extent, that Gov. Wolcott, considers 'an investigation of the causes which produce it as by far the most important subject which can engage the attention of the legislature.' " *Supporter*, Aug. 12, 1817.

[30] *Niles Register*, IX, 149, 165.

[31] To Gore, Nov. 5, 1816. King, *Life of King*, VI, 32-34. His forecast was probably a factor in the decision of his son Edward to settle in Chillicothe, Ohio, where he began to practice law at the close of the war.

duction of the farmer became more than sufficient for the requirements of his own family. An agricultural surplus meant the possibility of exchange by the farmer for the products of the labor of others; it meant the possibility of distant commerce and of local division of labor, and in a measure it resulted in both. Isolation affected the West, however, much as commercial restrictions and war did the old states; or to vary the comparison, it was equivalent to high duties on imported goods. The vast distances which separated the new settlements from the markets of Europe and the Atlantic coast, and the mountain barrier which interposed along the direct routes to the East, made all intercourse with the rest of the world so difficult that the West was compelled so far as possible to manufacture for itself.[32]

With this differentiation of economic activity, exchange began between town and country, the farmer finding a home market in supplying the needs of men of other occupations, and receiving in his turn the products of the craftsman. Thus the West entered the second stage of its economic development. The first manufactures were, as the term literally implies, handicrafts, but the application of power to machinery appeared early in the form of mills for grinding wheat and corn, driven by wind, water, or horsepower. By the beginning of the War of 1812, factories were rising in the upper Ohio Valley. Even as early as 1809 Cincinnati had two cotton mills, and at about that time a factory was erected there for the production of cotton and woolen machinery.[33] Within a half-dozen years its output became considerable, and mills for the manufacture of various fabrics, operated by steam power, were

---

[32] Early observers found in the isolation of the West an omen of prosperity. Harris, who visited the West at the beginning of the nineteenth century, commented: "So circumstanced they will be provident of their use of foreign articles, they will prevent their need of many of them by setting up various manufactures, the raw materials of which they so abundantly possess, and thus supply other places without needing or being able to receive any return but specie. The consequence will be that this interior country must every year become more independent of other countries, more prosperous, and more happy." *Journal of a Tour into the Territory Northwest of the Alleghany Mountains*, 1803, in Thwaites, *Early Western Travels*, III, 180.

The West, like the East, felt to some extent the impulse due to the artificial restrictions on foreign commerce in the form of the embargo and non-intercourse acts, as may be seen from the message of Governor Huntington, of Ohio, in 1810, directing attention to the benefits of home manufactures: "The embarrassments imposed on our commerce by foreign nations, has [*sic*] turned the attention of the people in many of the states to domestic manufactures. Some establishments for that purpose have been commenced in this state . . . ." Message printed in *Supporter*, Dec. 22, 1810.

[33] Goodwin, F. P., "The Rise of Manufactures in the Miami Country," in *Amer. Hist. Rev.*, XII, 768.

built throughout the Valley from Pittsburg and Steubenville to Lexington and Cincinnati.[34]

Within a decade of the close of the war, the manufactures of the region attained considerable proportions and variety, including steam engines, agricultural implements, carriages and wagons, milling machinery, hats, caps, cloth and clothing, hardware, nails, copper, tinware, glass, pottery, brick and lime, soap and candles, flour, leather, lumber, liquors, packed meats, linseed oil, paints and cordage.[35] Large quantities of these products were marketed not only in Ohio, Kentucky, and Indiana, but in the lower Mississippi Valley,[36] and engaged a considerable percentage of the population in the more advanced communities.[37]

This extension of the scope of western industry ushered in what we have called the provincial era, covering roughly the decade following the war. The contemporary expansion of the plantation system in the South enlarged the market for the produce of western farms, and gave the means with which to command goods imported from quarters of the globe where the West sold nothing. The western attitude towards industry and trade at the beginning of this epoch is indicated by the opinion of one of Cincinnati's leading residents: "To convert into manufacturers the hands engaged in clearing and improving a new country, would be a mistaken policy. . . . . In the case in which a new country is contiguous to an older, of dense population, which can exchange manufactures for subsistence, it may even be advisable to defer manufacturing in the former to a late period. But where a new country must transport its surplus agricultural production to a great distance, and import the necessary manufactures from shops equally remote, it may be advisable to commence manufacturing much earlier. It must not, however, attempt to convert its farmers into tradesmen. They should be imported instead of their manufactures. The ranks of agriculture would then remain entire; the simple process of

---

[34] Lippincott, Isaac, "Pioneer Industry in the West," in *Journal of Political Economy*, XVIII, 269 *et seq.* Gephart, W. F., *Transportation and Industrial Development in the Middle West*, 90-94.

[35] *Ibid.*, and Goodwin, "Rise of Manufactures," 764.

[36] *Ibid.*, 762.

[37] The census of 1820 divided persons in gainful occupations into three classes: those engaged in agriculture, commerce, and manufactures. In the counties of the Miami Valley the percentage of the industrial population engaged in manufacturing (probably including household as well as shop industries) varied from eleven in Preble County to twenty-five in Butler. *Ibid.*, 774.

barter at home be substituted for expensive and hazardous commercial operations; and the immigrating manufacturers with their
increase become an addition to the population." [38]

As early as 1810 Governor Huntington of Ohio had declared
in his message: ". . . . The heavy charges attending the introduction
of foreign manufactures, so far into the interior, all point out the expediency of making every public, as well as private, exertion, to
establish, on a permanent-foundation, such manufactures, at least,
as are of first necessity. . . . . Manufactures would afford a market
for the productions of our soil, and enable us to do without the merchandise of other countries. . . . ." [39] "The enormous price which
everything of foreign growth or manufacture bears at the present
day must convince us that we cannot too soon commence our independence of other nations by growing and manufacturing for ourselves," wrote a newspaper contributor in 1814.[40] "If for the solid
products and labor of the country exported, and far beyond it, articles of luxury and superfluity are introduced into the country, the
necessary tendency is, to impoverish and weaken it. . . . . What we
do manufacture is better generally than that which we import . . . .
and when we consider further that whatever is manufactured
among ourselves is free of the expense of duty and transportation,
it is our duty . . . . to examine our own resources and bring them
into action and use." [41]   So wrote the Governor of Ohio in 1817.
He admits, indeed, that "if in our intercourse with other nations,
we could on our part give in exchange such articles as we can grow
or manufacture most advantageously, for such others as our own
comfort and circumstances may require, such a course of change
would operate beneficially." But he held that such is not the situation of the West, and concluded that "as far as circumstances will
permit, every community should rely on its own resources." The
evil of buying more than the exports from the western country paid
for, hinted at in this message, involved the additional evil of payment of trade balances in specie, much to the embarrassment of the
circulation in the West. To these economic motives favoring western manufactures were joined at the close of the war patriotic considerations derived from the British origin of most of the imported

---

[38] *Ibid.*, 770, quoting Drake, *Natural and Statistical View of Cincinnati*, 3.
[39] Printed in *Supporter*, Dec. 22, 1810.
[40] *Western Spy*, cited by Goodwin, "Rise of Manufactures." (Issue of January 29.)
[41] Gov. Worthington. Message printed in *Supporter*, Dec. 9, 1817.

goods. "How shall we find a remedy for this ruinous British trade, which .... drains us of our specie," became the cry, and the Cincinnati writer who voiced it was ready with the answer: "We can manufacture almost every article of British manufacture that we drag over the mountains at such enormous expense. .... Put in operation in Cincinnati manufactures for woolen cloth, for cotton cloth, for .... every article which .... can be manufactured in Cincinnati. Let the money which we send over the mountains be paid the manufacturers in Cincinnati." [42]

These expressions of opinion are evidence of the desire for an economy adjusted to the stage of development which had been reached by the provincial West. The inconvenience of intercourse with the East created a desire for self-sufficiency, and local manufactures lessened the hardships of semi-isolation. The banking and currency system conformed to the provincial situation. In the West as elsewhere numerous state banks sprang up after the refusal of Congress to recharter the United States Bank, in 1811, and in view of the scarcity of specie, the nearest approach to a sound currency possible was the issues of these banks, on the basis of specie reserves. Lax as were the current laws regulating banking operations, there was a general appreciation of the importance of maintaining a sufficient supply of specie to support the paper of the banks, and bankers who endeavored to conduct their business in good faith did not venture to issue paper in excess of two or three times the amount of specie held in reserve. The states usually imposed some such restrictions upon the banking corporations holding charters,[43] but institutions of various descriptions circulated notes without authority of government, and in practice the test of the soundness of the issuing concern was payment of its notes in specie on demand.[44] Such a currency served fairly well, on the whole, in transactions in the neighborhood of the issuing banks, but the inconvenience and cost of exchange in distant trade relations added to the other impediments in the way of such trade, and to the reasons for confining trade within the western country.

---

[42] Goodwin, "Rise of Manufactures," 769.

[43] *E. g.*, the Ohio law of 1816 limited debts, including notes, above deposits, to three times the paid-in capital stock, of which one-half at least must be specie.

[44] *Cf.* Huntington, C. C., *A History of Banking and Currency in Ohio before the Civil War*, 37, 65-66. Near the end of the war, specie payments were suspended by the western banks, but normal conditions, according to contemporary standards, were restored soon after the war closed and lasted for a short time. *Ibid.*, 52, 55.

The provincialism of the West was intensified, too, by the fact
that the governments of the new states were often interested in
the operations of the chartered banks and shared in their profits
under various plans.[45]

The attacks of western states on the branches of the Second
United States Bank resulted from this provincial attitude. The
branches were accorded a˘lukewarm welcome at first, because it
was believed that they would bring into the country large sums
in specie to provide the basis of their note issues. It was soon
rumored, however, that the capital of the branches consisted chiefly
of the notes of local banks, and that the specie for their operations
was obtained by presenting these notes for redemption. The con-
tinual presentation of local bank notes for payment in specie and
the remittance of it eastward in settlement of trade accounts was
taken as proof that the Bank and its branches was a mechanism for
draining the interior states of their specie; the contraction of the
local bank circulation made necessary by the specie drain made it
more difficult to obtain accommodations and was believed to have
an adverse effect upon prices and trade conditions in general; and
the lack of any profit in or control over the operations of the
branches by the state governments aroused a hostility which was
well-nigh universal, and led to the attempts of Ohio and Kentucky
to tax.[46] Contemporary criticisms of the Bank remind us that the
Ohio Valley bore a relation to the seaboard in financial matters in
1818-1820 similar to that held by the "back settlements" in the
eighteenth century.[47] From this time can be traced, too, the beginnings of a "hard money" sentiment in the Ohio Valley which
was to be a factor in the history of Jacksonian Democracy in the
thirties.[48] Early in the twenties the West began to realize that
the bank was not the cause of the drainage of specie to the eastward, and to attribute it to the unfavorable course of trade. With

---

[45] The common rate of profit varied from 7 to 9 per cent., while states could borrow
at 5 and 6. Kentucky, Tennessee, Indiana, and Illinois at one time or other sold bonds and
invested the proceeds in bank stock. The Ohio legislature, by an act of 1816, offered to extend
the charters of those banks which would transfer to the account of the state one share in
twenty-five of their stock. Callender, "Early Transportation and Banking Enterprises," 161;
Huntington, *History of Banking*, 45.

[46] Chillicothe, where one of the branches was located, was a storm center in the
period of contest, and the story of the war on the bank can be followed to advantage in the
columns of the local papers, such as the *Supporter*, beginning about 1818. Of especial interest are the essays of "X. Y.," running through the summer of that year. The question was
an issue in state politics that year and the next.

[47] *Cf.* communication of "Logan," in *Supporter*, Sept. 16, 1818.

[48] *Cf.* communications of "A Countryman," in *Supporter*, July 29 and Sept. 2, 1818.

this the opposition to the Bank ceased,[49] leaving, however, an aftermath of ill-will that proved injurious to Clay in the campaign of 1824, and might have warned him against making re-charter the issue in the election of 1832.[50]

But the hope of western self-sufficiency could not be made a reality. During the handicraft stage the West did, indeed, to a large extent import artisans instead of goods, supplying the equipment for its primitive industries by the labor of immigrant smiths, wheelwrights, carpenters, and tanners.[51] But the abundance of cheap land was the lure which drew the great majority of the newcomers, and despite the notable growth of manufacturing activity it did not keep pace with the expansion of agriculture.[52] Although the needs of newcomers before their own lands became productive added measurably at times of large immigration to the demand for the agricultural surplus, at no time did the surplus find the local market sufficient, and the desire for an adequate market made war upon the ideal of self-sufficiency. In spite of the obstacle of distance, almost from the beginning the surplus flour, grain, tobacco, and meat of Kentucky sought an outlet by way of the Mississippi to the West Indies and Europe, and from an early date grain found a way out also in the form of the easily transported whiskey. Cattle and hogs, too, could be driven across the mountains, and this phase of western commerce became of great volume.[53] Up the river came specie in payment for these exports, and notwithstanding the heavy cost of transportation, over the rough mountain roads lum-

[49] "You never would hear a word about the mismanagement of the Bank of the U. States, if it had not been for the exportation of specie. . . . . The real pure, and uncontaminated source of the ruin that is involving our country, is the permission by government of a trade that impoverishes the country, and a total neglect of manufactures. . . . ." "A Friend to His Country," in *National Intelligencer*, quoted by *Supporter*, April 7, 1819. *Cf.* quotations from *Pittsburg Gazette*, in issues of December 9, 1818, and April 14, 1819. Governor Brown, in his message of 1820, informed the legislature of Ohio that "money, rather than security, will probably continue to be required in negotiations, till the payment [of debts due to the eastward] shall be nearly completed." Then credit will revive and hoarded coin be placed in circulation. *Supporter*, Dec. 14, 1820.

[50] See *below*, 135.

[51] By 1799, Cincinnati newspapers carried the cards of blacksmiths, millers, saddlers, hatters, dyers, tanners, bakers, potters, gunsmiths, and cabinet-makers. Goodwin, "Rise of Manufactures," 761.

[52] "The attraction of the laboring class to the vacant territory . . . . is the great obstacle to the spontaneous establishment of manufactures, and will be overcome with most difficulty wherever land is cheapest, and the ownership of it most attainable." Madison to Clay, April 24, 1824. *Works of Clay* (Federal edition), IV, 91.

[53] Cattle were driven overland from Ohio to Baltimore as early as 1804. Gephart, *Transportation and Industrial Development*, 85. By 1810, 40,000 hogs were driven annually from the state to the east. *Ibid.*, 103, quoting *Kilbourne's Ohio Gazetteer for 1818*. *Cf.* Pitkin, *Statistical View*, 534 *et seq.*

bering wagons carried many imports to fill the debit side of the trade account. But the disadvantage under which the West carried on all trade with distant parts even of the United States may be seen from the cost of freight. To eastern Ohio the rates overland from Philadelphia and Baltimore, and by way of the Mississippi from New Orleans, were about the same, averaging nearly $7 per hundred weight.[54] Such rates forbade the transportation of bulky articles by land to the cities of the Atlantic coast. Down river freights were much lower, and yet at times prohibitive in view of prices obtainable for produce in the New Orleans market.[55] The obstacles to river navigation resulted in an alternate dearth and glut of the market, attended by great fluctuations in prices and misleading quotations. The bulk of the exports of the upper valley regularly arrived at about the same time, with the spring rise of the water, and often so depressed the market as to occasion loss to the shippers.[56] Even these precarious trade opportunities were accessible only to those whose farms lay near navigable streams, for the cost of carrying grain over unimproved country roads consumed its value in a short haul.[57]

The cost of transportation reduced the price of all western exports and increased that of all imports. The disadvantage of the West in such exchange was reduced by contemporaries to the estimate that it required four bushels of corn to buy at Cincinnati what one bushel would command at Philadelphia.[58]

Yet the abundance of the fruits of the soil seemed to mean the power to command the wealth of the world if the natural im-

---

[54] The following are typical rates, compiled by recent secondary writers:
Philadelphia and Baltimore to Lexington, 1802, $7 to $8.
New Orleans to Zanesville, 1818, $6.50.
New Orleans to Pittsburg, 1786-1815, $6.75.
New Orleans to Shawneetown, 1817, $4.50.
Shawneetown to Pittsburg, $3.50.
New Orleans to Louisville, 1818, $6.25.
Philadelphia to Cincinnati, average $7 to $8.
[55] Lippincott, "Pioneer Industry," gives the rate from Shawneetown to New Orleans in 1817-1818 as $1.00 per cwt. In 1819 the rate of 25 cents per bushel on corn from Vincennes to New Orleans absorbed all profit.
[56] The *Supporter*, issue of Jan. 13, 1819, quotes from a letter written at New Orleans: "Flour very scarce and is worth 15 and 20 dollars per barrel . . . ." The following May flour was worth in the New Orleans market $5 to $5.50 per barrel. *Ibid.*, June 16, 1819.
[57] "About the year 1805, the usual price of carriage over the country roads was stated to have been 50 cents for 100 pounds for every twenty miles. At this rate corn, which before 1835 rarely sold for as much as 35 cents per bushel, would not stand the expense of moving twenty-five miles, even tho' it had been produced without cost. On the same basis, the area in which wheat could be sold at a profit to the farmer was limited to a radius of from fifty to seventy-five miles." Lippincott, "Pioneer Industry."
[58] Goodwin, "Rise of Manufactures," 768.

pediments to commerce could but be overcome. The one town of Circleville, located near the head of navigation on the Scioto, sent down the river in the year 1822 exports worth approximately one hundred thousand dollars, and according to local opinion, the community could have supplied ten times the amount with proper facilities for transportation.[59] Eleven years earlier the neighboring town of Chillicothe sent off fifty loaded boats in the month of February, occasioning the declaration that "If the rivers were improved so that a market could be reached the supply of corn, wheat, cattle, hogs, and hemp which could be furnished by the region would be enormous."[60]

The conditions in these two towns are typical of those which prevailed for many years in every surplus-producing area of the maturer West. The insufficient local market did not supply an adequate incentive to stimulate the farmer to the maximum productive effort, and indolence as well as poverty resulted. "Notwithstanding the great fertility of our soil," wrote Governor Worthington of Ohio in his message of 1816, "if the surplus produced from it, beyond our own consumption, does not command a price sufficient to reward the husbandman, the spring to industry is in a great measure destroyed." [61]

The obvious remedy seemed to be the improvement of transportation facilities in order that western produce might cheaply reach the distant market. "If we would raise the character of our state by increasing industry, and our resources, it seems necessary to improve the internal communications; and to open a cheaper way to market for the surplus produce of a large portion of our

---

[59] Gephart, *Transportation and Industrial Development*, 103, quoting *Olive Branch*, March 18, 1822.

[60] *Ibid.*, 101.

[61] Printed in *Supporter*, Dec. 10, 1816. *Cf.* speech of P. B. Porter in Congress, 1810: "The great evil, and it is a serious one indeed, under which the inhabitants of the western country labor, arises from the want of a market. There is no place where the great staple articles for the use of civilized life can be produced in greater abundance or with greater ease, and yet as respects most of the luxuries and many of the conveniences of life the people are poor. They have no vent for their produce at home, and, being all agriculturists, they produce alike the same article with the same facility; and such is the present difficulty and expense of transporting their produce to an Atlantic port that little benefit is realized from that quarter. The single circumstance of want of a market is already beginning to produce the most disastrous effect, not only on the industry, but on the morals of the inhabitants. Such is the fertility of their land that one-half their time spent in labor is sufficient to produce every article which their farms are capable of yielding, in sufficient quantities for their own consumption, and there is nothing to incite them to produce more. They are, therefore, naturally led to spend the other part of their time in idleness and dissipation." *Annals*, Eleventh Cong., 1 and 2 sess., 1385 *et seq.* Similar views are to be found in western newspapers. See, *e. g.*, "Julius" to "Edwin," in *Supporter*, May 18, 1811.

fertile country," declared Governor Brown, Worthington's successor, in 1818.[62]

For the next few years it is doubtful if any single policy so united sentiment in the Ohio Valley as the policy of internal improvements. It is the constant theme of editors, newspaper writers, legislators, and governors, who discuss it in all phases, local, state, and national. The coming together of the diverse elements of the Ohio population in opinion concerning the interests of the western country is one of the best evidences of the real fusion of Federalists and Republicans.[63] In the late twenties the National Republicans and Democrats of Indiana were still in accord on the question of internal improvements within the state.[64]

The western population contemplated the benefits to be derived from access to the world's markets with an enthusiasm which was for some time unchecked by any doubt of the power and readiness of those markets to absorb all the produce it could offer. The steamboat promised relief from the high freight charges on imports brought by wagon, and its advent was hailed with delight. "The improvement of our barges and steamboats insure [sic] within two years the total supply by the Mississippi and Ohio Rivers of many articles which are now wagoned from Baltimore and Philadelphia, and our exports will then be commensurate with our imports. Our flour, pork, tobacco and whiskey will return in calicoes, hardware, coffee, cotton, sugar, bartered for at New Orleans. There was never such a prospect for improvement and trade at one time on any portion of the globe as that which is now exhibited to western America." [65] These great expectations were doomed to suffer a measure of disappointment. The steamboat did, indeed, reduce the time required to bring freight from New Orleans to Louisville from about three months to a week or eight days, with a corresponding lowering of charges,[66] but the full realization of its benefits was postponed for a time by the contests over the mo-

---

[62] *Supporter*, Dec. 23, 1818.

[63] See *above*, 61-62.

[64] Esarey, *History of Indiana*, 304. *Cf.* interest of the seaboard in improving means of communication with the interior for the sake of its trade. New York, Philadelphia, and Baltimore became rivals in the race for the commerce of the Ohio Valley. Even Virginia had hopes of competing with the northern states by connecting the James and Kanawha rivers. An ardent advocate of this project was Thomas Ritchie, of the *Richmond Enquirer*. Ambler, *Ritchie*, 64-65.

[65] Gephart, *Transportation and Industrial Development*, 79, quoting *Brownsville Telegraph*, Aug. 14, 1815.

[66] Lippincott, "Pioneer Industry," quoting *Edwardsville Spectator* of June 5, 1819, and March 22, 1825.

nopoly claimed by the inventors, and the abandonment of their claim about 1818, although the number of steamers plying the Ohio and Mississippi increased for a year or two, was followed by hard times which prevented rapid expansion of the river trade.[67]

The project of a canal connecting the lakes and the Hudson likewise aroused great interest in the Ohio Valley, but especially in the northern half of Ohio. In 1812 the New York legislature appealed to Ohio and other western states for aid,[68] and in 1816 renewed the invitation to Ohio by means of a letter from DeWitt Clinton to Governor Worthington, which the latter transmitted to the Legislature with the recommendation that investigation be made as to the practicability and expense of the scheme. If the results of the investigation were satisfactory, he thought "it will become the duty of the people of Ohio to give all the aid in their power towards effecting an object in which they are so deeply interested." [69] Although Ohio did not join in the building of the Erie canal, the prospect of the completion of the New York waterway awakened interest in the construction of a connecting system between Lake Erie and the Ohio River, and started an agitation which culminated in the undertaking of a state system in the late twenties.[70]

Thus, as in the case of the steamboat, realization of benefit was postponed for some time, but meantime interest was maintained by the newspapers and by reports of the canal commissioners

---

[67] Gephart, *Transportation and Industrial Development*, 74, 81.

[68] *Ibid.*, 110-111; Phelan, *Tennessee*, 276 *et seq.*

[69] *Supporter*, Dec. 17, 1816.

[70] McClelland and Huntington, *History of the Ohio Canals.* Enthusiasm for an Ohio system was by no means confined to the northern portion of Ohio, but extended to the river towns. The *Cincinnati Inquisitor Advertiser* for July 24, 1820, has a two-column editorial on the progress of the Erie work, the certainty of success, the benefits to result, the effects on Ohio, and the desirability of canals connecting the lake and river. The article is noteworthy because of the recognition that economic unity of Ohio and western New York would result. Western New York, Pennsylvania, and Virginia have much in common with the Ohio Valley throughout the period. In the issue of August 8 is another editorial on the same lines, in which occur the following words: "Should Ohio . . . . imitate [New York] . . . . we should be able to send the immense surplus produce from nearly every part of our rich and fertile territory to the city of New-York at less expense than we can now transport it to New-Orleans, and be able to return with groceries and other heavy articles of common necessity at one-third of the expense we are now compelled to pay for the transportation of the same up the Mississippi and Ohio rivers . . . ."

Soon after this an article appeared in the *Louisville Public Advertiser*, inspired by canal editorials in the *Inquisitor*, picturing in glowing terms the benefits Ohio will derive from a canal across the state. "In a few short years we calculate on seeing the extensive forests and plains between the town of Delaware and the mouth of Sandusky, abounding with well cultivated farms." "Instead of being confined in their trade to a single port, they will be able to select a market." Quoted by *Inquisitor*, Aug. 22, 1820.

setting forth the advantages expected. In the report for 1822, for example, it was estimated that the cost of shipping flour by canal to New York City would be $1.70 per barrel, whereas the rate to the New Orleans market was $4.50. With flour worth $3.50 at Cincinnati and $8 at New York, it was believed that the producer would profit by a large part of the reduction in cost of transportation, and that the output of Ohio fields would be increased many fold. Imports, too, for the entire Ohio Valley, it was thought, would come chiefly from New York by way of the canals.[71] But the delay in the construction of canals thus left central Ohio in the mid-twenties still without means of transporting its surplus to market, save in the form of animals on the hoof. The lack of means of communication left the produce of abundant harvests to rot in the fields, while the farmers lacked money sufficient to pay taxes.[72]

This period of hope deferred was a period of conflicting aspirations for the West. While the desire for internal improvements to promote the marketing of the surplus of the interior was a virtual confession of the inadequacy of the home market, yet the continued lack of easy means of transportation and the high price of imported articles maintained the interest in local manufactures. In truth the West was held back in the provincial stage of her development by actual conditions, while aspiring to improvements which would facilitate intercourse with other sections of the country and inaugurate the national economy.[73] It was a period, more-

[71] Gephart, *Transportation and Industrial Development*, 113-114, quoting Journal of the House of Representatives, 1822. As a matter of fact, the Ohio canals proved to be feeders for both the Erie canal and the Ohio-Mississippi route, and while the east-bound traffic grew with relative rapidity, it was not until the railways united the Northwest and the coast in the fifties that the river trade felt severely the competition of the artificial routes. *Cf. ibid.*, 118-119.

The interest which the Erie canal excited in the West was felt as far South as Tennessee. The request of New York that the legislature instruct the representatives of the state in Congress to support measures favorable to the Erie project turned attention in the direction of congressional action in the Southwest. Phelan, *History of Tennessee*, 276 *et seq.*

[72] Callender, "Early Transportation and Banking Enterprises," 123.

[73] Extreme emphasis was sometimes placed on the ideal of national self-sufficiency. " . . . . From the vast extent of the dominion of the United States, the variety of climate, soil and produce, there can be no doubt but all the necessaries of life and many of the luxuries may be procured without the assistance of any other country under heaven. . . . . We think [commerce] . . . . should be [confined] to our own country." *Cincinnati Inquisitor Advertiser*, Feb. 12, 1823. "So long as Europe shall continue in the present state of slavery and degradation, there is more danger of intercourse with its nations having a demoralizing [than good] effect upon our citizens. When these U. States may be ripe for cutting off all intercourse with foreign nations for commercial purposes, we may willingly and readily resign all pretensions to their improvements in arts, sciences and literature—and be perfectly contented with such improvements as we are ourselves capable of making in those matters.

"Let us endeavor to turn our territory into a world for our own use. Let us make it subservient to commercial purposes, by promoting inland navigation, constructing bridges,

over, during which the views of the West were rapidly being shaped by experience into harmony with the new nationalism. We have seen how Governor Worthington, though a Republican of Virginia stock, along with other leaders of western thought, repudiated the *laissez faire* principles of Jefferson, and advocated government care for manufactures.[74] The problem of internal improvements exerted a similar influence. In response to the appeal of New York in 1812, the Ohio legislature passed a resolution in favor of construction of the Erie canal by the federal government, as a means of "rendering the produce of our country more valuable, the price of foreign commodities cheaper," and the bonds of the union firmer.[75] The delay in inaugurating the work on the Ohio canal system was due in part to the hesitation to entrust a task so closely involving the public welfare to a private company.[76] Besides, it was doubtful whether a private corporation would be able to finance so vast an undertaking. This form of industrial organization, while well known, had hitherto been employed chiefly in banking, and the work of internal improvements required a far greater capital than had yet been brought together in any industry in this country. Only public securities could command the confidence of the owners of loanable capital, at home and abroad, for such sums.[77] For these reasons the preponderance of opinion favored the con-

---

and making roads by which internal intercourse may be facilitated." *Ibid.*, Feb. 15, 1823. The antagonism between the western farmer and the merchant engaged in European commerce is emphasized still more in a third article in this series, in issue of Feb. 22, 1823.

[74] See *above*, 96; *cf.* Gov. Huntington's views, *ibid.* Also see *below*, 107.

[75] Gephart, *Transportation and Industrial Development*, 110-111.

[76] Bills for the incorporation of a canal company were considered by both houses in 1818. Commenting on the senate bill a Columbus newspaper correspondent remarks: "There is no man who has reflected on the incalculable advantage that would result to this, and the adjoining states, by a canal uniting the waters of Lake Erie and the river Ohio, but must ardently wish for the accomplishment of so great and beneficial a work—but whether the plan of a private company, with power, exclusively, to navigate the canal, when made, be expedient, is, to say the least, extremely doubtful.—The plan of a canal . . . . forms an important link, to my view, in the chain of our future prosperity, and should be entered upon with caution." *Supporter*, Dec. 10, 1818.

The impolicy of private construction is urged later in the report of the state canal commissioners: "Nothing can be more interesting to the whole community than the great navigable highways through the State from the lakes to the Ohio River. . . . . It does not consist with the dignity, the interest, or the convenience of the State that a private company . . . . should have the management and control of them. The evils of such management cannot be fully foreseen, and therefore cannot be fully provided against. . . . . A private company will look only to the best means for increasing their profits. The public convenience will be regarded only as it is subservient to their emolument." Report of 1825, quoted by Callender, "Early Transportation and Banking Enterprises," 155.

[77] *Ibid.*, 131-152.

struction of the canals by the state.[78]   But even the state, in those days of partially developed resources, hesitated to incur the necessary financial obligations until it felt confident of federal aid in the form of land grants.[79]

A similar lesson was taught by the efforts to improve the navigation of the Ohio by a canal at the rapids near Louisville, where transshipment of cargoes was necessary except in the case of boats of light draft or during high water. The delay and expense at this point early aroused the interest of the adjacent population in canal projects. State jealousies, however, prevented the co-operation which might have brought success. About 1820 rival companies were incorporated by the legislatures of Indiana and Kentucky, for the construction of canals on opposite sides of the river. The interest of Ohio was no less than that of either of these states, but being indirect in that the river did not touch her territory at the rapids, she was at a loss what course to pursue, inclining to the view that the great cost of the undertaking called for federal action.[80]

---

[78] *Cf.* the opinion of an "Ohio Citizen," in *Supporter* for Dec. 30, 1824: "Great public works, whether the fruit of individual or of national enterprize, have hitherto in all *modern* states, been the result of the accumulation of redundant capital." After discussing the success of New York in building the Erie canal when no great surplus of capital existed and interest rates were high, he concludes with the hope that Ohio may imitate her example. "This state, which for some years past, has made such noble and generous exertions in the same way has now filled the whole public mind with the most ardent hopes that an undertaking on the same colossal scale, and of the same permanent utility, will be accomplished by herself . . . ." The *Cincinnati Inquisitor Advertiser* for Aug. 29, reprinted an article from the *New York Statesman* on the prospect of an Ohio canal, which held that Ohio was abundantly able to undertake the work. "She has people, enterprise, industry, and credit. The whole work would be within herself—not a cent of capital carried beyond her borders, and all the expenditures, for an undertaking that will hereafter render her rich, flourishing, and powerful, be made to her own citizens."

[79] McClelland & Huntington, *History of the Ohio Canals*, 35.

[80] Gephart, *Transportation and Industrial Development*, 107-110. "H" in the *Cincinnati Inquisitor Advertiser* for Oct. 30, 1821, urged the need of federal activity in river improvements in these words: "The immense benefit that would arise to the nation from an unobstructed navigation of these two immense rivers of the Western country, the Ohio and Mississippi, is so palpable to every person acquainted with the geography of our country and with the state of the population west of the Alleghany mountain [*sic*], that I should suppose the subject worthy of the consideration of congress. . . . . [The West] must now look to the enlightened advocates of internal improvements in the national legislature for assistance." The demand for federal action is coupled with a statement of western grievances in the comment of "Dion" on "The Interests of the West," in the *Liberty Hall and Cincinnati Gazette* during the summer of 1819: "Let any person cast his eye on the map and trace the line formed by the Apalachicola, and the Allegheny [Mountains], into Pennsylvania, and thence to lake Erie, and he will see at once what proportions of country *pay* and what *receive* the national revenue —On the one side are cities, harbors, roads, public works of every description, and an old, well cultivated country; on the other, an immense wilderness, interspersed with a few infant, tho' flourishing towns, but generally peopled by emigrants yet struggling with the hardships of first settlements, felling the forests around them, building their rude cabins, toiling industriously for subsistence, with no money to spare even for the comforts of domestic life, much less for those public improvements so important to the prosperity of any country. From every

Thus experience exerted a powerful influence upon the views of the western people. Under the stress of poverty and the need of improved communications the belief in the sufficiency of private initiative, which Jefferson had made a part of the creed of the early Republicans, gave way generally to a demand for government action, and even the jealousy for state rights yielded to the necessity of federal aid.[81]

The breakdown of the ideal of western self-sufficiency and the espousal of the "American System" came in the early twenties with a larger knowledge of the state of the European markets. For several years previously, however, local economic thinkers had been perplexed by the excess of imports over exports, which they were inclined to attribute to the speculative tendencies of importing merchants and the lack of proper facilities for transporting the produce of the West. Internal improvements and greater encouragement of exportation they thought to be the remedy.[82] Here and there it began to be perceived that without selling the West could not buy. "To enrich a country by trade, much more must be exported, than imported. . . . . Neither ought we to deal with any people, who will not barter for, or purchase our surplus produce . . . ."[83] Hard times drove home the lesson that abundant production does not mean prosperity in the absence of a market. ". . . . Produce never was greater in quantity and so low in value," declared the *Columbus Gazette* in 1820. "Oats and corn and hay will not defray the labor of harvesting and bringing to market. The best of pork was sold in market last Saturday for two cents per pound. Land has fallen fifteen per cent in value . . . ."[84] "It is alarming to reflect on the present condition of our state. The country is overrun with produce, and destitute of a market," wrote "Franklin" in the *Muskingum Messenger*. "We cannot obtain

corner of both these sections the public revenue is collected, and where is it distributed? . . . . This we do expect, and have a right to claim, that some part of the revenue shall be employed on public improvements among us . . . ."

[81] "The pioneers were very anxious to have the national government open up the streams and help build roads."—Esarey, *History of Indiana*, 250.

[82] "We are at this time able to produce from the soil, a surplus of provision ten times greater than that which we could have *spared* ten years ago: if this is the fact, we ought at this time to command the wealth of a foreign market, in the same ratio." "Let us unite in giving encouragement to those who will undertake the transportation of domestic produce . . . ." "Socrates," in *Supporter*, Aug. 5 and 12, 1818.

[83] "A Farmer," in *Supporter*, June 9, 1819.

[84] Quoted in *Scioto Telegraph*, Oct. 12, 1820. *Cf.* prices in Cincinnati market, as given by the *Inquisitor Advertiser* May 29, 1821: Flour, $1.00 per cwt. Eggs 4c per dozen. Hams 4c per pound. Beef, choice pieces, 4c per pound; inferior pieces 2c. Butter 8c. Corn meal, bushel, 20c. Lard 4c. Pork, choice pieces, 3c; inferior pieces 2c.

money for our commodities, so how are we to purchase the luxuries or even the necessaries of life?" [85]   A favorite proposal was to practice self-denial, " to purchase no foreign goods, and to abstain, as far as possible, from the use of all articles which are not produced or manufactured" at home.[86]   "Every day we see merchants' advertisements exhibiting the most costly and unnecessary articles; such however as have been and still are in general use.   If you purchase these articles, you must pay for them in specie money, and where is this money to come from. . . . . Every cent of good money that falls into the hands of the merchants, is immediately transported to the Atlantic states, and from thence shipped to foreign countries for more luxuries. . . . . The sooner we abolish the traffic in foreign goods, the sooner will the dark cloud which is now lowering over our state be driven away. . . . ." [87]   The progress of home manufactures was watched with great interest, and many a calculation was made which showed, on paper, the substantial profits to be realized from capital so invested.   A writer in the *Philanthropist* proved that fifty acres of hilly land, unsuitable for grain raising, if used as pasture for merinos, could be made to yield sixteen hundred dollars at prices paid for wool at the Steubenville Woolen Factory and elsewhere.   "The larger factories," he urged, "must be looked to as the great engines for turning the balance of trade in our favor.   The difficulties under which we labor at present, are probably greater than was [sic] ever experienced in the United States before.   The cause lies in the wrong application of labor and money." [88]   Exhortations to use domestic manufactures were made on every hand.   "Domestic manufactures, are in every body's mouth—but not on every body's back.   Less talk and more action would look better.   He that wears a suit of homespun, does more to encourage domestic manufactures than the whole

---

[85] Quoted in *Scioto Telegraph*, May 12, 1821.

[86] *Ibid.*

[87] *Ibid. Cf.* article entitled "Our Soil," in *Pittsburg Mercury*, quoted by *Scioto Telegraph*, Aug. 25, 1821: "Flour per bbl. $1; whiskey 15 cents per gallon, good merchantable pine boards 20 cents per 100 feet, sheep and calves one dollar per head. . . . . One bushel and a half of wheat will buy a pound of coffee, a barrel of flour will buy a pound of tea; 12½ barrels will buy one yard of superfine broadcloth. Foreign goods are plenty, laid in on the best terms. They are sold at a very moderate profit and very cheap. The merchant is very sorry he has it not in his power to take produce in payment. He cannot remit it to Philadelphia; but if the farmer will sell his flour, bacon and whiskey to somebody else, and procure the cash, the goods can be had at almost first cost for specie and par money, but at a very small advance if paid in current paper. This is the condition of the western country. This is the prospect of the farmer under our present system."

[88] Quoted by *Scioto Telegraph*, Feb. 12, 1821.

herd of scribblers, who write so zealously on the subject," wrote one zealous scribbler, who proposed the organization of clubs for the purchase of the cloth output of local mills. This "would be of more real advantage to society, than all the abuse that could in a year be heaped on agents, brokers and merchants, by those who wear their stuffs, and pay them exchanges, carriages and profits." [89] "This looks like doing business," said the *Supporter* by way of comment. "The purchaser will have the proud satisfaction of wearing the native product of his own country, and of doing more towards establishing its *real* independence, than he could by killing a myriad of its enemies. . . . . It will be the only *effectual* way to prevent our money travelling over the mountains for English cloths —and will teach the storekeepers, through the medium of their *interests*, that it will be better for them to sell domestic cloths than none. . . . ." [90]

"The proud satisfaction of wearing native products" did not prove to be an adequate motive to create a demand for the products of the home manufacturer, and not all of the tirade against the merchants who dealt in foreign goods served to drive them out of business, as the advertisements in any contemporary newspaper will show.[91] The lack of foreign demand continued to mean a plethora of farm produce at low prices, while the fashion for foreign goods interfered with the growth of manufactures on a scale sufficient to absorb the agricultural surplus. Then at last came the conviction that the growth of agriculture had too far exceeded that of manufactures, and that a more equal balance should be brought about between them.[92] "For the interest of the farmer to be pro-

[89] *Greensburgh Gazette,* quoted by *Supporter,* Oct. 6, 1819.

[90] *Ibid.*

[91] Such advertisements as the following may be found in almost any paper in any issue of the period: "McCoy & Culbertson . . . . have just received an assortment of Spring and Summer Goods, of which they are anxious to dispose Wholesale or Retail." Among the goods are "fancy Ginghams, Leghorn Bonnets, Tortoise Combs, French Prunella Shoes, Morocco shoes, ribbons, Damask crape shawls, Real Merino shawls, silk umbrellas, figured gauze, painted feather fans, superfine Russia drilling and Angola cassimere, for summer pantaloons," etc. *Supporter,* May 3, 1820.

[92] Some of the plain people would have turned back to the days of the self-sufficient household. Says "Dorothy Thrift": "I want him [her husband] to raise flax and less rye. . . . . [He] is in debt for this trash [India cottons], and his rye won't pay his debts, even if he could raise ever so much. Year after year he will persist in this fatal practice; and every year our stock of sheep and cows diminishes, and we grow poorer and poorer; my girls are idle for want of wool and flax." She compares this situation with that of her own girlhood, when she and her sisters were busy daily with spinning the raw materials furnished by the father, who "was delighted to see us clothed in the fabrics of our own industry, and his house furnished with substantial homespun in abundance. . . . . I will scold and fret to see my girls idle, hardly decent in dress, my house furnished with cotton cobwebs and rags, and all going to loss and ruin, for want of flax and wool, and wheels, merely for want of materials. . . . ." *Plough Boy,* quoted by *Scioto Telegraph,* Oct. 12, 1820.

moted, it is not only necessary to procure merchants to export his produce, but it is also necessary to find a market where it can be sold.   In the present state of the world, the latter is the most difficult point to be gained.   Plenty of merchants can be found, but only few markets; consequently the surplus produce lies heavy on the hands of the agriculturist.· . . . ."   This writer argues that foreign countries receive only such of our exports as they must have, and would pay for them if we took no goods in exchange.   If, then, we produced our own manufactures, the export trade would not suffer, and a favorable balance would result.   Referring to the former views of Jefferson, he continues, "The day is past when it was prudent for America to have her work shops in Europe, and the principal arguments in favor of that system are done away.   'You have neither capital nor knowledge sufficient to be your own manufacturers,' said the political economist of that day: 'you have millions of acres of fertile and productive land, and while your woods continue to be uncultivated your business is agriculture, and you have no business with manufacture which is only suitable for countries of dense population.'   This reasoning would well apply provided our manufacturing shops were to be supplied with provisions exclusively by us—but since we cannot obtain admission for our produce in provisions into those shops, except in times of great scarcity or famine—when they will not exchange with us their manufactures for our corn, our flour, and our pork—and since the manufactures which we import far exceed the amount of such raw material as we export, the balance must be paid in money, very much to our disadvantage. . . . . We have more land under cultivation than is necessary for the subsistence of our own citizens, and more produce than we can find a market for in foreign countries.   We have accumulated a capital greater than we can find employment for either in agricultural or commercial pursuits—and our population has at least doubled within twenty years. . . . . Who can say then . . . . that it is not full time for us to remove our workshops from Europe to America, and endeavor to do that for ourselves which we have to pay other nations for doing for us.   We may boast of our liberty and independence in a political light, but if we are independent of a British government, we are still dependent on a British people—and that dependence must continue so long as we suffer our workshops to remain in England." [93]

[93] *Cincinnati Inquisitor Advertiser,* April 2, 1822. *Cf.* article in issue of Jan. 27, 1823: "It appears pretty evident that there is already too much land under cultivation, witness the

Such was the economic doctrine which gripped the whole Ohio Valley in the early twenties. Governors of states aided in its dissemination. William Findlay, of Pennsylvania, in his message of 1820, declared: "The limited demand for, and consequent low prices of, our agricultural products in foreign markets, cannot fail to suggest the necessity as well as the policy of promoting domestic manufactures, which, if properly encouraged, would provide a sufficient home market for all our surplus produce . . . ." [94] Governor Jonathan Jennings, of Indiana, anticipated the sentiment of the Pennsylvania executive by a few days.[95] Little by little the belief in the necessity of home manufactures, and of the fostering care of the government in order to obtain them, took hold of the minds of the great majority of the people of the West.[96]

---

price of its produce. What use can there be in cultivating land when its produce cannot find a market? . . . . Does it not prove, to a moral certainty, that the time is arrived that they [the people of the United States] should turn their attention to manufactures, when it evidently appears that the produce of what land is already under cultivation cannot command a market to advantage? Is it not plain to any unprejudiced person that when as much land is under cultivation as to reduce the profits of the husbandman to nearly nothing, when as much can be produced in one year as can be disposed of in two, that the same effect must be produced as if there was not another acre of land to cultivate. Is it not plain, we say, that something ought to be done to find a market for this redundancy of produce, and to find employment for that portion of our population which must eventually be thrown out of employment when the agriculturists relax in their exertions, a relaxation which is naturally to be expected when they cannot have their produce taken off their hands? Yes, we say, now is the time for the ranks of the manufacturer to increase. Agriculture has been pursued to its acme. The number employed in it is disproportionate to that of the mechanical branch—and the true interest of the whole community will be promoted by producing an equilibrium between them—the want of employment, (to use the terms of the sensible writer before hinted at) has driven mechanics into the wilds to make farmers of them—by which instead of customers have become rivals to agriculturists. And by this means the farming business is overdone. . . . ."

[94] *Scioto Telegraph*, Dec. 21, 1820.

[95] ". . . . The surplus produce of the state, increasing in quantity and reduced in price, has been greatly deficient in the amount of its proceeds, to meet the demands upon us which have been created by the consumption of foreign objects of merchandise. . . . . To retrace these errors, however fascinating, which national pride or false ambition may have produced; and directing the future by a strict scrutiny of the past; by curtailing our consumption of foreign articles, by the application of active industry, not less to domestic manufactures of every description, than to the soil . . . . we may ere long be reinstated in our former independence. . . . ." *Ibid.*, Dec. 28.

[96] Light is cast on the process of education by the following extract: "A Farmer" writes to the editor of the *Western Herald*: "Being over the other day at the Squire's and happening to get into conversation about the tariff and the support of domestic manufactures, both of which I confess I was not disposed to encourage, on the ground that it would have a tendency to interrupt our commercial relations with England and would perhaps cause them to retaliate on us by throwing obstacles in our way, the squire informed me that there was a regulation for some years past, which prevented our flour and grain from entering their market. Now Mr. Wilson, I want to make enquiry through the medium of your paper if any such restriction does exist. (I think he called it a corn law) . . . ." If correctly informed by the "squire," the "Farmer" declares he will become a supporter of "all such measures as will have a tendency to counteract such restriction, and if we can not obtain a market abroad will encourage the system which will afford a market at home." The editor confirms the "squire's" information, and asks: "Such being the case, the question arises, Ought we to receive the

When it was realized that Europe could not or would not receive the surplus products of western agriculture, that fact was accepted as the explanation of the "hard times," and a new significance was imparted to the old demand for a home market. The inadequacy of the local western market had long been admitted by implication, and with the new light in regard to the foreign demand came new stress upon a domestic market as wide as the United States. In the theory of a national economy which now replaced the provincial economy in the contemplation of the West, internal improvements held, of course, an essential place; but the protective tariff was relied upon as the means of redressing the balance between agriculture and manufacturing, and by encouraging the latter, of diverting a sufficient proportion of the population from agriculture to render the two interests reciprocally supporting.[97]

3. DIVERGENCE OF WEST AND SOUTH

Clay and Calhoun, with all their efforts to embrace nation-wide interests in their thought, spoke as exponents of the West; that is, their scheme of national policy fell in with the local interests of the western section. Calhoun, representing a constituency in that piedmont region from which so much of the western population had sprung, and which was in 1816 still partly a region of farms; and Clay, from the state which was the first fruit of the trans-

---

products of any nation that will not take our products in exchange? Every farmer can answer this question." *Western Herald*, April 10, 1824.

Laissez faire arguments are rare indeed but appear occasionally. Witness the following: "American manufactures will flourish without any alterations of the present tariff, as far *as it is the general interest or the interest or* HAPPINESS of the great mass of our fellow citizens that they should flourish." "I wish not to see the happy population of the New-England states reduced to the level of a British weaving population. . . . . I wish not to see the increased and overgrown population of cities and towns, which is the sure causes [sic] of vice, disease and poverty . . . ." The writer cites Jefferson's "Notes on Virginia," and adheres to the former views of the author regardless of the change in the circumstances of the United States and the western country. He also cites similar opinions held by Franklin. *Liberty Hall*, quoted by *Supporter*, July 21 and 28, 1819.

[97] The intimate relation between western prosperity and the American system, and the dependence of the West upon Federal action are illustrated by the complaint of the *Western Herald*: "Unless the western country can prevail upon the government to promote means for transporting its surplus agricultural produce to a certain and safe market, and unless their manufactures be so protected as to be placed on a permanent footing, property will continue to depreciate, and poverty and misery will be our constant companions." Feb. 7, 1824.

"More foreign products has (*sic*) been imported than can be paid for. . . . . A few years will be sufficient to correct the evil, the correction may be expedited or protracted as our national legislature is wise or improvident, and as manufactures are hastened or delayed. The doctrine that inculcates the propriety of letting commerce and manufactures find their own level, and of, depending on themselves, is nonsense; manufactures never succeeded in any country without artificial aid . . . ." *Supporter*, May 12, 1819, quoting *Pittsburg Gazette*.

montane migration, derived their enthusiasm concerning the nation's future from the very fact that it was developing so rapidly in the West. "We are great, and rapidly—he was about to say fearfully—growing. This . . . . is our pride and danger—our weakness and our strength . . . . Whatever impedes the intercourse of the extremes with this, the centre of the Republic, weakens the Union. . . . . Let us then . . . . bind the Republic together with a perfect system of roads and canals." [98]   Calhoun's advocacy of western interests in this famous speech on the Bonus Bill was incidental to his argument for national unity; but Clay soon afterwards spoke avowedly as a western man, representing a new country which needed means of communication as it did the breath of life, although in almost the same breath he declared he spoke as a citizen of the Union, looking forward to a great destiny, so closely were the welfare of the West and of the nation associated in his thinking.[99] In all, of his advocacy of the American System, in fact, Clay appears to the historian as the champion of the West, engaged in an effort to persuade the other great sections into the belief that their interests are in harmony with his great scheme of policy.[100] The reciprocal relation of the farmer and manufacturer was sufficiently obvious, but in vain did he seek to reconcile the ship owner and the planter to the idea of a national economy. The westward movement in this period represented directly the progress of the farming and planting interests. In the Southwest the planter

---

[98] *Annals*, Fourteenth Cong., 2 sess., 853.

[99] March 13, 1818. *Works of Clay* (Federal edition), VI, 116 *et seq.*

[100] "I am aware that on two subjects I have the misfortune to differ with many of my Virginia friends—internal improvements and home manufactures. My opinion has been formed after much deliberation, and my best judgment yet tells me that I am right. . . . . I believe Virginia and the Southern States as much interested, directly or indirectly, as any other parts of the Union in their encouragement. When the Government was first adopted we had no interior. Our population was inclosed between the sea and the mountains which run parallel to it. Since then the west part of your State, the western parts of New York and Pennsylvania, and all the Western States, have been settled. The wars of Europe have consumed all the surplus produce on both sides of the mountains. Those wars have terminated and emigration has ceased. We find ourselves annually in possession of an immense surplus. There is no market for it abroad; there is none at home. If there were a foreign market, before we, in the interior, could reach it, the intervening population would have supplied it. There can be no foreign market adequate to the consumption of the vast and growing surplus of the produce of our agriculture. We must, then, have a home market. Some of us must cultivate; some fabricate. And we must have reasonable protection against the machinations of foreign powers. On the sea-board you want a navy, fortifications, protection, foreign commerce. In the interior we want internal improvements, home manufactures. You have what you want, and object to our getting what we want. Should not the interests of both parties be provided for?

"It has appeared to me, in the administration of the general Government, to be a just principle to inquire what great interests belong to each section of our country, and to promote those interests, as far as practicable, consistently with the Constitution, having always an eye

pressed hard upon the heels of the pioneer farmer. Under the stimulus of the growing demand of European factories for cotton, "black belts" were forming everywhere in the alluvial lands of the Gulf states by the mid-thirties. Capitalism as represented by the plantation system outbid the small farmer at the land auctions, or bought him out if already established, in either case sending him onward to the new frontier or crowding him back into the hills to swell the ranks of the "poor whites." [101] Indirectly the westward movement involved also the fortunes of the other two great interests, maritime commerce and manufactures. The first had suffered severely during the period of non-intercourse and war, while the same events had stimulated domestic industry. In the succeeding years ocean commerce continued to be affected adversely by the forces which promoted manufactures. On the economic side, in brief, the half-generation following the war of 1812 witnessed a revolution in the relations of the great economic interests and in the relations of the sections where their chief strength lay. The farming interest, growing by leaps and bounds through the rapid settlement especially of the Northwest, was growing in political power almost in the ratio of its territorial expansion. Much the same was true of the planting interest in the Southwest. Manufactures and ocean commerce, the one growing, the other declining, the one capable of spreading over the Northwest the other localized on the coast, held their futures subject in large measure to their economic and political relations with the other interests.

The key to the national politics of the period 1815-1825 is to be sought in the rivalries and shifting alliances of these interests and of the sections where they centered. The "piedmontese" expansion of this era was a continuation of the movement which had

---

to the welfare of the whole. Assuming this principle, does any one doubt that if New York, New Jersey, Pennsylvania, Delaware, Maryland, and the Western States, constituted an independent nation, it would immediately protect the important interests in question? And is it not to be feared that if protection is not to be found for vital interests, from the existing systems, in great parts of the confederacy, those parts will ultimately seek to establish a system that will afford the requisite protection? I would not, in the application of the principle indicated, give to the peculiar interests of great sections *all* the protection which they would probably receive if those sections constituted separate and independent States. I would, however, extend some protection, and measure it by balancing the countervailing interests, if there be such, in other quarters of the Union. . . . ." Clay to Francis Brooke, Aug. 28, 1823. *Works*, IV, 78 *et seq.*

[101] Phillips, "Origin and Growth of the Southern Black Belts." *Cf.* the typical experience of Thomas Dabney, who removed from Virginia to Mississippi about 1835, where he acquired a plantation of four thousand acres by purchasing the land of half a dozen small farmers. Callender, *Economic History*, 642, quoting Smedes, *Memorials of a Southern Planter*.

won the early West for Republicanism in its race with the Federalist party. Superficially it seemed to insure the continued dominance of the triumphant party. On the side of party history, then, the meaning of the period is to be sought in an answer to the question, whether the Republican name and organization could continue to hold together in fact the old party elements, now so altered in their relations.

A divergent drift of the South and West, both professing the Republican name, became apparent while Madison was still president. With a regard for the letter of the constitution worthy of the original traditions of the party, he vetoed the Bonus Bill, a measure inspired in part by his own recommendation of the policy of internal improvements.[102] Monroe, following in his footsteps, announced to Congress in his first message his disbelief in their right to promote such works without an amendment altering the constitution.[103] To the leaders of the New School such literalism seemed to make of the constitution itself a bar to the country's progress. "If we permit a low, sordid, selfish, and sectional spirit to take possession of this House . . . . we will divide [disrupt the Union]," cried Calhoun, not indeed in reply to Monroe's message, but combatting a similar narrowness. The constitution "ought to be construed with plain, good sense," and the uniform sense of Congress and the country had approved the power of appropriating money for the improvement of the means of communication.[104] Clay referred to the views of the administration group as a "water-gruel regimen," an interpretation which would construe the Constitution to a dead letter and reduce it to an inanimate skeleton. The rule of construction, he urged, must not "forget the purposes of the Constitution, and the duties you are called on to fulfill, that of preserving the union being one of the greatest magnitude." Was the Constitution, with its grant of power to establish post offices and post roads and to regulate commerce between the states, made for the Atlantic margin of the country only? "Every man who

---

[102] Richardson, *Messages of the Presidents*, I, 584. A hint of his constitutional scruples was contained in the message of 1815, but was unheeded by Congress: "It is a happy reflection that any defect of constitutional authority which may be encountered can be supplied in a mode which the Constitution itself has providently pointed out." *Cf.* Jefferson's recommendation in messages of 1806 and 1808 (Ford, *Writings of Jefferson*, VIII, 493; X 224); and comments on Madison's veto in contemporary correspondence (*ibid.*, X, 80, 91, *et passim*).

[103] Richardson, *Messages*, II, 18. *Cf.* Madison to Monroe, Dec. 27, 1817; *Works of Madison* (Congress edition), III, 55-56.

[104] *Annals*, Fourteenth Cong., 2 sess., 853 *et seq.*

looks at the Constitution in the spirit to entitle him to the character of a statesman, must elevate his views to the height which this nation is destined to reach in the rank of nations. We are not legislating for this moment only, or for the present generation, or for the present populated limits of the United States; but our acts must embrace a wider scope,—reaching northwestward to the Pacific, and southwardly to the river Del Norte. Imagine this extent of territory covered with sixty, or seventy, or an hundred millions of people. The powers which exist in this government now will exist then; and those which will exist then exist now." [105]

Believing that Congress possessed adequate powers under the constitution as it stood, Clay and his supporters refused to jeopardize the rights of the national legislature by referring them to the hazard of an amendment which might not carry.[106]

Thus differing with Monroe over what Clay regarded as fundamental, it is hardly necessary to refer the leadership of the opposition, which presently fell to Clay, to personal pique over the appointment of Adams instead of himself as secretary of state. Indeed, the clash over constitutional construction between the Old School presidents and the leaders of the New Republicanism was the first appearance of a breach which was to become permanent, and which was to widen until the party was hopelessly divided. The vetoes by presidents on constitutional grounds of measures of which they approved when judged on their intrinsic merits represented an attitude which was presently replaced by an opposition to nationalizing measures *per se,* and which assumed the doctrine of strict construction as a convenient weapon of defence.[107] In

---

[105] *Annals,* Fifteenth Cong., 1 sess., I, 1165 *et seq. Cf.* speech of Henry St. George Tucker, one of the New School Republicans from Virginia, *ibid.,* 1116. On the negative side, see speeches of Senator James Barbour, of Virginia, *ibid.,* Fourteenth Cong., 2 sess., 893; Fifteenth Cong., 1 sess., I, 1151; and proposed amendment, *ibid.,* 21-22.

[106] *Works of Clay,* VI, 117. *Cf. Tucker:* "But why, it is asked, not amend the Constitution? The answer is easy. Those who do not believe we possess the power, are right in wishing an amendment. Those who believe we have it, would be wrong in referring it to the States; and as the Committee were of this opinion, they could not recommend an amendment. For, if an amendment be recommended, and should not be obtained, we should have surrendered a power which we are bound to maintain if we think we possess it." *Annals,* Fifteenth Cong., 1 sess., I, 1119. For efforts to amend, see *ibid.,* 21-22 (Barbour); Seventeenth Cong., 2 sess., 200 (Smith); Eighteenth Cong., 1 sess., I, 134 *et seq.* (Van Buren).

[107] As late as 1824 Jefferson's objection to internal improvements was academic—lack of constitutional power. "I suppose," he wrote, "there is not a State, perhaps not a man in the Union, who would not consent to add this to the powers of the general government." To Edward Livingston, April 4, 1824. Ford, *Writings of Jefferson,* X, 300. Yet he was ready (1825) to have the state legislature declare internal improvement legislation null and void. *Ibid.,* X, 359.

other words, behind Presidents Madison and Monroe was the seaboard South, which became the seat of a marked reaction against
the nationalism which dominated the country at the opening of the
era, the seat of a revived insistence upon sectional interests and
state rights. This reaction had its mainspring in antagonism to
the American System and the nationalism toward which the West
was so steadily tending.[108]

The cotton-raising region was hopelessly out of the range of
the benefits expected from the development of the home market.
In 1816 the argument for protection to develop home manufactures
of necessaries as a means of national defence won a measure of
acquiescence in the South. Lowndes, of South Carolina, as chair-

---

[108] In Virginia the reaction paralleled the decline of the influence of the state in federal
affairs. The retirement of the Old School leaders gave place for a group of younger men who
broke with the New School led by Clay and Calhoun, and attacked their nationalizing tendencies. Judge Spencer Roane, of this group, became conspicuous for his criticism of the
decisions of the supreme court. (Articles signed "Algernon Sidney," in *Richmond Enquirer*,
March-August, 1821. See comment of John Quincy Adams, in *Memoirs*, V, 364). P. P. Barbour and John Tyler were of this party, and John Randolph acted with them. Their agitation
did much to revive and disseminate the old dogmas of strict construction and state rights.
Jefferson reverted to his former views in these years of controversy. *Cf.* Ambler, *Ritchie*, 73,
82-83. John Taylor contributed to the reaction by his writings on government. Of *Construction
Construed*, published in 1820, Jefferson wrote: "It is the most logical retraction of our governments to the original and true principles of the constitution creating them, which has appeared since the adoption of that instrument." Washington, *Works of Jefferson*, VII, 213. The
next year (1825) Jefferson proposed to Madison a protest by Virginia against the policy of
the administration in the matter of internal improvements, to be made in terms of the resolutions of 1798. Ford, *Writings of Jefferson*, X, 359.

Madison did not follow the reaction to its extreme. His views in this period are quite
consistent with his nationalism in the days of the formation of the constitution. See *Works*
(Congress edition), III, 246, 325, 483 ; IV, 19, 210, 296, *et passim*. Monroe also took a middle
ground. *Cf.* document accompanying his message of 1822, vetoing the Cumberland Road Bill.

The great decisions of the supreme court (notably Martin v. Hunter's Lessee, 1816; Mc-
Culloch v. Maryland, 1819 ; Dartmouth College v. Woodward, 1819 ; and Cohens v. Virginia, 1821),
under the dominance of the powerful mind of the former Federalist John Marshall, were in
such striking harmony with the constitutional views of the New School Republicans that Jefferson referred to the latter as "pseudo-republicans but real federalists" (Washington, *Writings
of Jefferson*, VII, 278), and described the judiciary as the "subtle corps of sappers and miners
constantly working under ground to undermine the foundations of our confederated fabric
. . . . construing our constitution from a co-ordination of a general and special government
to a general and supreme one alone." Letter to Ritchie, Dec. 25, 1820, *ibid.*, VII, 192. *Cf.* 212,
223, 294. "The original objects of the federalists were, 1st, to warp our government more to
the form and principles of monarchy, and, 2d, to weaken the barriers of the State governments
as co-ordinate powers. In the first they have been so completely foiled by the universal spirit
of the nation, that they have abandoned the enterprise, shrunk from the odium of their old
appellation, taken to themselves a participation of ours, and under the pseudo-republican
mask, are now aiming at their second object, and strengthened by unsuspecting or apostate re-
cruits from our ranks, are advancing fast towards an ascendancy." To Judge Johnson, June
12, 1823. *Ibid.*, 293. Contrast Madison's views as shown by comment on McCulloch v. Maryland,
in letter to Judge Roane, Sept. 2, 1819 (*Works*, Congress edition, III, 143 *et seq.*) ; and on
Cohens v. Virginia, in letter to same, May 6, 1821 (*ibid.*, 217 *et seq.*) See *Niles Register*, XVII,
311; XX, 118; XXI, 404, for Virginia legislature on supreme court.

man of the Ways and Means Committee, introduced the tariff bill
of that year, and it had no more ardent supporter in any section
than Calhoun. The South cast twenty-three votes in favor of the
bill. Two members of the South Carolina delegation besides
Lowndes and Calhoun supported it on its passage.[109] Yet these lost
their seats at the next election, and Calhoun was charged by residents of his district with having sacrificed his state to his presidential aspirations.[110] In fact, the South cast thirty-four of the
fifty-four votes against the measure, the rest coming from the commercial regions of the northern coast. John Randolph, refusing to
be persuaded by the arguments of the nationalists, insisted upon
presenting the case in its sectional aspects. "It eventuates in this:
whether you, as a planter will consent to be taxed, in order to hire
another man to go to work in a shoemaker's shop, or to set up a
spinning jenny. For my part I will not agree to it, even though
they should, by way of return, agree to be taxed to help us plant
tobacco; much less will I agree to pay all, and receive nothing for
it. No, I will buy where I can get manufactures cheapest, I will not
agree to lay a duty on the cultivators of the soil to encourage ex-
otic manufactures; because, after all, we should only get much
worse things at a much higher price, and we, the cultivators of the
country, would in the end pay for all." [111] The case of the planter
could hardly be more concisely stated, and if he would not sacrifice himself for the good of the whole country, it was not to be
expected that he would become reconciled to the protective policy
when its aim ceased to be primarily associated with the national
defence. In relation to the market at home and abroad the position of the planter was essentially different from that of the farmer.
He suffered from no such lack of market in Europe as that which
depressed grain farming. On the contrary, as the producer of a
raw material which could not be grown in Europe, nor anywhere so
advantageously as in the rich, cheap lands of the Gulf Plains, he
enjoyed the control of a monopolist over a commodity for which
the demand was increasing. While the countries of Europe, ad-
justing themselves to peace conditions after the downfall of Napoleon, were resuming cultivation and placing restrictions upon
the food supplies exported from the United States, they were wel-

---

[109] *Annals*, Fourteenth Cong., 1 sess., 1352.
[110] Houston, D. F., *Critical Study of Nullification in South Carolina*, 5.
[111] *Annals*, Fourteenth Cong., 1 sess., 687.

coming southern cotton. Especially in England, manufacturing methods, a generation ahead of continental processes, thanks to the inventive genius of the eighteenth century and to the fostering care of the government, were expanding the textile industry so rapidly as to tax the productive capacity of the westward-moving plantation area of the southern states. Under such conditions the cotton region had but slight interest in the development of the textile industry at home as it would add inconsiderably to a demand already ample. On the contrary, the cost of manufactured goods consumed by the staple states would be increased by the tariff, whether imported or purchased from the domestic manufacturer. Nor was the prosperity of the cotton belt uniform. Although increased production caused lower prices, the decline did not seriously depress the grower on the newer lands, while many of those who occupied the impoverished or less fertile soils of the coast states found themselves on or below the economic margin. On these the tariff laid a serious burden. Thus the South, while agreed in its dislike of the tariff, was divided in the degree of its opposition, the chief antagonism springing from the seaboard.[112]

The growth of the opposition to the tariff may be traced by means of memorials to Congress, resolutions of state legislatures and other bodies, and speeches of southern members of Congress. Beginning as an agitation against the proposed law of 1820, they increased in number and vehemence until the climax was reached in the attempt at nullification. In general, they elaborated the economic argument which has been outlined, appealed to the theory that government should not interfere with the natural course of industry, especially where such interference favors one interest at the expense of others, attacked the constitutionality of protection, and pointed out the dangerous political tendencies of federal activity. A few examples drawn from the literature of opposition will serve to illustrate the harmony of sentiment which prevailed from Virginia to Georgia. A meeting at Petersburg, Virginia, in 1820, passed resolutions declaring: " . . . . The idea of coercing a people to manufacture among themselves articles which they can

---

[112] The situation of the tobacco, rice, and sugar planters should be differentiated from that of the cotton planters, but in general they acted together, and further discrimination would be an unnecessary refinement for the purposes of this study. For anti-tariff analysis of the American System in the tobacco-growing district, see editorials of the *Richmond Enquirer*. Other anti-tariff memorials are printed in *Annals*, Eighteenth Cong., 1 sess., II, App., 3075 *et seq.*

purchase abroad at a much lower price than they can produce them at home, we conceive to be equally repugnant to justice, to policy, and to the principles of the constitution. . . . . The powers necessary to execute such measures we consider as too despotic to have been delegated by the American people to their Government, and such as we cannot suspect our representatives of wishing to assume, by the instrumentality of inference or construction." [113] The Roanoke Agricultural Society memorialized Congress asking to be let alone. "Identity of feeling and interest is the cement of our Union. Without it, the component parts of our confederacy must hang too loosely together to withstand the jars to which it must be exposed. That identity would be destroyed by a rigid system of prohibitory duties. In the nature of man, it cannot be expected that the agricultural [planting] and commercial portions of the Union could experience any other feeling than that of the bitterest hatred towards the manufacturing interest, by whom they would be burdened to the utmost of their power to bear; they would cease to feel as members of one great family.

"We have no favors to ask at the hands of Government. All we require is, to be left to ourselves, and to our own resources. As we desire not to interefere with others, we hope and trust not to be interfered with." [114]

In Congress Mr. Tatnall of Georgia spoke for the lower South. "We do not complain upon slight occasion. No, sir, the Southern States have never been querulous in their character. Whenever the national benefit has been the object, they have freely yielded up all that you have required. . . . . But it is impossible the Southern planter can ever afford to give you the price at which you offer at present to furnish your goods. To compel him, therefore, to buy at your market, is tyranny; and the taking advantage of his necessities to exact from him a higher price than the value of the article, is robbery; and robbery of the most impudent kind! . . . . Are you prepared, by passing this infernal bill, to add to a poverty which is already wearing one portion of our country to the bone, for the purpose of supplying the appetites of a few pampered nabobs? Such a policy is disgraceful to a free people. It is incon-

---

[113] *Ibid.*, Sixteenth Cong., 2 sess., 1490.

[114] Dated Clarksville, Mecklenburg Co., Va., Dec. 7, 1820. *Ibid.*, 1522. See petition also of delegates of the United Agricultural Societies of Prince George, Sussex, Surrey, Petersburg, Brunswick, Dinwiddie, and Isle of Wight Counties, Va. *Ibid.*, 1517.

sistent with our institutions, and will be destructive of our happiness. And is it thought that we will tamely submit to this treatment? No, sir, we cannot. By Heaven, sir, we will not! . . . ." [115] A memorial of a meeting of citizens of Charleston set forth the objections of South Carolinians as held in 1820. "The great plea for taxation advanced in this case is, that domestic manufactures will make us independent of foreign nations. This is certainly important in itself; but, when advanced as a ground for forcing artificially the production of everything we want, the plea is every way fallacious. . . . . If, under a new system, the surplus labor of an individual will procure for him but one-half of the articles of consumption which he has hitherto been accustomed to receive for the same labor, what compensation will it be to him to know that this diminished supply was produced in his own country, or even on his own farm? . . . . How much more simple and wise is it for each nation to raise or manufacture those articles which are most congenial to its soil and to the habit of the people, and exchange its superfluous productions for the productions of other climates and other conditions of society. . . . . Neither should it be forgotten how hostile to the general spirit of our Constitution is every system of restriction, of monopoly, or particular privileges. . . . ." The impossibility of developing manufactures within the state is then mentioned to explain why it must continue to devote itself to planting, and the effects of the protective system upon the planter are analyzed. "It is, therefore, peculiarly our interest that our interchange with the world should be free. . . . . It is equally our interest that the articles we are compelled to consume should be procured on the most advantageous terms." [116] Four years later a committee of Charleston citizens renewed the protest of 1820, viewing with alarm the tendency towards a permanent system of protectionism. The state was now feeling the strain of competition with the new cotton lands, with low prices prevailing in the European market. While the former objections still held, the former prosperity was gone. While the citizens of the State might formerly have regarded protective measures, if not without disapprobation, at least without dismay, and have acquiesced without much murmuring, certainly without violent resistance, matters now stood very differently, owing to the glut of cotton in the

---

[115] Jan. 30, 1823. *Ibid.*, Seventeenth Cong., 2 sess., 756.
[116] *Ibid.*, Sixteenth Cong., 2 sess., 1505.

European market and the low price. "It is manifest that the extraordinary prosperity which South Carolina, in common with the other Southern States, enjoyed some years ago, is gone forever, and it will require all the skill and industry of our agriculturists, in future, to maintain their place in the market, even at the most reduced prices of produce." They regarded the occasion as so alarming as to call for an emphatic declaration that the proposed tariff measure violated the spirit of the constitution, and proceeded to discuss the nature of the Union and the powers of Congress under the constitution, at some length.[117]

In the declining price of cotton the West found reason to hope that the South might make common cause in support of the American System, in order to create a home demand. "Late occurrences in the European market induce us to believe our plans will not be so strenuously opposed in the southern section of our country," remarked a western paper in 1819. "The price of their produce must continue to fall, and it will soon be their interest to encourage a consumption of the raw material at home. . . . ."[118] The two great obstacles which prevented Congress from giving proper support to manufactures, according to Matthew Lyon, addressing the *Kentucky Reporter*, were the influence of the commercial region on the northeast coast, and the low estimate placed by the South on domestic manufactures. "The people [of the South] are afraid if domestic manufactures were encouraged by prohibitive or protecting duties, they would have to give a cent or two a yard more for cloth manufactured in New England . . . . than they now do for cloth manufactured in Old England, and they would begrudge it, although the New England cloth should be four cents a yard the best—and although the time cannot be far distant when the principal market for their cotton must be derived from American manufacture. . . . ."[119] Gloomy paragraphs in the southern press contributed to this illusory hope. "Cotton, our staple article of export," the *Milledgeville* (Ga.) *Journal* is quoted as saying, "is daily declining in price, and will, in a short time not be worth the cultivation. The *consumption* of cotton manufactures has already arrived at its utmost extent; but the *production* of the article itself may be increased a thousand fold. This circumstance

---

[117] *Ibid.*, Eighteenth Cong., 1 sess., App., II, 3075.
[118] *Pittsburg Gazette*, quoted by *Supporter*, May 12, 1819.
[119] Quoted by *Supporter*, Oct. 6, 1819.

will keep down our market *generally* . . . . but there is another cause that will operate on the market of the southern states. The English are encouraging its cultivation in their East India colonies judiciously and extensively. It is true it is not so good as ours, but the manufacturers say it is good enough for their purposes. Hence our trade in it will be destroyed just as certain as our *indigo* trade was destroyed in the year 1779 by the same policy." [120]   "The cotton planters of the southern states seem to have great antipathy to domestic manufactures," says the *Cincinnati Inquisitor Advertiser*, "lest their encouragement should operate against commerce, and thereby affront their customers the English. But we should think that they ought to be the first that would encourage them, in order to procure customers at home for their produce that is now become a mere drug in the British market. We should suppose that when upland cotton has been reduced to about 9 cents per lb., after all the expense of freight and insurance— that they might be among the first to call out for encouragement for domestic manufactures in order to find customers for that redundancy of cotton which has so powerfully operated to bring down the price. . . ." [121]

The spread of cotton culture westward expanded the market for the food products of the farms of the Northwest, and the growing intercourse between that section and the South fostered the faith of the former in the practicability of the sectional reciprocity aimed at by the American System.[122]   But the South persisted in its way of thinking. The milder tone of the more prosperous state of Alabama, but at the same time the clear perception by the southerners of the sectional alignment on the tariff question, is shown by the speech of Owen in the House of Representatives, on the bill of 1824: "He summed up the policy of the bill as amounting to this, that the East and the West must co-operate, and the South must submit and contribute. He reprobated this policy as not calculated

---

[120] *Scioto Telegraph*, July 7, 1821. *Cf.* statements in same article concerning conditions as set forth by the *Montgomery Republican*.

[121] January 27, 1823.

[122] "The state of North Carolina, heretofore noted for the quality and excellence of its Pork, sent chiefly to the Virginia markets, is now indebted for large supplies of this article to Kentucky and Tennessee. The cultivation of cotton in this state has produced this new order of things." *Cincinnati Inquisitor Advertiser*, Jan. 13, 1823, quoting *North Carolina Register*. *Cf.* Callender, "Early Transportation and Banking Enterprises," 126; also Callender, *Economic History*, 290 *et seq.*

for the benefit of the whole Union." [123]   The territory adversely affected was defined by Randolph in the course of this debate. "Here is a district of country extending from the Patapsco to the Gulf of Mexico, from the Allegany [mountains] to the Atlantic, a district which . . . . raised five-sixths of all the exports of this country that are of home growth . . . . I bless God that, in this insulted, oppressed, and outraged region, we are, as to our counsels in regard to this measure, but as one man, that there exists on the subject but one feeling and one interest." [124]   His further words show the growing violence of the opposition. "We are proscribed, and put to the ban; and if we do not feel, and feeling do not act, we are bastards to those fathers who achieved the Revolution; then shall we deserve to make our bricks without straw . . . . I do not stop here, sir, to argue about the constitutionality of this bill . . . . I have no faith in parchment . . . . I *have* faith in the power of that Commonwealth, of which I am an unworthy son, in the power of those Carolinas, and of that Georgia . . . . which went with us through the valley of the shadow of death, in the war of our independence. . . ." [125]

The southern seaboard developed likewise an opposition to the other important feature of the American System, that is, the policy of national aid to internal improvements. Before the spread of the plantation system into the interior of the South Atlantic states, considerable interest had been displayed in local roads and canals to afford access for the farmers of the interior to the seaport towns. Before the close of the eighteenth century, the Santee canal, by connecting Charleston with the river which gave the canal its name, had shortened the distance between the inland farms and the city, affording the one a readier market and the other cheaper supplies. The Chesapeake and Ohio and James River Canal projects were likewise designed to tap the uplands and ultimately the Ohio Valley.[126] But while Baltimore held its own with Philadelphia for a time, the southern states soon fell hopelessly behind the northern in the competition for the trade of the transalleghany

---

[123] *Annals*, Eighteenth Cong., 1 sess., I, 1550.

[124] *Ibid.*, II, 2360.

[125] *Ibid.* A very temperate criticism of the protective policy, from the viewpoint of the Old School Republican, is made by Madison in a letter to Clay, dated April 24, 1824, written in acknowledgment of a copy of the latter's speech on the tariff of 1824. Cited *above*, 99, *f. n.* 52.

[126] Phillips, U. B., *Transportation in the Eastern Cotton Belt*, 15, 16.

region. The higher mountains precluded all possibility of canal connection, and not until the advent of the railroad were the conditions north and south somewhat equalized. Meantime, with the advance of staple growing in the interior interest even in the local roads and canals declined in the eastern cotton belt. The marketing of cotton could be done when teams were idle, for the crop did not suffer from long hauls over poor roads. The planters considered the loss of time less serious than the cost of toll on the turnpikes, and the roads constructed at an earlier date fell into disuse during the twenties.[127] The western South showed more interest in the proposals of national turnpikes and improvements in water courses, and as late as 1824 Governor Troup of Georgia wrote to President Monroe urging the claim of his state to a share of the benefit under the survey act, and suggesting canals to connect the Savannah with the Tennessee and the St. Marys with the Suwanee.[128] Tennessee was the scene of similar agitation.[129] In this matter as in the tariff question, the South was not wholly united, but as the association of the two policies in the American System became clear, the seaboard, lacking any positive interest to enlist its support for the policy of improvements, placed both equally under the ban of its disapprobation.

It is clear to the historian that by 1824 the basis of the old party system was gone. The Federalist organization, quitting the field in 1816, had left the Republicans in undisputed possession. But as the growth of the West had destroyed the one, so now it had in turn destroyed the other. The Republicans retained, it is true, the old party name and the semblance of an organization. But the two geographical sections which shared the name were as wide-

---

[127] *Ibid.*, 12.

[128] Phillips, U. B., *Georgia and State Rights*, 114. The western portion of the tobacco states showed considerable interest in improved means of communication with the coast. See petition of Virginians asking co-operation of the federal government in the James River Canal project, *Niles Register*, XIII, 125. Politically this portion of Virginia, so long in conflict with the tidewater, inclined strongly to affiliate with the Ohio Valley, as did also western Pennsylvania and New York. This fact gave Clay a real basis for expecting support in the campaign of 1824. For the same reason Virginia was divided somewhat in its attitude towards the Adams administration. Ambler, *Sectionalism*, and *Ritchie*. As late as 1832, the *Lynchburg Virginian*, discussing "the constant migration to the great West of our most substantial citizens . . . . and the declension of our business," remarked: "It is idle to talk of the blasting effects of the Tariff system. We suffer most from our failure to keep pace in building internal improvements." Commons, John R., *et al.*, *A Documentary History of American Industrial Society*, II, 196-197. The reactionary Virginian party opposed the federal policy of internal improvements vehemently. See Ames, *State Documents*, 140-143.

[129] See *above*, 103, *f. n.* 68 ; 104, *f. n.* 71.

ly separated as the poles in their views of national policy, in their votes on specific measures, and in their interpretation of the constitution.[130] They knew that they were at odds; nothing remained of the party, indeed, but the name.[131] The decade following the War of 1812 was, in short, a period of disintegration for both of the old parties, during which their several elements, with the addition of the elements contributed by the growing West, were poured into the melting pot to emerge in new forms and combinations.

---

[130] *Cf.* Ambler, *Ritchie*, 82-83.

[131] "How long shall we be compelled to suffer by that contracted view of our public interests, which can.embrace only the growth of cotton and tobacco, and the necessary means to provide for these articles, a profitable foreign market, we pretend not to say." *National Republican and Ohio Political Register*, March 4, 1823.

"The question is not now whether this candidate or that is a democrat or a federalist, but whether he is a friend or an opponent to domestic industry and internal improvements." *Western Herald*, quoted in *Supporter*, Aug. 2, 1823.

CHAPTER V

TENDENCIES TOWARDS REALIGNMENT OF PARTIES

The main task for which this study was undertaken has now been completed; that is, to show that both the Federalist and Republican parties, based on conditions connected with the geographical development of the United States up to the beginning of the constitutional period, were destroyed before 1825 in consequence of the changes incident to further geographical development. But the decade ending in 1825 was a period of party reformation as well as disintegration, and by the close of it the new party alignment was becoming fairly distinct. We can not fitly end our study, therefore, without a survey of the chief forces which shaped the new parties.

It seemed for a time that the contest over the admission of Missouri might lead to a new organization of parties on the basis of the slavery issue.[1] The opposition to the admission of the new state sprang from two sources. The distrust of the West which the Federalists had shown survived the party and, when the Missouri question arose, still appreciably affected portions of the East;[2] the growing dislike of slavery affected the whole Northwest as well as the East, and tended to unite the Republicans of that region with the former Federalists in common antagonism to the spread of the institution.

Most prominent among the opponents of the new state was Rufus King, at this time senator from New York. His speech of February, 1819,[3] became the arsenal from which congressmen,

---

[1] Hockett, H. C., "Rufus King and the Missouri Compromise," in *Missouri Historical Review*, II, 211-220.

[2] See *above*, 67, *f. n.* 63; 75, *f. n.* 93. The tone in which easterners commonly referred to the people of the West is indicated by the following: "How do the *wild men of the west* relish a treaty that . . . . does not provide for the extinction of the Indians and the assumption of the 'uppermost' Canadas?" James Emott to Rufus King, Feb. 19, 1815. King, *Life of King*, V, 472. [Italics mine.]

"A gentleman of intelligence informs us, that a most singular and sudden change has taken place in the minds of the inhabitants of our cities with respect to the western country [because of the pressure of hard times, which turned the thoughts of many towards the West.] The name but lately was associated with everything disagreeable and uncomfortable; it was *used in nurseries for the purpose of frightening children*." [Italics mine.] *Supporter*, May 12, 1819, quoting *Pittsburg Gazette*.

Cf. the description of the emigrants and their motives, in Dwight's *Travels*, II, 458 *et seq.*

[3] *Niles Register*, Dec. 4, 1819.

127

newspaper writers, and other agitators drew their arguments during the whole contest. So marked was the effect of the movement in uniting the Federalists and Republicans throughout the North and West, and so central a figure was King, that many persons believed, with John Quincy Adams, that King had set on foot a concert of measures which should form the basis of a new alignment of parties.[4] This opinion was supported by the stress which King placed upon the injustice of extending the political power of slavery, which seemed to outweigh in his mind its moral evils. Slave representation, he pointed out in his senate speech, already gave the southern states twenty representatives and twenty presidential electors more than their white population would entitle them to. The constitutional provision for such representation was an ancient settlement which faith and honor were bound not to disturb. But it was a settlement between the thirteen original states, and its extension to the new states which Congress might now be willing to admit would be unjust and odious. The states whose power would be abridged could not be expected to consent to it. The right of Congress to provide for the gradual abolition of slavery in Missouri he found to be implied in the constitutional provision that "Congress may admit new states."

The antecedents of King's views are easily recognized. In the denunciation of the extension of southern power through the admission of new states in the West, we encounter again the old prejudice shown by Federalists in the constitutional convention, and at the time of the Louisiana Purchase and of the admission of the State of Louisiana. In the constitutional argument, too, we find an attempt to give to that instrument an interpretation according with the wishes of Gouverneur Morris and his associates, of whom King was one, when they framed the clause to which appeal was now made.[5] Notwithstanding the well-nigh universal favor with which the anti-Missouri program met for awhile in the North, the country presently recognized the association of these doctrines with Federalism. Nor did the fact that King had been a leader of that party and the recipient of the last electoral votes which it cast, serve as a disguise for this association. The Republicans therefore grew suspicious, deeming the agitation a "federalist movement, accruing to the benefit of that party," and believing

---

[4] Adams, *Memoirs*, VI, 529.
[5] See *above*, 46-50, 69-71, 73-75.

that King hoped to organize a sectional party on anti-slavery principles, under Federalist leadership, and strong enough to dominate the Union.[6] That such was his conscious purpose is unproven and unlikely, but the belief seems to have caused a defection of both Republicans and Federalists from the anti-Missouri phalanx;[7] and the vote of northern members for the compromise may find its explanation in this way. There is even evidence that President Monroe was induced to forego his contemplated veto of the compromise bill, at the risk of forfeiting the endorsement of Virginia for a second term as president, by a conviction that the compromise would defeat the machinations of King.[8]

Here, then, was a question, originating in the process of westward expansion, which shows a new tendency— a tendency for the Northwest to sever its alliance with the Old South and to form a connection with that eastern section which had formerly been the seat of antagonism to it. With the progress of the frontier, in short, the Northeast was forgetting its earlier antipathy to the Ohio Valley, and stretching out its hands to it in common hatred of the type of institution which was appearing beyond the limits of the territory to which the Ordinance of 1787 applied.[9] South as well as north of the river, besides, the course of western economic development, which had brought it into conflict with the planting region, had given it affinity for the new industrialism of the Northeast. "The West," said the *Western Herald* in 1823, "has no interest distinct from the interest of the grain growing and manufacturing states to the east." [10] The stage was set for a political revolution.

---

[6] Benton, Thomas H., *Thirty Years' View*, I, 10. "Let Missouri continue her efforts . . . . and a reaction may be produced which will prostrate those *Hartford Convention men* who now predominate in the north, and give the victory to the friends of the union and to the *republicans* of the *Jeffersonian school*." [Italics mine.] *St. Louis Enquirer*, quoted in *Niles Register*, XVIII, 371 (Feb. 3, 1821).

[7] Gore to King, Jan. 28, 1820, King, *Life of King*, VI, 259.

[8] *Congressional Globe*, Thirtieth Cong., 2 sess., App., 63-67. See also Barbour Correspondence, in William & Mary College *Quarterly*, X, 5-24. Cf. Ambler, *Ritchie*, 78-79.

[9] "I shall not be at all surprised if the Mo. affr. shd. strew the seeds of a new state of things agt. the next 4 yrs. after Mr. Monroe's next term. . . . ." R. H. Goldsborough, a Maryland Federalist, wrote to King, March 13, 1820. King, *Life of King*, VI, 307. "It does appear to me that the country has not so soon recovered from the Missouri question, and that the Eastern States, if they find the South and West too strong, will be inclined to cry out 'No Slavery,' and by these means compel Ohio and the Western free states to abandon their choice [Clay for president] and unite in this policy." Edward King to Rufus King, Jan. 23, 1823. *Ibid.*, 497.

[10] March 1.

The adoption of the Missouri Compromise practically removed the slavery issue as a factor in the reshaping of parties, although some echoes of it were heard during the campaign of 1824, leaving the chief role in the readjustment of the political relations of sections to be played by economic questions. Only on the surface was the campaign of 1824 a personal contest among men holding "common Republican principles." The persistence of the old party name has served to disguise the wide divergence in the views of the candidates, and the colorless character of the statements made on behalf of some of them has tended the same way. In reality such statements usually emanated from the prudence which perceived the antagonism of sectional interests and knew that clean-cut pronouncements would destroy the chance of general support. It was necessary, so far as possible, to make each candidate acceptable everywhere, which really meant that the voters in each section must be satisfied that the candidate was friendly to the interests of that section.

The period had arrived when the West was ready to assert itself. Keenly conscious of its interests and its strength, it laid claim to the highest office in the land, and to a determining influence in shaping the national policies. The growth of the West, having proven the decisive factor in sapping the foundation of the old parties, was now to assert an equally important influence on the evolution of the new.

For a glimpse at the formative influence of the section in this respect we cannot do better than to take Ohio. Ohio had attained fourth place among the states of the Union, and was first in the West. Having no candidate of its own, as did Kentucky and Tennessee, its vote represents a more impartial judgment than that of either of these; while the newer states, just because they were new, played a relatively unimportant part in this election. The mixed character of the population of Ohio, moreover, which was far more representative of the several older regions than was the case in either of the neighboring states, made it a fair battleground for all of the candidates, and gave its attitude toward their respective claims unique significance.[11]

---

[11] In collecting material on Ohio, I have been aided by the work of students in my graduate seminar. I am especially indebted to Mr. E. H. Roseboom, scholar in American History in Ohio State University, 1915-1916, who made, under my direction, a study of Ohio in the Presidential Campaign of 1824, in connection with his candidacy for the degree of M. A. This study appears in *Ohio Archaeological and Historical Quarterly*, XXVI, 153-224.

In the early stages of the state campaign the slavery question seemed likely to be again prominent.[12]   Sentiment in Ohio had been practically united in opposition to the admission of Missouri as a slave state, and to the end of the campaign many persons felt that slavery should be regarded as the paramount issue.   In general, however, it was felt that the Missouri question should be considered as settled, and many of those who had been most ardent in their wish to prolong the fight against slavery yielded to the view that economic interests should be ranked first.[13] As to what were the economic interests of the West there was no disagreement.[14] It is equally clear that the people regarded the election as an oppor-

---

[12] *Cf.* Charles Hammond's expectation concerning the influence of the Missouri question: "A new state of parties must grow out of it. Give me a Northern President, whether John Quincy Adams or De Witt Clinton, or anybody else, rather than that things should remain as they are." Smith, W. H., *Charles Hammond and his Relations to Henry Clay and John Quincy Adams*, 32. See also letter of Edward King to his father: "If the Missouri question should present itself, in the contest, Ohio probably would leave her favorite [Clay] and support Mr. Adams." November, 1822. King, *Life of King*, VI, 487.

[13] "The ignis fatuus 'western interest,' is like to absorb every sound moral and political consideration." *Ohio Monitor*, quoted by *Delaware Patron*, Sept. 16, 1823.

James Wilson, editor of the *Western Herald and Steubenville Gazette*, opposed Clay on anti-slavery grounds until it became evident that the slavery issue was subordinate to economic questions. Then he turned to Clay. *Western Herald*, issues March 1 and 22, 1823, and April 24, 1824. Clay himself believed in February, 1824, that Ohio would vote for "no man residing in a slave state but me, and they vote for me because of other and chiefly local considerations." Letter to Francis Brooke. Colton, *Life of Clay*, IV, 86.

[14] "It will be recollected that the promotion of domestic measures is the ground we assume as the criterion of our choice. Those candidates who are unfavorable, or not known to be favorable to these measures we throw out of the question. . . . ." *Liberty Hall*, Nov. 14, 1823.

"So far as we have been able to learn the sentiments of the editors of this state, we believe, however they may differ on other subjects, that they pretty generally agree in this one important point:—that we ought to support that man for the Presidency, other things being equal, who will most effectually encourage domestic manufactures and internal improvements." *Ibid.*, Jan. 6, 1824.

Friendliness to domestic industry and internal improvements "is a *sine qua non*—an article of faith, to which every political aspirant must subscribe, before he can expect to be honored with their [Ohio voters'] suffrages." *Supporter*, March 25, 1824.

"Mr. Clay will in all probability . . . . be the first choice of Ohio; but in case it shall be found that he cannot become one of the *three highest* in votes, it will become our duty . . . . to turn our attention to the candidate who shall come the next nearest to our standard in point of qualification. This standard is—(1) Encouragement to domestic industry. (2) Internal improvements, by roads and canals. (3) Inflexible integrity." *Western Herald*. The *Herald* had favored making slavery the chief issue. See *above, f. n. 13*.

In announcing the founding of a new paper, *The Ohio Journal*, the publishers disavow any intention of establishing a party organ, but to "prevent misapprehension of our sentiments and of the course we intend to pursue [we] declare ourselves desirous of seeing a man elected whose policy will cause us as a nation to be respected abroad and will foster at home those two great main stays of a free and independent people—Domestic Manufactures and Internal Improvements." *Hamilton Intelligencer and Advertiser*, Aug. 16, 1824.

See similar announcement of the *Western Statesman*, in *Supporter*, Dec. 20, 1824.

tunity to translate their economic views into political action.[15] Monroe's vetoes of measures which would have benefited the western country led to insistence upon the election of an executive of broader constitutional views and keener sympathy with the growing portion of the Union.[16]

To the several candidates Ohio voters applied the two tests mentioned, namely, attitude on the question of slavery and towards the protective tariff and internal improvements which together constituted the American System.   Calhoun enjoyed a degree of popularity because of his early record, although his fidelity to his former views was brought under suspicion by the growing opposition of South Carolina to the tariff.[17]   At best, however, he was hopelessly overshadowed, as an advocate of the American System, by Clay, and from the moment that he lost the support of Pennsylvania for the first place his cause was dead in Ohio.   The chief newspaper which had supported him transferred its influence to Clay, because of his relation to the interests of the section,[18] while the friends of Jackson endorsed Calhoun for the vice presidency on the ground of his friendliness to the tariff and internal improvements.[19]   The liking for Calhoun in Ohio, in short, was due to the belief that he favored the American System.

Crawford, with the support of the congressional caucus, represented the remnants of the democratic organization and depended rather upon the appeal made by the "regularity" of his candidacy than upon an avowal of his principles.   His record did not speak unmistakably of his attitude on the questions of the day, as did those of Calhoun and Clay, and it seemed likely that his views accorded with those of the Old South where his strength centered. These facts were sufficient to condemn him in Ohio, for the state

---

[15] "We indulge a hope that the proceedings of the present congress [in defeating the tariff bill] will awaken a spirit of universal inquiry among the people, and produce such a change in the federal administration as will insure to it that wisdom which can discern the necessities of the country." *National Republican and Ohio Political Register*, March 4, 1823.

[16] "There is a party of politicians at Washington, whose consciences are so tender, or whose minds are so contracted, that no general system of internal improvements can be anticipated, from the councils of the nation, until there is a radical change in the Executive departments." *Ibid.*, July 23, 1823.

[17] *Supporter*, Feb. 26, 1824. At this time Calhoun's views were still fairly consistent with his earlier opinions. *Cf.* speech at Abbeville, May 27, 1825; *Niles Register*, XXVIII, 266. Two years later his correspondence begins to betray the change which carried him into the southern party and made him the chief of the nullifiers. See *below*, 143, *f. n.* 58.

[18] *Liberty Hall and Cincinnati Gazette.*

[19] Address of the Jackson State Committee, September, 1824. *Hamilton Intelligencer*, Sept. 27 and Oct. 4, 1824.

was resolved to support no candidate whose position with regard to western interests was uncertain. It is significant that the most damaging charge brought against Clay was that he intended, at the last, to throw his influence in favor of Crawford, which would have meant the subordination of western interests to southern.[20]

Both Calhoun and Crawford were unacceptable in Ohio, too, because of their residence in the slave section. An added objection to both was their membership in Monroe's cabinet. The West was growing impatient and alarmed at the practice of "cabinet succession."[21] Even more odious was the caucus system to which Crawford owed his nomination.[22] Never popular, and now discredited by the defection of nearly all congressmen but those who favored Crawford, it had come to stand in western opinion for that type of political manipulation which jeopardized the rule of the people.

It seemed for awhile that DeWitt Clinton would make a strong showing in the state. He was popular both as an opponent of the expansion of slavery and as the champion of the Erie canal and a connecting system of internal improvements. He was the favorite with many anti-slavery men in the regions where the New England stock was numerously represented, and in the Cincinnati region, where the friends of internal improvements were offended by Clay's connection with the United States Bank.[23] The Clinton movement collapsed for want of support in New York.

Adams fell heir to most of Clinton's following in the eastern and northern portions of Ohio, where his opposition to slavery was sufficient to determine the choice of many of the descendants of New England.[24] Where economic questions were considered uppermost he suffered from a non-committal policy. His views, like Crawford's, were not to be deduced with certainty from his public record, and although friendly to the American System he believed it possible to harmonize sectional interests, and made efforts to

---

[20] See *below, f. n.* 42.

[21] Resolutions of Clay Convention, July 15, 1824, published in *Columbus Gazette*, July 22; Address of Jackson State Committee, published in *Hamilton Intelligencer*, Sept. 27 and Oct. 4, 1824.

[22] *Cf.* criticisms of the caucus, for example, in *Columbus Gazette*, Feb. 26, 1824; *National Republican*, Feb. 27, 1824; *Delaware Patron*, March 4, 1824.

[23] For example, Clinton was supported in the southwestern quarter by the *National Republican*, because of his leadership in internal improvements, and in the eastern portion by the *Western Herald*, on anti-slavery grounds.

[24] See files of leading Adams papers: *Ohio Monitor, Delaware Patron*. Most of the old Federalists probably supported him, although, in meeting the charge that he was a Federalist the *Patron* pointed out that the Federalist leaders—Judge Burnet, Elisha Whittlesey, General Beecher—were supporting Clay. Issues of October 7 and 21, 1824.

persuade Virginia that his policies would accord with the desires of the people there. He succeeded in convincing "many of the old school . . . . that he was a true friend of the doctrines of 1798," [25] but his cautious statements in some degree defeated the purpose for which they were made.[26] In the West he made no statement; it would have been difficult to satisfy the West of his devotion to its interests and at the same time seem consistent. An avowal of friendship for western policies, however, coupled with his anti-slavery principles, would have strengthened him in Ohio and might conceivably have given him a plurality in the electoral college. The addition of Ohio's sixteen votes would have given him the lead over Jackson, and the "plurality doctrine," of which the latter's friends made so much later, would have been unavailable for the opposition.[27] However, he refused even to allow his friends to make an authoritative statement of his principles, thus losing the support of an unknown, but certainly large, number of voters who considered certainty of attitude towards western interests a *sine qua non* for their support.[28] This handicap allowed prejudice to

---

[25] Ambler, *Ritchie*, 89, commenting on Adams's Address in reply to General Smyth's public statement of reasons why he would not support Adams for the presidency. Adams's address is printed in *Richmond Enquirer*, Jan. 4, 1823. Jefferson and a majority of the Old School Republicans of Virginia preferred Adams to Jackson. Ambler, *Ritchie*, 98. See Adams, *Memoirs*, IV, 353. Also note statement of Adams to James Barbour, senator from Virginia, in the interval between the election and the House balloting (Dec. 22, 1824) : "I was satisfied with the tariff as now established . . . . if the tariff should be found to bear hard upon the agricultural and commercial interests, I should incline to an alleviation of it in their favor. As to internal improvements . . . . since the Act of Congress establishing the Cumberland road, there had been no constitutional question worth disputing about. . . ." *Ibid.*, VI, 451. In this interview Barbour assured Adams that he was the second choice of the Virginia delegation, and, he believed, of the people of the state. *Ibid.*, 450.

[26] On the Smyth incident Ritchie remarked editorially : "Is Mr. A. really a friend to the limited interpretation of the constitution—does he stick to the doctrines of Virginia—is he opposed to the Bank of the U. S.—to a general system of internal improvement? We cannot make out from his address. . . . ." *Richmond Enquirer*, quoted by *Cincinnati Inquisitor Advertiser*, Feb. 15, 1823.

[27] The Address of the Jackson State Committee, issued in September, 1824, predicted the selection of Jackson by the House of Representatives because of "the general impression which prevails, that that body would elect the candidate who had received the greatest number of electoral votes, and not incur the responsibility and obloquy of selecting one less popular with the people." *Hamilton Intelligencer*, Sept. 27 and Oct. 4, 1824.

[28] Postmaster-General McLean's brother was on the Adams electoral ticket in Ohio. In response to an inquiry, Adams wrote a letter to the Postmaster expressing views favorable to internal improvements. McLean's purpose in making the inquiry was to obtain an expression of Adams's opinion which his brother might use in the campaign, but Adams requested that the letter be kept from the newspapers. *Memoirs*, VI, 323. Despite the efforts of friends to prove his position with insufficient evidence, the opposition press continued to exploit the fact that his views were doubtful. Thus the *Supporter* brushes aside the charge of Socinianism on the one hand and the praise of his talents and character on the other as irrelevant: "The people of Ohio and of the middle states although ready to acknowledge his merits will not support him for President until they shall have ascertained beyond the possibility of a doubt

play havoc with his prospects. His personal character could not offset his lack of satisfactory views and popular qualities; rather, it contributed to the estimate of him as an aristocrat and former Federalist—a New Englander, and by that token a natural enemy of the West.[29] Like Calhoun and Crawford, he suffered also from the western dislike for the succession of cabinet members, the succession of the secretary of state being regarded as especially obnoxious.

Clay appeared from the first to be the logical candidate for Ohio to support. He was a western man, and more thoroughly identified than any other with what the West regarded as its essential interests. On the tariff and internal improvement policies his record left nothing to be desired, and in the last session of Congress before the election his voice had been lifted more eloquently than ever in behalf of western rights. The position of other candidates might be uncertain but not Clay's. Such considerations governed the action of the legislative caucus which endorsed him in January, 1823.[30] Against him the anti-slavery element urged a friendliness for slavery, as shown by his conduct during the Missouri contest,[31] while the antagonism to the United States Bank, centering in the southwestern portion of the state, prevented him from becoming at any time the favorite in that quarter.[32] The most

---

that his sentiments on the great political questions which now agitate the country coincide with their own." The sentiment of Congress and the West is for internal improvements and a president is wanted who will co-operate and not thwart their wishes. "We never can—we never will countenance the pretensions of any man, however meritorious he may be in other respects, whose sentiments on the questions at issue may be considered doubtful. We will put nothing to hazard." March 25, 1824. *Cf.* summary of irreconcilable claims made for Adams in issue of Sept. 16. At the very close of the campaign the *Supporter* remarked: "It has been proved beyond the possibility of a doubt that he always has been, and now is, decidedly hostile to internal improvements and the protection of national industry." Issue of Oct. 31, 1824.

Similar objections were made in Indiana. The *Western Sun* for July 24 said: "The chief objections to Adams are, 1 He is still at heart a Federalist, 2 He is opposed to a tariff and to Internal Improvement, ..." Quoted by Esarey, L., "The Organization of the Jacksonian Party in Indiana," in Mississippi Valley Historical Society *Proceedings* for 1913-1914, 227-228.

[29] *National Republican*, Aug. 28 and Sept. 3, 10, and 29, 1824; *Supporter*, March 25, April 29, June 24, Aug. 5, Sept. 9, Oct. 21, Nov. 4, etc., etc.; *Mad River Courant*, quoted by *Columbus Gazette*, May 29, 1823; *Hamilton Intelligencer*, July 26, 1824, quoting *Boston Statesman*.

[30] *Columbus Gazette*, Jan. 9, 1823.

[31] *Ohio Monitor*, Feb. 22, 1823. *Western Herald*, Mar. 22, 1823.

[32] Clay had acted as attorney for the Cincinnati branch, and in that part of the state was held responsible for its pressure on debtors to the point of foreclosure in many instances. *Hamilton Intelligencer*, Feb. 24, 1823; *National Republican*, Aug. 13 and 17, and Oct. 15 and 22, 1824. The charge was repeated elsewhere in the state (*Ohio Monitor*, March 1, 1823; *Western Herald*, Mar. 22, 1823) but without serious consequences save where the bank's conduct had aroused great feeling. Charles Hammond, Clay's manager, had been chief counsel for the state during the attempt to tax the branches.

damaging attack upon him, however, was the charge already alluded to, that he was in secret favorable to the success of the candidate who represented the southern interest.[33]

Jackson's campaign in Ohio was late in developing but made rapid progress.[34] It found its basis in the growing antipathy to the machine politics of the time, as embodied, in the popular estimate, in caucus nominations and succession of cabinet members, and to aristocratic control of the Federal Government as represented by the traditional regard for birth, social standing, and special training as essentials for the filling of public office.[35] Jackson's personal qualities made him immensely popular, and were believed to be a guarantee of reform of these practices.[36] But it is perfectly clear that notwithstanding all this, he could not have commanded any considerable support had it not been believed that he was "sound" in his views on western policies.[37] His orthodoxy

---

[33] See *above*, 133.

[34] *National Republican*, April 27, 1824. Webster, H. J., *History of the Democratic Party Organization in the Northwest*, 8 *et seq*.

[35] Address issued by Jackson Corresponding Committee of Cincinnati and Hamilton County, in *National Republican*, May 18, 1824; Address of Committee appointed by Jackson State Convention, in *Hamilton Intelligencer*, Sept. 27 and Oct. 4, 1824.

[36] See, for example, articles in *Hamilton Intelligencer* for Jan. 20, 24, April 13, 20, 27, May 25, Oct. 4, *et passim; Delaware Patron*, Oct. 29, 1823.

[37] A typical plea for Jackson is that published in the *Westmoreland* (Pa.) *Republican*. After adverting to the need of simplicity in government and the dangerous tendencies of the secretarial succession, it declares that the people desire a president "who would extend equal and impartial protection and support to the three great national interests—who would foster our resources, encourage domestic industry, promote internal improvements, and divested of sectional prejudice or party feeling, labor for the public good alone. General Jackson, we believe, combines these requisites in his character, and in this faith we have united in support of him." Quoted by *Cincinnati Inquisitor Advertiser*, Feb. 22, 1823.

"Jackson was considered a 'good tariff and Internal Improvement man' in all three of his campaigns in Indiana. Any intimation that he was not sound on both of these issues would have been resented by his Indiana friends."—Esarey, "The Organization of the Jacksonian Party in Indiana," *loc. cit*.

Cf. Address of Hamilton County Committee, which declared that "ill-founded constitutional scruples" had intervened to prevent appropriations for national purposes. Also Address of the State Committee, which deplored Clay's candidacy as dividing those holding the same sentiments as to a national policy, and declared Jackson's "views of public policy, as to internal improvements and protection to domestic manufactures, eminently qualify him for the chief seat in our national councils."

Cf. Jackson himself, in letter to Col. George Wilson, April 17, 1824: "It is well known that I am in favor of the general principle of the [tariff] bill," etc. Parton, *Life of Jackson*, III, 42. See also the letter to L. H. Coleman, April 26, 1824: "Where has the American farmer a market for his surplus product? Except for cotton, he has neither a foreign nor a home market. Does not this clearly prove, when there is no market either at home or abroad, that there is too much labor employed in agriculture, and that the channels of labor should be multiplied? Common sense points out at once the remedy. Draw from agriculture this abundant labor; employ it in mechanism and manufactures, thereby creating a home market for your bread stuffs, and distributing labor to the most profitable account, and benefits to the country will result. In short, sir, we have been too long subject to the policy of British merchants.

in this regard was taken for granted, and the attacks upon him were based on his unfitness for the presidential office.[38]

The friends of both Clay and Jackson deplored the division of support between two western candidates. Each group urged that the division endangered the influence of the West in the election and charged the other with the blame. Jackson's friends urged the withdrawal of Clay, but there was at no time any hope of a union of the two groups.[39] It was also perceived that the cause of the West could triumph only through union with the Northeast or South. A union with the Northeast could be effected, however, only by accepting an eastern candidate;[40] while southern votes for a western man could be had, if at all, only at the price of subordination of western interests.[41] The friends of both Crawford and

It is time we should become a little more *Americanized*, and, instead of feeding the paupers and laborers of England, feed our own, or else, in a short time, by following our present policy, we shall all be rendered paupers ourselves. . . . ." *Ibid.*, 34 *et seq.*

The *Hamilton Intelligencer*, June 29, and *National Republican*, Aug. 24, 1824, contain typical articles designed to prove Jackson's friendliness to western interests. An occasional doubt appears, *e. g.*, *Liberty Hall* questioned the sincerity of his protectionism in view of the fact that his strength was so great in the South (April 27, 1824), and was sure that the American System had a thousand better friends. Quoted in *Supporter*, Aug. 12, 1824.

[38] *Liberty Hall*, Sept. 2, 14, 21, 24, Oct. 1, 1824; *Supporter*, Feb. 26, Oct. 21, 1824. See *below*, 139, *f. n.* 48. The situation in Indiana was similar, in a general way, although being still in the pioneer stage, Jackson's following was proportionately stronger. "The sympathies of the pioneers were for the rough and rugged Jackson. It was known that Jackson opposed the banks, and, on that ground, received the support of great numbers of financially embarrassed settlers who attributed the scarcity of money to the manipulation of bankers. . . . . The business men and the well-to-do farmers usually favored Clay on account of his position on the tariff and internal improvements. . . . . Adams stood well with the lawyers and other professional men and was the favorite among the Quakers and other settlers on the Whitewater. . . . ."—Esarey, *History of Indiana*, 250 *et seq.*

[39] Address of the Jackson State Committee, *loc. cit.*; Resolutions of Clay Convention; *Cincinnati Inquisitor Advertiser*, Feb. 7, 28, March 3, Sept. 11.

[40] "The eastern and northern states from the important part they took in achieving our independence and establishing the form of gov't under which we live, & from which we derive such incalculable benefits, have an undoubted right to be a little tenacious of the honor of furnishing the next President; and courtesy & *reciprocity of benefits* should induce the other *sections* to accord to them that honor, provided the candidate offered possesses equal qualifications with the other competitors." *Delaware Patron*, March 18, 1824. The *Patron* favored Adams.

[41] "If a western interest is intended to effect the election of a president, as is proposed by all who speak of the feasibility of electing a western president, it must include all the southern states, and one or more of the middle states, and if a western candidate is elected by such votes he must be governed by their policy." *Ohio Monitor*, Feb. 15, 1823. Like the *Delaware Patron*, the *Monitor* favored Adams.

Clay indulged a hope of winning the support of Virginia, his native state, and visited friends there in 1822 to promote his candidacy. Ambler, *Ritchie*, 87-90. His cordial reception encouraged his hope, but at times he perceived its vanity. See correspondence with Francis Brooke, especially letter of August 28, 1823, quoted *above*, 113, *f. n.* 100. The conclusion of this letter, as to his own prospects in Virginia, is gloomy: "You will oppose my election, I suppose, in Virginia. I have no right to complain." And he perceives clearly the reasons why he cannot expect the desired support. "You will oppose me because I think that the interests of all parts of the Union should be taken care of; in other words, that the interests of the

Clinton sought to promote coalitions in behalf of their candidates. So far as Crawford's hopes are concerned, they were impossible of realization because of the incompatibility of the sectional interests concerned, and the overtures of his friends were rejected without hesitation.[42]   The Clintonians pled with more reason that Ohio should join with the Northeast in support of their candidate rather than a western man, upon the basis of common opposition to slavery expansion and common desire for internal improvements and protection.[43]   As later events proved, there was an excellent basis for a union of the Ohio Valley and those eastern states which favored the American System, in support of Adams.   But none of the schemes for coalition made any headway.   In default of common support of a candidate for the presidency, the next best step in the direction of new sectional alliances was to support candidates of different sections for the presidential and vice-presidential offices.   From this angle, the acceptance of Calhoun as the candidate for the second place by the western friends of Jackson is significant.   While it did not at the time mark a personal alliance of the two men, it foreshadowed it, and the union of their followers in opposition to the administration during the term of Adams. Similarly, the Clay men, although refusing to forsake their favorite at the suggestion of the friends of either of the northern candidates, resorted to the strategy of bidding for the support of the Northeast by nominating Sanford, of New York, for the second

---

interior, on the two subjects mentioned, as well as that of the maritime coast, ought to be provided for." In a later letter to Brooke, however (Feb. 23, 1824), he argues that the caucus nomination has destroyed Crawford, that Virginia will have to choose between Jackson and himself, and urges a demonstration in his favor. Colton, *Life of Clay*, IV, 86 et seq. A few days later he suggests that any appeal to the people in his behalf should be "temperate and conciliatory." To Brooke, March 6, 1824. *Ibid.*, 88.

[42] The desire of Crawford's friends to win support for him in the West (Ambler, *Ritchie*, 94 et seq.) was the source of the charge of coalition with Clay. (See *above*, 203, 210). Clay's opponents used it quite effectively, asserting that to support Clay meant eventually to aid Crawford. *Delaware Patron*, Aug. 6, 1823, June 24, July 15, and Sept. 15, 1824 ; *National Republican*, March 30, April 2, 16, June 1, 22, and Aug. 13, 1824. Clay gave the proposal no countenance, unless we can so construe his suggestion to Brooke, March 6, 1824, that his friends at Richmond should not clash with those of Crawford. Colton, *Life of Clay*, IV, 88. He insisted that the vote of the northwestern states would go for Adams as their second choice. To Brooke, Feb. 23, 1824. *Ibid.*, IV, 86. The mutual friends of Clay and Crawford, in Virginia, sought to force a vice-presidential nomination upon the former. Said one: "As to consulting Mr. Clay it is injudicious. Let him not be consulted, and the force of circumstances must urge him into an acquiescence. . . . . When New York elects electors favorable to Mr. Crawford her Legislature ought to nominate Mr. Clay as vice-president." Ambler, *Ritchie*, 94 et seq. Clay's friends took great pains to deny the charge of coalition with Crawford. *Columbus Gazette*, Jan. 22, 1824 ; *National Republican*, April 2, 1824 ; *Supporter*, April 15 and Sept. 30, 1824. The whole incident affords interesting collateral evidence of the incompatibility of their sections.

[43] *National Republican*, Sept. 19, 1823.

place.[44]   The Adams group made an attempt of the same kind by advocating in Ohio and elsewhere for a time the nomination of Jackson as the New Englander's running mate.[45]   All of these devices are significant as indications of the tendencies to realignment, but none of them were practically effective in securing intersectional co-operation to a sufficient extent to determine the election. The continuation of the four leading candidates in the field to the end of the contest insured, as was foreseen, a resort to the House of Representatives for the final choice.[46]   In this campaign the race for the electoral vote served as an elimination event, to be followed by coalitions of the kind which could not occur before the election. The way was thus cleared for the union of the West and Northeast which had been advocated in vain before the election.   The interval between the election and the balloting of the House was the period in which these coalitions took form, and they were shaped by the same forces which we have found at work during the campaign. It was inevitable that the influence of the eliminated candidate should be a prime factor in determining the final result.

The motives of Clay in deciding to support Adams rather than either of the other candidates are no longer a mystery.   They are in entire accord with his long-established views.   Agreeable as Crawford was to him as a man, his policies, even if the unfortunate stroke of paralysis had not cast doubt upon his physical capacity for office, were such that Clay could not possibly have supported him.[47]   As to Jackson, however satisfactory his views with regard to public policies, Clay's conviction of his personal unfitness is not to be doubted.[48]   Adams, on the other hand, although never

[44] Report of Clay Convention, at Columbus, in *Columbus Gazette*, July 22, 1824.

[45] Adams, *Memoirs*, VI, 253 ; *Delaware Patron*, April 8, 1824.

[46] Clay's chance of coming before the House depended largely upon his ability to command electoral votes in the South. But although his western friends endeavored to make it appear that his candidacy was based on broad national grounds (*Cf.* Address of Clay Convention at Columbus), he failed in the South as Crawford failed in the West, and for the same reason, *viz.*, that each represented the interests of his own section, and they were irreconcilable. In western Pennsylvania and New York, where sentiment was in harmony with Clay's policies, it was made to accrue to the benefit of other candidates.

April 26, 1823, the *Western Herald* remarked that all of the candidates were sectional, and sectional influences would prevail in the House election.

[47] Clay to Hammond, Oct., 1824 (Smith, *Hammond*, 37) ; to F. P. Blair, Jan. 8, 1825 (*Works of Clay*, Federal edition, IV, 109 *et seq.*) ; to Francis Brooke, Jan. 28, 1825 (*ibid.*, IV, 111.)

[48] See letters to Blair and Brooke, cited in preceding note; also to Rutgers, June 4, 1827, *ibid*, 163. *Cf.* Hammond: "It is their [Clay's friends'] sincere and honest conviction that he does not possess the political intelligence and judicial information indispensable in a

in cordial relations with Clay, was respected for his ability and known by him to be in sympathy with the American System.[49] Besides, Clay and his friends believed that Adams was the second choice of the West.[50] In fact, instead of determining the western delegations in their choice, Clay seems to have followed rather than led; and in supporting Adams the West was pursuing its true economic interest.[51]

The union of forces foreshadowed by the aid of Clay's friends in electing Adams was carried towards its consummation by the appointment of Clay as secretary of state, and the final result was

---

president." *Cincinnati Inquisitor Advertiser*, Sept. 11, 1824. For Hammond's more intimate opinion see Smith, *Hammond*, 35. See also John C. Wright to Ephraim Cutler, in Cutler, *Life of Cutler*, 185.

[49] "He wished me, as far as I might think proper, to satisfy him with regard to some principles of great public importance." Adams's record of interview with Clay on Jan. 9, 1825. *Memoirs*, VI, 464.

[50] The *Supporter* declared, July 8, that Clay's rumored withdrawal, if it took place, would give Ohio to Adams. See letter of Hammond (signed "L.") in *Cincinnati Inquisitor Advertiser*, Sept. 11, 1824: He believed Clay's withdrawal would give Ohio, Indiana, New York, and New Jersey to Adams. The drift of Clay's friends towards Adams became noticeable as soon as the result of the fall election was known. The caustic comment of the Jackson press really bears witness to a natural preference for Adams: "It is really amusing to observe with what facility some of the chief men of the Clay party in Ohio, men who have pretended to be the champions of a liberal and enlightened policy for the protection of Domestic Manufactures, can veer about, as interest or ambition may dictate, and become the humble supporters of a man notoriously opposed to 'domestic measures.'" *National Republican*, Dec. 28, 1824. In the issue for March 4, 1825, the *Republican* refers to Clay as the "Arnold of the West." The Clay men who supported Adams were better informed than their critics as to his real views. Clay wrote to Blair (letter cited *above*, 139, *f. n.* 47): "What has great weight with me is the decided preference which a majority of the delegation from Ohio has for him over General Jackson." In the House election ten of the Ohio delegation voted for Adams, two for Jackson and two for Crawford. Clay's reasons for his course are summed up in his *Address to his Constituents: Niles Register*, XXVIII, 71 *et seq.* Clay had declared Adams to be the second choice of the Northwest in February, 1824. Letter to Brooke, cited *above*, 139, *f. n.* 47.

[51] *Cf.* letters of members of the Ohio delegation, published in the *Address of Henry Clay to the Public*, Appendix, 30-61, for statements showing that Adams's support was due to the recognition of the community of interest between the West and the Northeast, and suspicion of Jackson because of his personal limitations and the support given him in the South. See also letter of W. Creighton, of Chillicothe, Ohio, approving of Clay's union with Adams, on the assumption "that Mr. A. will pursue a liberal policy, and embrace within its scope the great leading policy that you have been advocating." Colton, *Life of Clay*, IV, 118. Similar motives influenced members of the delegations of other western states. See letter of David Trimble, of Kentucky, to the editor of the *Mount Sterling Spy*: ". . . . My own opinion was founded on the facts as I knew them to exist, and upon considerations referable to the general *interests of the union*, and of the *western states as a part of it*. Apart from personal feeling, it was as clear a case as I ever had before me. . . . ." Quoted in *Niles Register*, XXVIII, 69. *Cf.* letter of Francis Johnson *To the Public*, March 7, 1825, *Niles Register*, XXVIII, 25; Brent, of Louisiana, to the editor of the *Attakapas Gazette*, *ibid.*, 134; and numerous others, *ibid.*, 203 *et seq.* Gazlay, one of the two Ohio representatives who voted for Jackson, said that he talked with three other Ohio members, two of whom said that it would not do to vote for Jackson, as he was the enemy of internal improvements; the third was ready to risk violating the wishes of his constituents.

the National Republican party, the platform of which was the American System.

The Democratic party grew out of the opposition. It must be recalled that the Republican party had from the beginning embraced antagonistic elements in the coastal aristocracy of planters and the farming democracy of the back settlements. Although the planter pressed close after the pioneer farmer in the Gulf region, we have seen that down to 1825 the movement of population to the west of the Alleghanies was predominantly a migration of the democratic stock of the piedmont. It was this element of the Republican party which had colonized the Ohio Valley, and ten years after the close of the War of 1812 the transalleghany region was still in large measure the child of that Old West of the eighteenth century which had challenged the political supremacy of the coast. The sweep of this pioneer stock into Indiana, Illinois, Mississippi, and Alabama carried into practice the democratic ideals for which they had struggled in their old homes, for although white manhood suffrage did not invariably prevail, the basis of apportionment was white population, even in the new slave states. Thus expanding democracy won on its new field the cause for which it had fought in vain in the old states.[52]

The growth of the number of new states, democratically governed and enjoying equal rights in the Union, foretold the early triumph of democratic principles in national politics. One might expect to find the western democracy turning upon the planting class. But suffrage and apportionment continued to be matters under state control, and the contest within the original states went on unaffected by the growth of the West save as the attraction of the lands and more liberal institutions there resulted in concessions to prevent migration. It was only in the national arena that the West could exercise its political power. The breach between South and West, in short, took place on economic grounds, and that portion of the West which placed economic interests first followed Clay into the coalition with Adams which formed the National Repub-

---

[52] By 1820, all of the states in the Northwest (except Ohio) and Missouri, had established manhood suffrage for whites. In the Southwest the same rule held except in Louisiana and Mississippi: in the former voters must be taxpayers or purchasers of public lands; in the latter enrollment in the militia or payment of taxes were alternatives. In Tennessee even free negroes voted until 1824. Maine, New Hampshire, Vermont, Maryland, and South Carolina had adopted white manhood suffrage by 1820.

lican party.[53] The democratic impulses of the West tended, however, in quite another direction. The aristocratic practices prevalent heretofore in the national administration were equally odious whether pursued by the northern or southern representatives of the coastal oligarchy; yet of the two old coastal parties it was the Republicans who had steadfastly upheld the equal political rights of the people in the new western communities, while the Northeast was historically associated with jealousy of popular ideals of government. The circumstances under which the National Republican party was born unfortunately gave offense to these sentiments, and enabled the friends of Jackson to promote his cause in the name of popular rule. The efforts which his group had made during the campaign to arouse the people against the methods of the politicians were redoubled when the House disregarded the indication of the popular choice afforded by the plurality for Jackson in the electoral college, because, as they charged, of a corrupt bargain between Adams and Clay, by which the latter received the appointment as secretary of state in return for his support.[54] The "defeat of the will of the people" by this "corrupt" pro-

---

[53] The earlier writers were inclined to see in the National Republican party a revival of Federalism. Thus Parton says of the Adams administration: "Federalism supposed to be dead, was living, rampant, and sitting in the seat of power." *Life of Jackson*, III, 89. According to Benton, the election of Jackson was a "triumph . . . . of the democracy over the federalists, then called national republicans. . . . . For although Mr. Adams had received confidence and office from Mr. Madison and Mr. Monroe, and had classed with the democratic party during the fusion of parties in the 'era of good feeling,' yet he had previously been federal; and in the re-establishment of old party lines which began to take place after the election of Mr. Adams . . . . his affinities, and policy, became those of his former party. . . . ." *Thirty Years' View*, I, 111-112. Such a statement ignores the new force in the establishment of party lines, i. e., the West. The phenomenon under observation was not the "re-establishment of old party lines," as Jefferson perceived at the time. A letter written by him relative to the Clay-Adams coalition bears witness to this and to his disappointment at the revolution in the relations of the sections: "I fear with you all the evils, which the present lowering aspect of our political horizon so ominously portends. . . . . And what is still less expected was that my favorite western country was to be made the instrument of that change. I have ever and fondly cherished the interests of that country, relying upon it as a barrier against the degeneracy of public opinion from our original and free principles. But the bait of local interests . . . . has decoyed them from their kindred attachments to alliances alien to them. . . . ." To Ritchie, quoted in Ambler, *Ritchie*, 102-103. *Cf.* letter to W. F. Gordon, Jan. 1, 1826; Ford, *Writings of Jefferson*, X, 358. Jefferson's grief over the West's apostasy was somewhat unnecessary, inasmuch as National Republicanism, instead of rejecting popular principles of government as Federalism had done, united Federalist nationalism with Republican confidence in the people. Such, indeed, was the happy implication of the party name.

[54] *Cf.* effect in Virginia of the rumor that Clay had agreed to support Adams in the House in return for the appointment: "The good people are run mad here about the presidential election. I was with some of our great men at Dr. Brockenbrough's the other night and found them all universally denouncing Clay and Adams. They . . . . said that they would take Jackson and any body now in preference to Adams." Betsy Coles to Andrew Stevenson, quoted by Ambler, *Ritchie*, 99. Ritchie now "turned the guns prepared for Jackson upon Adams." *Ibid.* See also 106-107, 112-113.

cedure, and the necessity of electing Jackson to vindicate the right of the people to rule, were the arguments employed with greatest effect by the managers of the campaign which brought Jackson to the White House. It was exactly calculated to rally the western population and the newly enfranchised classes in the old states.[55] The rule of intriguing politicians in the nation's capital became the object of attack much as aristocratic domination had been attacked by the interior democracy of the original states.[56]

But this does not afford a complete explanation of the triumph of the "Old Hero." The planters felt no enthusiasm for popular government such as inspired all this acclamation and yet they continued in alliance with the democratic element of the West and formed the second factor in the Jacksonian Democracy in the period of its inception, as they had done in the Jeffersonian Republicanism. The explanation lies in their opposition to the economic policy of the Adams administration. The inaugural address and first message of the new president revealed that the South had nothing to expect from the National Republicans,[57] and gave the basis for renewed union with a part of the West in common opposition to the party in power.[58] In their disregard of the policies which Jack-

[55] "The election of John Q. Adams by the House of Representatives welded the dissatisfied democrats of Indiana into the Jacksonian Democratic Party. There was a fierceness in their resentment of the treatment of Jackson which was little short of warlike. They referred to the election of Adams as 'the theft of the presidency.' All believed that Clay had sold his influence to Adams for the appointment as Secretary of State, a bargain and sale of the government which they thought far more dangerous than Burr's Conspiracy."—Esarey, *History of Indiana*, 298.

[56] "The election of General Jackson was a triumph of democratic principle, and the assertion of the people's right to govern themselves. That principle had been violated in the presidential election in the House of Representatives in the session of 1824-'25; and the sanction, or rebuke, of that violation was a leading question in the whole canvass." Benton, *Thirty Years' View*, I, 111.

[57] Adams, *Memoirs*, VII, 105. "The declaration of principles [in the inaugural address] which would give so much power to the government, and the danger of which had just been so fully set forth by Mr. Monroe in his veto message on the Cumberland road bill, alarmed the old republicans, and gave a new ground of opposition to Mr. Adams' administration, in addition to the strong one growing out of the election in the House of Representatives. . . . . This new ground of opposition was greatly strengthened at the delivery of the first annual message. . . . ." Benton, *Thirty Years' View*, I, 54.

[58] The renewal of the alliance between the planters and the western democracy was deliberately engineered by the political managers. *Cf.* letter of Van Buren, dated Jan. 13, 1827, outlining the plan for such an alliance between "the planters of the South and the plain Republicans of the North," quoted by Ambler, *Ritchie*, 107.

Cf. J. C. Calhoun to his son, Aug. 26, 1827, in which he bases his opposition to the administration on the ground of the corrupt means by which it came to power, and the mistaken policy "of arraying the great geographical interests of the union against one another,"—that is, by the advocacy of the American System. Jameson, J. F., *Correspondence of John C. Calhoun*, 249-250. *Cf.* Benton, *Thirty Years' View*, I, 111. This letter of Calhoun's is one of

son would pursue when president, however, the southerners by aiding in his election, prepared to step from the frying pan to the fire. The natural antipathy of the planters towards the political self-assertion of the people, the measures of the new government, and the autocratic temper of Jackson as chief magistrate, combined to hasten a further readjustment of party groups, in which the breach between South and West was widened by the defection from the Democracy of that southern faction which, as State Rights Whigs, entered into mismated union with the National Republicans.[59]

---

the earliest evidences of the change of attitude which he was making. As late as May, 1825, he had reaffirmed his earlier views. See *above*, 132, *f. n.* 17.

Crawford did not accept the bargain charge as true, but wrote to Clay, Feb. 4, 1828, criticising Adams's course as president: "The whole of his first message to Congress is replete with doctrines which I hold to be unconstitutional." Even this, "although exceptionable," would not have driven Georgia under the banner of Jackson, Crawford thought, had it not been for Adams's Indian policy. Colton, *Life of Clay*, IV, 191. Clay replied: "Truth compels me to say that I have heartily approved of the leading measures of his administration, not excepting those which relate to Georgia." *Ibid.*, 192.

[59] See Phillips, U. B., "The Southern Whigs," in *Turner Essays in American History*, 203-229.

BIBLIOGRAPHY

1. PUBLICATIONS OF THE UNITED STATES GOVERNMENT

American State Papers. Washington, 1832-1861.

Annals of the Congress of the United States. 42 volumes. Washington, 1834-1856.

A Biographical Congressional Directory, 1774-1911. Washington, 1913.

Congressional Globe. 108 volumes. Washington, 1834-1873.

Ford, Worthington Chauncey, and Hunt, Gaillard, eds., *Journals of the Continental Congress, 1774-1789.* 15 volumes. Washington, 1904-1909.

Poore, Ben Perley, comp., *The Federal and State Constitutions, Colonial Charters, and other Organic Laws of the United States.* 2 volumes. Washington, 1877.

Richardson, James Daniel, *A compilation of the Messages and Papers of the Presidents, 1789-1897.* 10 volumes. Washington, 1896-1899.

United States, Bureau of the Census, Census Reports. . . . *Twelfth Census of the United States, taken in the Year 1900.* 10 volumes. Washington, 1901-1902.

United States, Bureau of the Census, Census Reports. . . . *Thirteenth Census of the United States, taken in the year 1910.* 11 volumes. Washington, 1912-1914.

United States, Bureau of the Census, *A Century of Population Growth from the First Census of the United States to the Twelfth, 1790-1900.* Washington, 1909.

2. MISCELLANEOUS SOURCES

Adams, Henry, ed., *Documents relating to New England Federalism.* Boston, 1877.

Ames, Herman V., ed., *State Documents on Federal Relations.* Philadelphia, 1906.

Benton, Thomas Hart, *Thirty Years' Views, or a History of the Working of the American Government for Thirty Years, from 1820 to 1850.* 2 volumes. New York, 1854-1857.

Callender, Guy Stevens, ed., *Selections from the Economic History of the United States, 1765-1850.* Boston, 1909.

Commons, John Rogers, ed., *A Documentary History of American Industrial Society.* 11 volumes. Cleveland, 1910-1911.

Cuming, F., *Tour to the Western Country, through Ohio and Kentucky: a voyage down the Ohio and Mississippi Rivers, and a Trip through the Mississippi Territory, and part of West Florida, 1807-1809.* (Volume IV of Thwaites, *Early Western Travels.*)

Farrand, Max, ed., *The Records of the Federal Convention of 1787.* 3 volumes. New Haven, 1911.

Faux, W., *Memorable Days in America; A Journal of a Tour to the United States to Ascertain the Condition and Probable Prospects of British Emigrants; 1819-1820.* (Volume XI of Thwaites, *Early Western Travels.*)

Flint, Timothy, *Recollections of the Last Ten Years.* Boston, 1826.

Harris, Thaddeus Mason, *Journal of a Tour into the Territory Northwest of the Alleghany Mountains, 1803.* (Volume III of Thwaites, *Early Western Travels.*)

Hart, Albert Bushnell, and Channing, Edward, eds., *American History Leaflets:*
> No. 11. *Jefferson's A Summary View of the Rights of British America.* New York, 1893.
> No. 22. *Documents Illustrating State Land Claims and Cessions, 1776-1802.* New York, 1895.

Hart, Albert Bushnell, *American History told by Contemporaries.* 4 volumes. New York, 1902-1903.

Hening, William Waller, comp., *The Statutes at large, being a Collection of all the Laws of Virginia from the First Session of the Legislature in the Year 1619.* 13 volumes. Richmond, 1819-1823.

Michaux, F. A., *Travels to the Westward of the Alleghany Mountains, in Ohio, Kentucky, and return to Charleston through the Upper Carolinas, 1802.* (Volume III of Thwaites, *Early Western Travels.*)

Thwaites, Reuben Gold, ed., *Early Western Travels; A Series of Annotated Reprints.* 32 volumes. Cleveland, 1904-1907.

3. NEWSPAPERS

Cincinnati Inquisitor Advertiser.
Columbus Gazette.
Delaware Patron. (Ohio.)
Hamilton Intelligencer and Advertiser.
Liberty Hall and Cincinnati Gazette.
National Republican and Ohio Political Register. (Cincinnati.)
Niles Weekly Register. (Baltimore.)
Ohio Monitor and Patron of Industry. (Columbus.)
Richmond Enquirer. (Virginia.)
Scioto Telegraph. Continued as the *Scioto Telegraph and Lawrence Gazette.* (Portsmouth.)
Supporter. Continued as *Supporter and Scioto Gazette.* (Chillicothe.)
Western Herald and Steubenville Gazette.

4. BIOGRAPHIES, MEMOIRS, AND WRITINGS OF PUBLIC MEN

Adams, Charles Francis, ed., *Memoirs of John Quincy Adams; Comprising Parts of His Diary from 1795 to 1848.* 12 volumes. Philadelphia, 1874-1877.
Ambler, Charles H., *Thomas Ritchie, A Study in Virginia Politics.* Richmond, 1913.
Barbour Correspondence, in William & Mary College *Quarterly,* X.
Bigelow, John, ed., *The Complete Works of Benjamin Franklin.* 10 volumes. New York, 1887-1888.
Clay, Henry, *An Address of Henry Clay to the Public Containing certain Testimony in Refutation of the Charges against Him made by General Andrew Jackson, touching the Last Presidential Election.* Washington, 1827.
Colton, Calvin, ed., *The Life, Correspondence, and Speeches of Henry Clay.* 6 volumes. New York, 1857-.
Colton, Calvin, ed., *The Works of Henry Clay Comprising his Life, Correspondence and Speeches.* 10 volumes. New York and London, 1904.
Crallé, Richard K., ed., *The Works of John C. Calhoun.* 6 volumes. New York, 1883.
Cutler, Julia Perkins, *Life and Times of Ephraim Cutler.* Cincinnati, 1890.
Ford, Paul Leicester, ed., *The Writings of Thomas Jefferson.* 10 volumes. New York, 1892-1899.
Ford, Worthington Chauncey, ed., *The Writings of George Washington.* 14 volumes. New York, 1889-1893.
Jameson, John Franklin, *Correspondence of John C. Calhoun,* in American Historical Association *Report* for 1899, II. Washington, 1900.
Jay, William, *The Life of John Jay.* 2 volumes. New York, 1833.
King, Charles R., *The Life and Correspondence of Rufus King Comprising his Letters, Private and Official, his Public Documents and his Speeches.* 6 volumes. New York, 1894-1900.
Lodge, Henry Cabot, *Life and Letters of George Cabot.* Boston, 1877.
Lodge, Henry Cabot, ed., *Works of Alexander Hamilton.* 9 volumes. New York and London, 1885-1886.
Madison, James, *Letters and other Writings of James Madison, Published by order of Congress.* 4 volumes. Philadelphia, 1865.
Massie, David Meade, *Nathaniel Massie, a Pioneer of Ohio. A Sketch of his Life and Selections from his Correspondence.* Cincinnati, 1896.
Morison, Samuel Eliot, *The Life and Letters of Harrison Gray Otis.* 2 volumes. Boston and New York, 1913.
Morris, Annie Cary, ed., *The Diary and Letters of Gouverneur Morris.* 2 volumes. New York, 1888.
Parton, James, *Life of Andrew Jackson.* 3 volumes. New York, 1860.
Pellew, George, *John Jay.* Boston and New York, 1890. (*American Statesmen series.*)
Rives, William C., *History of the Life and Times of James Madison.* 3 volumes. Boston, 1859-1868.
Smith, William Henry, *Charles Hammond and his Relations to Henry Clay and John Quincy Adams. An Address delivered before the Chicago Historical Society, May 20, 1884.* Chicago, 1885.

Smith, William Henry, ed., *The St. Clair Papers.* . . . . 2 volumes. Cincinnati, 1882.

Sparks, Jared, *The Life of Gouverneur Morris, with Selections from his Correspondence and Miscellaneous Papers.* . . . . 3 volumes. Boston, 1832.

Van Tyne, Claude Halstead, ed., *The Letters of Daniel Webster.* New York, 1902.

Washington, H. A., ed., *The Writings of Thomas Jefferson.* 9 volumes. Washington, 1853-1854.

5. STATE AND LOCAL HISTORIES

Ambler, Charles Henry, *Sectionalism in Virginia from 1776 to 1861.* Chicago, 1910.

Alexander, De Alva Stanwood, *A Political History of the State of New York.* 2 volumes. New York, 1906.

Benton, Nathaniel Soley, *A History of Herkimer County, including the Upper Mohawk Valley.* . . . . Albany, 1856.

Bradford, Alden, *History of Massachusetts.* 3 volumes. Boston, 1822-1829.

Bruce, Philip Alexander, *Economic History of Virginia in the Seventeenth Century.* . . . . 2 volumes. New York and London, 1896.

Burnet, Jacob, *Notes on the Early Settlement of the Northwestern Territory.* New York and Cincinnati, 1847.

Carter, Clarence Edwin, *Great Britain and the Illinois Country, 1763-1774.* Washington, 1910.

Craig, Neville B., *The History of Pittsburgh.* . . . . Pittsburg, 1851.

Esarey, Logan, *A History of Indiana from its Exploration to 1850.* Indianapolis, 1915.

Hammond, Jabez D., *History of Political Parties in the State of New York from the Ratification of the Constitution to December, 1840.* 2 volumes. Cooperstown, 1845.

Hart, Samuel, *et al.*, eds., *Connecticut as a Colony and as a State.* . . . . 4 volumes. Hartford, 1904. (In Bibliophile Library of Literature, Art, etc.)

History of Luzerne, Lackawanna, and Wyoming Counties, Pennsylvania. New York, 1890.

James, Charles Fenton, *Documentary History of the Struggle for Religious Liberty in Virginia.* Lynchburg, 1900.

Johnston, Alexander, *Connecticut.* Boston and New York, 1887. (*American Commonwealth series*).

Kercheval, Samuel, *A History of the Valley of Virginia.* Woodstock, 1902.

McElroy, Robert McNutt, *Kentucky in the Nation's History.* New York, 1909.

Meginness, John F., ed., *Official Report of Proceedings of the Centennial Anniversary of Lycoming County (Pa.).* Williamsport, 1896.

Phelan, James, *History of Tennessee.* Boston and New York, 1889.

Phillips, Ulrich Bonnell, *A History of Transportation in the Eastern Cotton Belt to 1860.* New York, 1908.

Randall, Emilius Oviatt, and Ryan, Daniel J., *History of Ohio.* . . . . 5 volumes. New York, 1912.

Sanford, Laura G., *The History of Erie County, Pennsylvania.* Philadelphia, 1862.

Shaler, Nathaniel Southgate, *A General Account of the Commonwealth of Kentucky.* Cambridge, 1876.

Taylor, William Alexander, *Ohio in Congress, 1803-1901* . . . . *with* . . . . *sketches.* . . . . Columbus, 1900.

Webster, Homer J., *History of the Democratic Party Organization in the Northwest. 1828-1840.* Columbus, 1915.

Whittlesey, Charles, *Early History of Cleveland, Ohio.* . . . . Cleveland, 1867.

6. ARTICLES AND ESSAYS IN PERIODICALS, ANNUALS, AND UNIVERSITY STUDIES

Adams, Herbert Baxter, "Maryland's Influence on the Land Cessions to the United States," in Johns Hopkins University *Studies in History and Political Science*, III.

Alden, George Henry, *New Governments West of the Alleghanies before 1780. Bulletin* of the University of Wisconsin, Historical Series, II, No. 1. Madison, 1897.

Alden, George Henry, "The State of Franklin," in *American Historical Review*, VIII.

Ames, Herman V., "The Proposed Amendments to the Constitution of the United States during the First Century of its History," in American Historical Association *Report* for 1896, II. Washington, 1897.

Anderson, D. R., "Jefferson and the Virginia Constitution," in *American Historical Review*, XXI.

Ballagh, James Curtis, "Introduction to Southern Economic History—The Land System—Part I," in American Historical Association *Report* for 1897.

Bassett, John Spencer, "The Regulators of North Carolina (1765-1771)," in American Historical Association *Report* for 1894.

Becker, Carl Lotus, *The History of Political Parties in the Province of New York, 1760-1776. Bulletin* of the University of Wisconsin, History Series, II, No. 1. Madison, 1909.

Callender, Guy Stevens, "The Early Transportation and Banking Enterprises of the States in Relation to the Growth of Corporations," in *Quarterly Journal of Economics*, XVII.

Caldwell, Joshua W., "John Bell of Tennessee," in *American Historical Review*, IV.

Cushing, Harry A., *History of the Transition from Provincial to Commonwealth Government in Massachusetts*. Columbia University *Studies in History, Economics, and Public Law*, VII. New York, 1896.

Esarey, Logan, "The Organization of the Jacksonian Party in Indiana," in Mississippi Valley Historical Society *Proceedings* for 1913-1914.

Farrand, Max, "The Compromises of the Constitution," in *American Historical Review*, IX.

Ford, Amelia Clewly, *Colonial Precedents of Our National Land System as it Existed in 1800. Bulletin* of the University of Wisconsin, History Series, II, No. 2. Madison, 1910.

Ford, Worthington Chauncey, "Jefferson's Constitution for Virginia," in *The Nation*, August 7, 1890.

Gephart, William F., *Transportation and Industrial Development in the Middle West*. Columbia University *Studies in Economics, History, and Public Law*, XXXIV.

Goodwin, Frank P., "The Rise of Manufactures in the Miami Country," in *American Historical Review*, XII.

Greene, S. W., "Scotch-Irish in America," in *American Antiquarian Society Proceedings*, X.

Haight, R. W., in *Milwaukee Sentinel*, November 25, 1900.

Henderson, Archibald, "Documents: The Origin of the Regulation in North Carolina," in *American Historical Review*, XXI.

Hockett, Homer C., "Rufus King and the Missouri Compromise," in *Missouri Historical Review*, II.

Houston, David Franklin, *A Critical Study of Nullification in South Carolina*, in *Harvard Historical Studies*, III. New York and London, 1896.

Hunt, Gaillard, "James Madison and Religious Liberty," in American Historical Association *Report* for 1901, I.

Libby, Orin Grant, *The Geographical Distribution of the Vote of the Thirteen States on the Federal Constitution, 1787-1788. Bulletin* of the University of Wisconsin, Economics, Political Science, and History Series, I, No. 1. Madison, 1894.

Libby, Orin Grant, *Review* of Beard, C. A., *Economic Origins of Jeffersonian Democracy*, in *Mississippi Valley Historical Review*, III.

Libby, Orin Grant, "A Sketch of the Early Political Parties in the United States," in *Quarterly Journal of the University of North Dakota*, II.

Lincoln, Charles Henry, *The Revolutionary Movement in Pennsylvania, 1760-1776*. University of Pennsylvania, *Series in History*, No. 1. Philadelphia, 1901.

Lippincott, Isaac, "Pioneer Industry in the West," in *Journal of Political Economy*, XVIII.

McKinley, Albert Edward, *The Suffrage Franchise in the Thirteen English Colonies in America. Publications* of the University of Pennsylvania, Series in History, No. 2. Boston and Philadelphia, 1905.

Morse, Anson Ely, *The Federalist Party in Massachusetts to the Year 1800*. Princeton, 1909.

Phillips, Paul Chrisler, *The West in the Diplomacy of the American Revolution*. University of Illinois *Studies in the Social Sciences*, II, Nos. 2 and 3. Urbana, [c1913.]

Phillips, Ulrich Bonnell, "Origin and Growth of the Southern Black Belts," in *American Historical Review*, XI.

Phillips, Ulrich Bonnell, *Georgia and State Rights*, in American Historical Association *Report* for 1901, II. Washington, 1902.

Phillips, Ulrich Bonnell, "The South Carolina Federalists," in *American Historical Review*, XIV.

Roseboom, Eugene H., "Ohio in the Presidential Election of 1824," in *Ohio Archaeological and Historical Quarterly*, XXVI, 153-224.

Schaper, William A., "Sectionalism and Representation in South Carolina," in American Historical Association *Report* for 1900, I. Washington, 1901.

Turner, Frederick Jackson, "The Diplomatic Contest for the Mississippi Valley," in *Atlantic Monthly*, XCIII.

Turner, Frederick Jackson, "Dominant Forces in Western Life," in *Atlantic Monthly*, LXXIX.
Turner, Frederick Jackson, "The First Official Frontier of the Massachusetts Bay," in Colonial Society of Massachusetts *Publications*, XVII.
Turner, Frederick Jackson, "The Old West," in State Historical Society of Wisconsin *Proceedings* for 1908.
Turner, Frederick Jackson, "The Significance of the Frontier in American History," in American Historical Association *Report* for 1893.
Turner, Frederick Jackson, "Western State Making in the Revolutionary Era," in *American Historical Review*, I.
"Virginia under Governor Gooch: Queries from the Lords of Trade to Sir William Gooch Governor of Virginia and his Answers Abridged," in *Virginia Magazine of History*, III.

7. GENERAL AND MISCELLANEOUS

Bancroft, George, *History of the Formation of the Constitution of the United States of America.* 2 volumes. New York, 1882.
Barrett, Jay A., *Evolution of the Ordinance of 1787.* New York, 1891.
Beard, Charles A., *An Economic Interpretation of the Constitution of the United States.* New York, 1913.
Beard, Charles A., *Economic Origins of Jeffersonian Democracy.* New York, 1915.
Becker, Carl Lotus, *Beginnings of the American People.* (Volume I of *The Riverside History of the United States.*) Boston, 1915.
Borgeaud, Charles, *The Rise of Modern Democracy in old and New England.* London and New York, 1884.
Dwight, Timothy, *Travels in New-England and New-York.* 4 volumes. New-Haven, 1821-1822.
Faust, Albert Bernhart, *The German Eleemnt in the United States. . . . .* 2 volumes. Boston and New York, 1909.
Ford, Henry Jones, *The Scotch-Irish in America.* Princeton, 1915.
Gordy, John Pancoast, *Political History of the United States, with special Reference to the Growth of Political Parties.* 2 volumes. New York, 1908.
Hanna, Charles Augustus, *The Scotch-Irish; or, The Scot in North Britain, north Ireland, and North America.* 2 volumes. New York and London, 1902.
Hockett, Homer C., "Federalism and the West," in *Essays in American History Dedicated to Frederick Jackson Turner.* New York, 1910.
Huntington, Charles Clifford, *A History of Banking and Currency in Ohio before the Civil War.* Columbus, 1915.
McClelland, C. P., and Huntington, Charles Clifford, *History of the Ohio Canals, their Construction, Cost, Use and Partial Abandonment.* Columbus, 1905.
McLaughlin, Andrew Cunningham, *The Confederation and the Constitution, 1783-1789.* (Volume X of *The American Nation.*) New York and London, 1905.
McMaster, John Bach, *A History of the People of the United States from the Revolution to the Civil War.* 8 volumes. New York and London, 1904-1913.
Mathews, Lois Kimball, *The Expansion of New England.* Boston and New York, 1909.
Merriam, Clinton Hart, *Life Zones and Crop Zones of the United States.* United States Department of Agriculture, Division of Biological Survey, *Bulletin* No. 10.
Osgood, Herbert L., *The American Colonies in the Seventeenth Century.* 3 volumes. New York, 1907.
Ostrogorskii, Moisei IAkovlevich, *Democracy and the Organization of Political Parties.* 2 volumes. New York and London, 1902.
Phillips, Ulrich Bonnell, "The Southern Whigs," in *Essays in American History Dedicated to Frederick Jackson Turner.* New York, 1910.
Pitkin, Timothy, *A Statistical View of the Commerce of the United States of America: including also an Account of Banks, Manufactures and Internal Trade and Improvements. . . . .* New Haven, 1835.
Roosevelt, Theodore, *The Winning of the West.* 4 volumes. (Standard Library Edition). New York and London, 1903.
Stanwood, Edward, *American Tariff Controversies in the Nineteenth Century.* 2 volumes. Boston and New York, 1903.

Turner, Frederick Jackson, *Rise of the New West, 1819-1829.* (Volume XIV of *The American Nation.*) New York and London, 1906.

Walsh, Correa Moylan, *The Political Science of John Adams.* New York and London, 1915.

Wildman, Murray Shipley, *Money Inflation in the United States.* . . . . New York and London, 1905.

Winsor, Justin, *The Westward Movement: The Colonies and the Republic West of the Alleghanies, 1763-1798.* Boston and New York, 1899.

INDEX

Adams, John, part in framing Massachusetts constitution of 1780, 26, note; on right of people to establish government, 33, note; philosophy of government, 35, and note; in peace negotiations of 1782, 42.

Adams, John Quincy, on acquisition of Louisiana, 100, note; 102, note; interpretation of Missouri contest, 128; presidential candidate in 1824, 131, note; 133-135; second choice of Northwest, 138 and note; 139-140; coalition with Clay, 140-142; planters alienated by policies as president, 143.

Addison, Alexander, judge in western Pennsylvania, 67.

Agrarian interest. See Agriculture, and Farmers.

Agriculture, development in "back country" east of Alleghanies, 12-13; sale of surplus produce, 15; basis of republican government, 37; Jefferson's views on, 48-50; effect of growth of West, 84; European restrictions on American, 90; home market for, 87, 88, 90-91, 99; decline in New England, 92; significance of surplus production in West, 94; outstrips manufacturing in West, 99, 109-111, 113, note; problem of market for western surplus, 99-102, 109-111; need of transportation facilities, 100-104; harmony of agricultural and manufacturing interests, 113.

Alien and Sedition Acts, effect on West, 52; on New York, 64.

American System, foreshadowed, 88; developed, 88-91; supplants preparedness program, 89; espoused by West, 107-112; Clay on, 89-91. 113, note; opposition of South, 117-125; upheld by Ohio in campaign of 1824, 131, and note; 132, 136, and note; Adams's views on, 133-134; Jackson's views on, 136, note; platform of National Republican party, 141.

Ames, Fisher, on reasons for adoption of constitution, 29; on Whiskey Rebellion, 67, note; member of Essex Junto, 71, note; attitude on secession of New England, 104, note.

Aristocracy, origin, 10-12; dominance in government of colonies, 16-20; loss of ground during Revolution, 23-24; control in framing state constitutions, 24-27; influence on federal Constitution, 29-33; Federalist Party affected, 33-35; 65, note; 80.

"Back country," settlement, 12-14; grievances, 14-19; characteristics, 20-22; petitions for redress, 21; influence during Revolution, 22-24; struggle for rights after Revolution, 27; impossibility of secession, 41.

Bacon's Rebellion, 10.

Banks and banking, in West, 97-99.

Barbour, Philip P., old school Republican, 117, note.

Burnet, Jacob, judge in Northwest Territory, a Federalist, 55; on separation of Michigan from Ohio, 58, note; on decline of Federalism in Ohio, 59, note; elected state judge, 59, note.

Burr, Aaron, influence over wavering Federalists of western New York, 65.

Byrd, William, interest in Virginia frontier, 10.

Cabot, George, on cure for democracy, 71; member of Essex Junto, 71, note; dislike of democracy, 71, note; attitude on secession of New England, 72, note.

Calhoun, John C., leader of "Young Republicanism," 85; preparedness program of 1816, 87-88; on home market, 88; speaks for West, 112-113; on Bonus Bill, 113; liberal constructionist, 115; presidential candidate in 1824, 132; vice-presidential candidate, 132, 138.

Canals. See Internal Improvements.

Capitalism, representation in federal convention, 29, 30; favorable to adoption of Constitution, 33, 35; a basis of Federalist party, 35, 80.

Clay, Henry, leader of "Young Republicanism," 85; preparedness program of 1816, 87-88; develops American System, 88-91; voices demands of West, 112-113; injured by friendship for United States Bank, 99, 135; liberal constructionist, 115-116; reasons for opposition to Monroe, 116; presidential candidate in 1824, 131, note; 135-139; hope of support of Virginia, 137, note; reasons for supporting Adams in House election, 139-140; appointment as Secretary of State, 140; bargain charge, 142.

Clinton, DeWitt, supported in Ohio in 1812, 62, note; in New York, 66, note; asks aid